Charles Augustin Sainte-Beuve, William Mathews

Monday - Chats

Charles Augustin Sainte-Beuve, William Mathews

Monday - Chats

ISBN/EAN: 9783741160851

Manufactured in Europe, USA, Canada, Australia, Japa

Cover: Foto ©Andreas Hilbeck / pixelio.de

Manufactured and distributed by brebook publishing software (www.brebook.com)

Charles Augustin Sainte-Beuve, William Mathews

Monday - Chats

WORKS
OF
WILLIAM MATHEWS.

GETTING ON IN THE WORLD; or, Hints on Success in Life. 1 volume. 12mo. Pages 374. Price $1.50

THE GREAT CONVERSERS, and Other Essays. 1 volume. 12mo. Pages 304. Price . . . 1.50

WORDS: Their Use and Abuse. 1 volume. 12mo. Pages 504. Price 2.00

HOURS WITH MEN AND BOOKS. 1 volume. 12mo. Pages 384. Price 1.50

MONDAY-CHATS. A Selection from the "Causeries du Lundi" of C. A. Sainte-Beuve, with a Biographical and Critical Introduction by the Translator. 1 volume. 12mo. Pages 386. Price 2 00

ORATORY AND ORATORS. 1 vol. 12mo. Pages 456. Price 2.00

LITERARY STYLE, and Other Essays. 1 volume. 12mo. Pages 345. Price 1.50

MEN, PLACES AND THINGS. 1 volume. 12mo. Pages 394. Price 1 50

WIT AND HUMOR: Their Use and Abuse. 12mo Pages 405. Price 1.50

MONDAY-CHATS,

BY

C. A. SAINTE-BEUVE,
OF THE FRENCH ACADEMY.

SELECTED AND TRANSLATED FROM THE "CAUSERIES DU LUNDI,"
WITH AN INTRODUCTORY ESSAY ON THE LIFE AND
WRITINGS OF SAINTE-BEUVE,

By WILLIAM MATHEWS, LL.D.,
AUTHOR OF "GETTING ON IN THE WORLD," "WORDS, THEIR USE AND
ABUSE," ETC. ETC.

Je n'ai plus qu'un plaisir, j'analyse, j'herborise, je suis un naturaliste des esprits. Ce que je voudrais constituer, c'est *l'histoire naturelle littéraire.*—SAINTE-BEUVE.

FIFTH EDITION.

CHICAGO:
S. C. GRIGGS AND COMPANY.
1891.

Sainte-Beuve, the finest critical spirit of our time.— MATTHEW ARNOLD.

Such admirable biographical essays in so small a compass are nowhere else to be found. They are miniatures of the most excellent workmanship — EDINBURGH REVIEW.

In point of literary execution and critical power the "Causeries" have challenged the admiration of all competent judges. There is nothing equal to them, in their line, in any language.—WESTMINSTER REVIEW.

We, in England, rarely undertake a subject, falling within the department of letters, that has attained to European interest, without turning first to see what Sainte-Beuve has said about it. . . . He was never provoked into coarseness. His thrusts were made with the small-sword according to the received rules of fence: he firmly upheld the honor of his calling, and in the exercise of it was uniformly fearless, independent, and incorrupt.— LONDON QUARTERLY REVIEW.

It is impossible to speak of literary portraits without mentioning M. Ste. Beuve. He has drawn an incredible number of them, all worked out in the most delicate and careful manner, and highly prized by amateurs. . . . A keen psychologist, he knows the secret links that bind things together; he has an unrivalled faculty for seizing the relative elements of truths and opinions; he identifies himself so thoroughly with those he judges that he forgets to judge them; he understands everything, adapts himself to everything, enters into everything. . . . There is nothing triumphant in his manner; it is all allusion and charm, the result of half-conscious, half-unconscious art.— EDMOND SCHÉRER, as translated in the *Westminster Review*.

To praise the talent of Sainte-Beuve would be a superfluous work: public opinion has slowly become accustomed to consider him as the first critic of our time.—VISCOUNT D'HAUSSONVILLE.

PREFACE.

IN selecting from the many volumes of the "Causeries du Lundi" the essays required for the present work, the translator has experienced no little difficulty. The difficulty, as every reader of Sainte-Beuve will readily suppose, has not been the dearth of material, but "the embarrassment of riches." The final decision has been influenced by two considerations,— a desire to choose themes of intrinsic and permanent interest, and a desire to give a due variety. That the translator has done justice to the original in this attempt to reproduce in English some of the masterpieces of modern French criticism, he is very far from flattering himself. If the best translation, even of a third or fourth rate author is inevitably but the "seamy side of the cloth," then he may well despair who has undertaken to convey in English the *curiosa felicitas*, the subtle graces, and the delicate refinements of Sainte-Beuve's style. Adequately to do so would imply a genius hardly inferior to that of Sainte-Beuve himself.

It is only necessary to add that the order in which the selections have been arranged (with the exception of the last two), is nearly chronological, and has no reference to the comparative interest of the themes,— the first paper being less interesting than many of the others,— and that a few of the translations of passages quoted in the Introductory Essay have been taken from a paper in the "Westminster Review" and other sources.

CHICAGO, October 1, 1877.

CONTENTS.

Introductory Essay on the Life and Writings of Sainte-Beuve, - - - - - ix–lxxxvi

Lewis the Fourteenth, - - - - 1

Fenelon, - - - - - - - - 22

Bossuet, - - - - - - - 44

Massillon, - - - - - - - - 84

Pascal, - - - - - - - - 123

Rousseau, - - - - - - - - 141

Madame Geoffrin, - - - - - - 162

Joubert, - - - - - - - - 185

Guizot, - - - - - - - - 205

The Abbe Galiani, - - - - - - 227

Frederic the Great, - - - - 248

Index, - - - - - - - - 291

THE
LIFE AND WRITINGS OF SAINTE-BEUVE.

ON a gloomy day in October, 1869, a small house in the suburban Rue Montparnasse, in the metropolis of France, was the scene of a public demonstration such as rarely occurs even in that city of spectacles, sights and sensations. France had just lost one of her chief literary stars,—one whose place in the galaxy of letters could be filled by no other, however large its dimensions or brilliant its beams. After a long and heroic struggle with a keenly painful disease, Sainte-Beuve, Senator and Academician, had passed away, and his fellow-citizens had come to testify their respect for his memory. The funeral ceremonies, if ceremonies they could be called, were in keeping with the simplicity of his character. In compliance with his last directions, none of the societies or learned bodies to which he had belonged took part in his burial; but a crowd of ten thousand persons, among whom were poets, historians, novelists, scientists, critics, artists, and journalists of every grade, together with a body of Parisian students, were present at the house, and followed the remains to the tomb. As he had also requested, his remains were not taken to a church, no religious rites were observed, and no discourse was pronounced over his grave. As the coffin was lowered into the vault, in the cemetery of Montparnasse, beside the grave of his mother, a wreath of violets was placed upon it; and Mons. Lacaussade, one of his executors, advancing to the head of the grave, uttered the words, "*Adieu, Sainte-Beuve! adieu, notre ami, adieu!*" then, turning to the crowd, he thanked them in the name of the buried man-of-letters for their attendance, and the ceremony was ended. Many friends and admirers, however, lingered awhile in groups in the burying-ground, to interchange thoughts and feelings on the sad occasion; and all, doubtless, felt that his departure had left a chasm not easily to be filled in the intellectual ranks of France.

Who was this man that thus in a christian city had asked for a pagan burial, and what had he done to be honored at his obsequies as few are honored who have been benefactors to their race? Why, if he was so illustrious at home, is he so little known in other lands? These questions we shall endeavor to answer. Let us say, however, in advance, that the task is not an easy one, and that we cannot flatter ourselves that we shall do it more than proximate justice. It would require, indeed, a subtlety of genius, a nicety and delicacy of touch, and a mastery of language, equal to his own, adequately to characterize what the London *Athenæum* rightly calls "this all-searching and ever-working intelligence." By the verdict of nearly all persons competent to decide, he was, what Matthew Arnold terms him, "the finest critical spirit of our time,"—perhaps it is not too much to say, the acutest and most brilliant critic of this century. The fineness of his workmanship, the brilliancy and exquisite delicacy of his style, his vast and varied knowledge, his catholic taste and comprehensive sympathies, and, above all, his rare sense and almost unerring judgment, have been confessed alike by friends and foes. Not only his compeers in Paris, but sagacious judges in England and America, who have weighed his claims, declare that it would be difficult to name another critic of our time who has lighted up such a variety of subjects, who has extracted and hived up the essence of so many masterpieces of genius and learning, who has with so admirable an instinct separated the golden ore of literature from the dross, and fixed on the best specimens of the true, the beautiful, and the good, as Sainte-Beuve.

Even those who may dispute these honors,—if such there may be,—will not deny that instances of such devotion to literature as his, such a ceaseless, persevering advance toward an ideal, are very rare. Sainte-Beuve did not leap at once to the topmost round of the ladder, but worked his way up slowly, gradually, by dint of patient, conscientious toil. His whole life was a progress, without one backward step, or one diversion from the natural path of his genius. Starting on his career with no other gifts than a naturally delicate taste, a rare good sense, and a marked intellectual subtlety, he reached, after twenty years of conscientious toil, the position which he held for twenty years more, in which his criticisms seemed not so much the fruit of investigation and thought as a kind of divination. Literature was his chosen mistress, his first love and his last, in devotion to whom he never for a day relaxed. To her he gladly sacrificed wealth, power, social influence, all other idols;

and though, as he passed from youth to age, he saw the hollowness of most objects of human pursuit,— though friends grew cold, popular admiration grew fickle, illusion after illusion vanished, and hopes and trusts were swept away into the abyss,— *she* never lost her charms. To him she was ever, in the language of Chaucer,

"Ruddy, fresh, lively-hued,
And every day her beauty newéd";

and so she held him with cords which grew tighter and tighter with age, and which were relaxed only with death.

Charles Augustin Sainte-Beuve, a posthumous child, was born on the twenty-third day of December, 1804, at Boulogne-on-the-Sea, a town previously noted as the birthplace of but one other eminent man, Daunou. It is a noteworthy fact that his father was fifty-two years of age when he married, and that his mother was then past forty. A few weeks after the marriage the father died; but, though Sainte-Beuve never saw his face or heard his voice, he believed, contrary to the popular judgment in such cases, that he owed his distinctive traits to the father rather than to the mother who watched over him from infancy, and who lived with him to her eighty-sixth year. The elder Sainte-Beuve, a Commissioner of Taxes, was a man of cultivated tastes, and left a considerable number of books, some of which he had annotated on the margin with discrimination and taste. A copy of Riouffe's *Memoirs* has been preserved, which he had enriched with notes and reflections upon the Reign of Terror; for example, the following, which would hardly have been disavowed by his son: "Public repose and tranquillity cannot be the habitual state of societies: the drop too much always comes." These books the son read,—the more thoughtfully, no doubt, as they afforded the only communion possible with the one whom he most revered as the author of his being. Of this father, whose habits of reading and of minute annotation he seems to have inherited, he thus speaks in one of his poems:

"Mon père ainsi sentait. Si, né dans sa mort même,
Ma mémoire n'eut pas son image suprême,
Il m'a laissé du moins son âme et son esprit,
Et son goût tout entier a chaque marge écrit."

In the official documents of the government, his father is denominated *de* Sainte-Beuve; but as the noble prefix was never used by his mother, the son dispensed with it. Perhaps he thought, also, of the pleasantries of which the poet *de* Béranger was the subject. "Not being noble," he says, "I did not wish to give myself the air of being so." Sainte-Beuve's mother was the daughter of an Englishwoman who had married a French sailor; and English writers are fond of tracing to her the keen predilection which her son betrayed for Cowper, Crabbe, and the Lake poets whose style of verse he tried to reproduce in the French tongue. No doubt such a crossing of the blood has often a happy issue, as may be seen in Montalembert and G. H. Lewes. M. D'Haussonville, Sainte-Beuve's biographer, says that Madame Sainte-Beuve was known to many persons in Paris, who declare that she was a woman *d'esprit, de bon sens, et de tact*. There is more reason, we think, for believing that she was simply a plain, warm-hearted, affectionate creature, who was more anxious about her son's material than about his intellectual wants. "He is always without socks," was the good soul's exclamation to a female friend. As he grew up, his literary yearnings troubled her; the career of a man-of-letters she naturally regarded as insufficiently lucrative, and she never felt easy till he was elected Academician.

Finishing at fourteen his rudimentary studies at Boulogne, Sainte-Beuve begged his mother to send him for a better education to Paris. There he was put to board with M. Landry, a mathematician, philosopher, and freethinker, and dined at his table, often with men of learning and eminence. "I was treated," says Sainte-Beuve, "as a big boy, as a little man." Attending successively the colleges of Charlemagne and Bourbon, he carried off several historical and Latin prizes, and received also from the government a medal as an exceptional recompense, after which he studied medicine for nearly three years,— a circumstance to which, perhaps, may be traced his early leaning toward materialism. He began life, he tells us, as a pronounced adherent of the most advanced form of eighteenth century philosophy,— the philosophy of Tracy, Daunou, and Lamarck; "there," he says emphatically, "is my true ground" (*mon fonds véritable*). The spirit of this school may be judged from the apostrophe put by M. Octave Feuillet in one of his dramas into the mouth of one of its chiefs: "How should I help believing in the immortal soul? I have touched it with my finger." It was almost inevitable, as the biographer of our critic rightly concludes, that a disposition like Sainte-Beuve's should be warped by such pursuits. "One must have, indeed, the soul and the intellect singularly inclined to spiritualism, not to feel an involuntary trouble in presence of the mysterious phenomena that physiological science reveals to our researches. When we see palpitating under the dissecting knife the organs in which life appears to be concentrated, we must sometimes be tempted to forget that the principle and the source of life are elsewhere." Not the least happy of the many inimitable touches in the Prologue to the "Canterbury Tales," is the portraiture of the physician, of whom we are told that

"His study was little on the Bible."

We must not, however, interpret too literally Sainte-Beuve's language touching his beliefs at this plastic period. He was too *spirituelle* (not to say, too spiritual), too poetic, to adopt the hard, chilling doctrines of the materialistic school without a long mental struggle; and we find him, at this very time, in a letter to his schoolfellow, the abbe Barbe, recognizing God as "the source of all things."

We may trace to this period of Sainte-Beuve's medical studies not only his philosophical views, but also, perhaps, the germ and first conception of the method which he inaugurated in literary criticism. No writer, in his critical judgments, has shown a profounder interest in the mysterious influence of material phenomena upon mental phenomena,— no one has been at more pains to show the action of the temperament upon the mind, of the physical nature upon the moral,— than Sainte-Beuve. No doubt, says D'Haussonville, that at that period, as he leaned over the dissecting table, his adventurous thought often wandered over the shadowy limits which separate the visible from the invisible world. " Besides, was not criticism, as he finally understood and defined it, 'a true course of moral physiology'? Did he not dissect the dead, and even the living? No doubt, at that date, the principles of his future method were confusedly germinating in the mind which literary curiosity had already invaded. Often does the genius thus grow and strengthen in secret without the knowledge of its possessor, and the matured man is astonished one day to find himself reaping the fruits which his unconscious youth has sown for him."

Sainte-Beuve had scarcely begun the practice of medicine when a struggle arose in his mind between its claims and those of the Muses. His pecuniary resources were very limited, and he was compelled to watch closely his smallest expenditures. Some years later, when his earliest books had already been given to the world, he wrote to a college friend: "I shall go and see you some Sunday in March, when I shall have received the bill which falls due at that date, and when twenty francs, more or less, in my pocket, shall be of no consequence." Literature, he was well aware, is a good staff, but a bad crutch; and though the world of letters seemed a far more enchanting one than that of medicine and dry facts, it was not till after a sharp mental conflict that Apollo and the Nine triumphed over Hippocrates and Galen. Though he threw aside his surgeon's case, he never ceased to be grateful to the noble profession he had left for the direction it had given to his mental development. To it he attributed the philosophical spirit, the love of exactitude and of physiological reality, the good method which characterized his writings; and when, four years later, the Faculty was attacked in the Senate, he nobly stood up and defended it. In 1824 M. Dubois, the Professor under whom he had studied at the Collège Charlemagne, founded the *Globe*, which soon became the most powerful literary journal in France. It was the organ of the *Doctrinaires* in politics, and in literature of that powerful intellectual movement which signalized the last years of the Restoration, and which seemed to be working a revolution in French literature and French thought. Jouffroy, Remusat, Ampère, Mérimée, and De Broglie were among its contributors, besides the glorious trio of the Sorbonne, as Sainte-Beuve called them, Guizot, Cousin, and Villemain; and though the journal was taunted with moderatism by the extremists of the Romantic school, its articles were full of freshness and originality, and won the praise of Goethe. "The editors," said the sage of Weimar, "are men of the world, lively, clear-spirited, and bold to the very highest degree. They have a way of expressing disapprobation which is fine and courteous. Our German savants, on the contrary, always think it necessary immediately to hate a person, if they don't happen to agree with him." To this journal Sainte-Beuve was invited to contribute; and, after he had penned a number of short articles under the direction of Dubois, the latter said to him one day: "*Now* you know how to write, and you can go alone."

It was at this time that he made the acquaintance of Victor Hugo, then in the heyday of his youth and genius, battling brilliantly for fame. Calling one morning upon Sainte-Beuve, M. Dubois showed him two volumes of *Odes and Ballads*, which he desired him to review. "They are by that young barbarian, Victor Hugo," said he, "who has talent, and who, moreover, is interesting on account of his life and character." The criticism which Sainte-Beuve wrote was a favorable one, though dashed with some strictures on the extravagances of that "*enfant sublime*," as Chateaubriand styled him; and it led to an introduction to the rising author. Gradually the acquaintance ripened into intimacy, and Sainte-Beuve, with his usual facility, became an enthusiastic admirer of the doctrines of the Romantic school and of the genius of its chief. The principal merit of this school was that, like that of the Lake poets in England, it was essentially a protest against artifice and conventionalism in poetry; the fault of the reformers was that they framed canons and shibboleths of their own as narrow as those against which they declaimed. Ere many months Sainte-Beuve became a member of *Le Cenacle* (the Guest-Chamber), a kind of Mutual Admiration Society of poets, painters, and sculptors in Paris, who had, each of them, according to his own story, a masterpiece in preparation or conception, and all of them together a monopoly of French genius. Among these self-reliant spirits were Alfred de Musset, Alfred de Vigny, Lamartine, and the brothers Deschamps, who, meeting constantly at Victor Hugo's, recited their new verses, and cheered each other amid the storm of criticism by which they were assailed. By degrees their intimacy so deepened that they called each other by their christian names; and, at last, the tone of familiarity became so general and so catching, that, we are told, M. Hugo was obliged to issue a peremptory ukaze, to prevent his wife from being addressed as Adèle. Sainte-Beuve was especially smitten with her charms, and it was to this, in part, that, later in life, he attributed that treason against the principles of sound criticism into which he was betrayed when he applauded her husband's innovations in poetry.

It was under the influence of Victor Hugo and his school that Sainte-Beuve made his first formal contribution to literature,— a work on the French poetry of the Sixteenth Century. The object of this work was twofold,— to find ancestors for the Romantic school in the early French literature, *de dresser leur arbre généalogique*, and to rescue from oblivion the poetry of the pre-classical period, which that of the *Grand Siècle* had overshadowed. By choice extracts and felicitous criticism, Sainte-Beuve showed triumphantly that Molière, Racine, Corneille, Boileau, and their successors, did not represent the sum total of French poetry; that, as there were brave men "before Agamemnon," so there were fine singers before the age of Lewis the Fourteenth.

Among the oddities or perversities of human nature there is none more unaccountable than the disposition of men who have a decided genius for a certain line of labor, to fancy that they were born to distinguish themselves in some wholly different pursuit. Canova, when his sculpture was praised, was sure to fetch a painting that he had just daubed, and display it with a smile of paternal pride. Douglas Jerrold, the wit, wanted to write a treatise on natural philosophy; Liston, the comic actor, who could not wink without provoking laughter, believed that tragedy was his true *rôle*; Girardet valued his verses far above his pictures; and David mourned the waste of his life in painting, when he was a born diplomatist, and, in place of depicting Napoleon scaling the Alps, might have revolutionized the politics of two hemispheres. Who has forgotten the havoc which that giant of classic scholarship, Bentley, made, when he turned from his proper field of criticism, and laid his hand on *Paradise Lost?* Sainte-Beuve's good sense did not save him from a similar weakness. His maiden work was pronounced by the "Revue Française" a marvel of criticism; but had his friends congratulated him on having found his true vein, he would have smiled, it is said, as painfully as did Alfred de Vigny, when, at the time he was meditating a rivalry of Milton, some female admirers cried out in chorus, "Oh, give us more *Cinq Mars;* that is your line." Like many other young men of that time, Sainte-Beuve not only had a strong taste for poetry, but fully believed that he was born to achieve immortality in verse. Burning to enter the lists with his brilliant associates, he made his poetical *entrée* in 1829 with the "Life, Poems, and Thoughts of Joseph Delorme."

It is said that the author had become an admirer of Wordsworth, Crabbe, and Coleridge, and was ambitious to naturalize in the French language poetry of the same simplicity, truthfulness, and subdued passion, drawn from natural scenery and types of every-day life. There is some analogy, perhaps, between the psychological, subjective manner of Sainte-Beuve and that of the English bards; and it may be admitted that he succeeded, to some extent, in avoiding like them the old, worn-out, conventional diction and threadbare mythological allusions of poetry. But, beyond this, the resemblance fails. There is no affinity between the themes that inspire the Frenchman's song and those of the singer of Rydal Mount, whose boast is that

> "In common things that round us lie,
>   Some random truths he can impart;
> The harvest of a quiet eye,
>   That broods and sleeps on his own heart."

Between the healthy, soul-bracing sentiments of Wordsworth's men and women and the sickly day-dreams, the fainting fits and frenzies of the moody, wayward Joseph Delorme, who abjured his religion because science had frozen the genial current of his soul; who refused to marry because "his rather rude philanthropy dreaded to be permanently imprisoned in too contracted affections, *un égoisme à deux personnes*"; and who, at one time, shut himself up in a garret, to die like the fabled swan, and at another thought of drowning himself with a lantern around his neck,— there is a gulf as broad as the distance between the poles. Health, vigorous, buoyant, sunny-tempered health is the salient characteristic of Wordsworth's genius,— the health that springs from communion with Nature and Nature's God; with him the love of nature is "an appetite," and "haunts him like a passion"; he sees and feels that behind the forms, hues, and sounds of the universe, there is something more than meets the external senses; and hence the meanest objects become to him full of mystery, and he finds subjects for his song in such humble themes as a pebble rounded and polished by the brook,— an exiled shell still echoing the sound of its native ocean,— a thorn on a hill-side overgrown with lichens,— the notes of the cuckoo,— the shadows of the falling leaves, dancing amid the sunshine,— a wagon lumbering and creaking along the dusty highway,— even a meek ass, grazing upon the common, and shaking his passive ears at the oaths and blows of his tormentors. In place of themes like these, Sainte-Beuve gives us a series of pictures drawn from the artificial life of Paris. In place of that unapproachable ideality, that "breath and finer spirit of all knowledge," which, in the Ode to Immortality, marks the highest limit which the tide of poetry has reached in this century, we have a diluted mixture of Byronism and Wertherism, of Sterne and Rousseau, of mawkish sentiment and diseased fancy, — verse in almost every page of which there is a taint of melancholy, an exhalation of the sick-room and the grave.

Sainte-Beuve's best excuse is that the psychological condition which his poem reveals was the malady of the age. Joseph Delorme, his hero, was of the same family of persons whom Melancholy had marked for her own, as the Werthers, Renés, and other imaginary beings whom Byron had made so popular by his Childe Harold.

It was a time when, as a reviewer has said, "a diseased liver, a heart complaint, a hectic cough, or chronic dyspepsia, was mistaken by preternatural self-conceit for an infallible mark of genius, and morbid self-consciousness sought notoriety, in default of fame, at the first grave check or mortification, in suicide." It was at the height of this mania that two young Parisians, on the failure of a theatrical piece which they had composed, put an end to their lives by charcoal. The melodious wailings of Joseph Delorme were well received by the Parisian critics, but did not meet with a very sympathetic response from the people. It is true it was no new gospel which he had preached. Chateaubriand had labored hard to propagate the worship of weariness and satiety; but the French are too lively a race, too sunny and merry-hearted, to take pleasure in being unhappy. Tell an Englishman that he is miserable,— that life is an illusion, and pleasure a snare,— that the world is going to the dogs, and he with it,— and that he has provocation enough to commit suicide,— and he will grasp your hand and thank you. But Johnny Crapeau has never learned the "luxury of wo"; he has no relish for the gospel of despair; and when Guizot ridiculed the lugubrious Joseph Delorme as "a Werther turned Jacobin and sawbones," the witticism was received with a shout of laughter which rang through Paris.

Just one year after the Poems of Joseph Delorme, appeared "The Consolations," a collection of lyrical pieces, closely resembling the former in style, but in its sentiments absolutely opposed to it. In place of cold materialism, of doubt, despair, and mocking scepticism, we have now a species of religious mysticism, and a monotony of piety which reminds one of Hood's line about persons who think that they "are pious, when they are only bilious." Never did a poet undergo a more startling revolution of sentiments in a twelvemonth. Victor Hugo, we are told, was the high-priest of this conversion, though, at a later day, Sainte-Beuve gives the credit with minute particularity to Lamartine. It is Hugo who has led him "to the source of all consolation"; who has led him to see that "the other waters dry up, and that it is only on the border of the celestial Siloe that one can be permanently seated and refreshed." Nevertheless, there are some rather strange passages in this work whose moral is that there is no happiness, above or below, except in faith. "The Confessions," undoubtedly the best poem of one who was no poet, was warmly welcomed by Hugo and De Vigny, and won much praise from the public. "Listen to your genius, sir!" was the characteristic plaudit of Chateaubriand. "I have wept, who never weep," was the tribute of the sentimental Lamartine, whose cambric was always wet with tears. The religious tone of the work, however, was distasteful to many; Merimée laughed in his sleeve at the joke, as he considered it; and Béranger could barely pardon what he called "that rag of worship thrown over a deist's faith,"—adding, in a letter: "When you use the word Seigneur, you make me think of those old cardinals returning thanks to Jupiter and all the gods of Olympus for the election of a new Pope." In spite of these gibes, we may believe in Sainte-Beuve's sincerity, and that, if he had not, he at least thought he had, a religious visitation during "those six celestial months of his life," as he terms them, when he dashed off the "Consolations." The change he underwent was only one of the various moral transformations which he, who, chameleon-like, took his hue from his latest associates, and was constant only in his inconstancy, passed through until he reached the last sad stage of blank unbelief, in which he died.

That Sainte-Beuve was a skillful poetic artist, we cannot doubt. Gustave Planche, by no means a partial critic, commends in both of Sainte-Beuve's poems "the truthfulness of the pictures and the thoughts," and the admirable clearness and transparency of the style. But it requires a good deal more than delicacy of taste and justness of perception to make a poet; and because he lacks the divine spark, the God-given afflatus, the mysterious something which we can all feel better than we can define,— because he *possesses* his genius rather than is possessed *by* it, and we feel that his conceptions are elaborated, and not that

"Across his sea of mind
The thought comes streaming like a blazing ship
Upon a mighty wind,"—

we must pronounce these volumes, products though they are of an ingenious, highly-cultured, and thoughtful mind, failures as poems.

The same may be said of his next effort, "August Thoughts," in which the author, after another moral somersault, again finds himself disenchanted, cries "All is vanity," and sits at the feet of Werther and yearns for death. This volume, fortunately, proved a perfect failure, and killed his poetical activity, so far as publication was concerned, though he never ceased to nourish the slumbering flame, and, to his latest hour, felt immeasurably less pride in his criticisms than in his rhymed prose. One of his latest effusions was a reply to some lines of Alfred de Musset upon a sentiment in one of Sainte-Beuve's essays,—"Every man contains a dead poet in his soul." That a critic of such insight should thus have been unable, in his own case, to discriminate between a merely engrafted talent of poetry and the true gift,—between the dainty rhetorical effects of great ability and the products of that genius which throws out masses of molten ore, and works as if by magic,—is a signal example of the blinding effects of self-love. By his latest failure he seems to have reluctantly discovered, that, in the public estimation, criticism, and not poetry, was his calling, and henceforth we find him pursuing the former with undiverted aim.

In 1829 the *Revue de Paris* was founded, and Sainte-Beuve began writing those critical essays which are the proudest monument of his genius, and which have no parallel in literature. His first article was on Boileau, and is a fair specimen of the "literary portrait," the peculiar combination of biography and criticism in which he has no rival. In 1830 came the July Revolution which overthrew the old monarchy, and the young generation of writers breaking up into antagonistic sections, Sainte-Beuve went back to the *Globe*, which became the organ of the Saint-Simonists. In the ferment of new ideas, old friends became estranged, and personalities were indulged in, which, it was thought, could be atoned for only by blood. One of the results was a duel between Sainte-Beuve and Dubois, in which the latter was the challenger. When the parties arrived on the ground it was raining hard. After the preliminaries were arranged, the principals took their places, but Sainte-Beuve took his with his pistol in one hand, and his umbrella over him in the other. When the seconds protested, he replied, "I am willing to be killed, but I am *not* willing to be wet" (*Je veux bien être tué; mais mouillé, non*). After four harmless shots, the seconds, neither of whom was a Sir Lucius O'Trigger, decided, against the remonstrances of the principals, that their honor was vindicated. Though a contributor to the Saint-Simonian organ, Sainte-Beuve took no stock in the doctrines of the "moonstruck" sect. Ever greedy of new intellectual pasture, he attended their religious services out of curiosity merely, to see a strange and interesting spectacle; "I may have smelt at the bacon," he said, "but was not caught in the trap."

Goethe has somewhere said that there is no more enviable situation for a man to find himself in, than between a love that is ending and a love that is beginning. A quarterly-reviewer thinks that if this be true of intellectual attachments, Sainte-Beuve must have been one of the happiest of men. In less than a decade, besides exchanging infidelity for faith, he had changed sides and systems three or four times. He had been the admirer or sat at the feet of Hugo, Leroux, Carrel, and Chateaubriand, and now was about to find a new Gamaliel in a prophet of Catholicism. One of his excuses, says the same uncharitable reviewer, "was that the critic was not yet born in him; but, tested by consistency, the critic was never born in him; he never attained fixity of any kind, either of head or heart; never, at least, till that period of life when, like the old coquet, he might be compared to the weathercock, which became fixed only when it was rusty." By others, again, Sainte-Beuve has been characterized as a sort of literary Don Juan,—a soul constantly on the look-out to espouse some other soul, and then, as soon as the espousals were consummated, as constantly looking out for reasons for divorce. His literary idols, when once his enthusiasm had cooled, became to him, apparently, like those of Wordsworth's youth, "as dead as a theatre fresh emptied of spectators."

In illustration of this fickleness a story is told of the way in which he treated the portrait of a popular novelist. Sainte-Beuve having commended his first novel, the author, in the first gush of gratitude, rushed with his portrait to the critic's house, and presented the picture to him. The portrait was hung conspicuously in Sainte-Beuve's study. Presently a second novel appeared, inferior to the first, and the portrait was banished to the ground floor. A third novel appearing by the same author, the portrait went out of the house altogether, and migrated from one friend's house to another's, till it vanished into regions unknown. So the words of idolatry with which Alfred de Vigny was almost apotheosized in the "Consolations" strangely contrast with the qualified praise of later years. He who, in that work, was the *chantre-élu*, the *ange*, the *séraphin*, the *apôtre* of his time, sank in subsequent essays into a common mortal. The truth is, Sainte-Beuve was one of those ardent, eclectic, impressionable spirits that cannot associate long with any great mind, or set of minds, without sympathizing with them, yet is too universally sympathetic to hold the same sentiments long. He had a boundless curiosity, an unquenchable thirst for knowledge, an insatiable appetite for new intellectual sensations. Expressed opinions,— the critical judgments at which he arrived from time to time,— seemed to him not the grave matters of faith they are with most men, but only temporary statements, to be modified from time to time by fresh facts and revelations. It is easy to call this openness and catholicity of mind, this watchfulness for and readiness to receive new ideas, inconsistency; but the word means nothing. Sainte-Beuve contended that this mobility of mind was essential to the complete study of the conflicting systems which he successively embraced. He persuaded himself, his biographer tells us, that he could see more of the edifice from within than from without; and if, to gain admittance to the consecrated enclosure, it was necessary to put on the gown of the neophyte, *n'importe*,— he did so without scruples or hesitation. "The plan of the localities once drawn, he throws away the gown, which he always wore loosely, and will wear it no more." Emerson calls a foolish consistency "the hobgoblin of little minds"; and it is certain that unless a man is to have cast-iron opinions, the same in youth, maturity, and old age, he must perpetually alter and modify his views with the acquisition of new and conflicting facts. The human mind is like a tree: when it has lost the power of organic growth, it is already beginning to decay.

The ten years from 1830 to 1840 was a period of transformation in Sainte-Beuve's life, and it was not until after the latter period that his sentiments crystallized, and took that unchanging form of rationalism which was the creed of his last thirty years. Various as were the changes through which his mind had passed, it had not yet reached the point where it was self-reliant and self-centred. Comprehensive, subtle, flexible, and facile as it had shown itself to be, it had not yet learned to do without external supports. He still required some master-soul on which to lean; and this time it is at the feet of the fiery Lamennais that he will sit. What it was that attracted him toward the priest whose narrowness and bigotry were so opposed to his own breadth and tolerance, we cannot tell; but probably it was the fiery earnestness, the intensity of conviction, which he half-consciously felt to be his own chief need. The time when this intimacy was formed, was when Lamennais had returned from Rome after a vain attempt to ally Romanism and democracy, and when the deadly struggle was beginning in his breast between his political views and his faith in Papal infallibility. "One was never bound to Lamennais by halves," said Sainte-Beuve; and when, after weeks and months of gloomy and anxious meditation, the priest determined to raise the standard of revolt,

Sainte-Beuve was already so deep in his confidence that Lamennais entrusted to him the care of seeing "The Words of a Believer" through the press. He softened the asperity of some passages; but the full import of the volcanic pamphlet was not revealed to him till the printer brought him the proofs, saying: "My very compositors cannot set it up without being, as it were, elevated and transported; the printing office is all *en air*." It was a vehement diatribe against kingcraft and priestcraft; strong enough, says a writer, to satisfy the philosopher who longed for the day when the last king should be strangled with the entrails of the last priest. Sainte-Beuve now cut loose from the apostate champion of Catholicism, saying bitterly: "Nothing, be assured, is worse than to invite souls to the faith, and then leave them without warning in the lurch." Afterward in conversation he said: "Lamennais has upset the coach into the ditch; then he has planted us there after taking good care to blow out the lamp before he took to his heels."

In the limited space allowed us, we can but hurriedly glance at the remaining points of interest in Sainte-Beuve's life and character, and then shall proceed to notice his last, best writings, the *Causeries du Lundi*. In 1831 was founded the *Revue des Deux Mondes*, to which Sainte-Beuve contributed at intervals, for thirty-seven years, articles which were one of its chief attractions. About the same time appeared his only novel, *Volupté*, the supposed autobiography of a priest,— a man of sensual, voluptuous temperament, who, after having made conquest of three women, to all of whom he brought sorrow, joins a religious order, and dies in the odor of sanctity in America. The story is well told, but has too much psychology for a novel, and lacks plot, passion, and power. Amaury, the hero, has been compared to a showman who exposes his moral ulcers, and then descants upon them in pious language. The confession, strange to say, is made for the improvement of a young friend prone to the vice which gives the title to the book,— a kind of impure defense of impurity, which tempts us to say to the author, in the words of the Duke to Jaques in *As You Like It:*

"Fie on thee! I can tell what thou wouldst do,—
Most mischievous foul sin, in chiding sin."

Few men, says Pascal, speak humbly of humility, chastely of chastity, or doubtingly of doubt. In spite of its faults, the book has reached a seventh edition, and Eugénie de Guerin speaks of having read it with great interest, finding in it "charming details, delicious miniatures, and heart-truths." In the appendix the author publishes some testimonials from its admirers, which suggest the criticism of an American bank president upon a note offered for discount: "This note" (looking at the signature) "is bad enough; but" (turning it over), "with these *endorsements*, it is absolutely good for nothing."

In 1837, and again afterward, Sainte-Beuve declined a distinction dear to Frenchmen, the Cross of the Legion of Honor. In the fall of the same year he made a tour in Switzerland, and being invited to become an Extraordinary Professor in the Academy of Lausaune, he accepted, and delivered eighty-one lectures on Port-Royal, which formed the basis of his work on that subject, the last volume of which appeared in 1859. In this great work, which cost him twenty years of research, and which is remarkable alike for the delicate beauty of its style and the scrupulous exactness of its facts, he has told the story of that religious revival in the seventeenth century known as Jansenism, as Gibbon has told the story of Rome's Decline and Fall,— for all time. Though intrinsically the subject is somewhat dry and forbidding, giving no scope for brilliant and picturesque handling, yet no one can read this account of the Catholic Puritans whom Lewis XIV so dreaded and detested,— whose opinions he hated even more than deism or atheism,— and whose vain but heroic struggle shook the very pillars of the fabric of Roman supremacy,— without deep interest in the story, and profound admiration of the genius that could disentangle it from the perplexities in which it was involved. The third volume, on Pascal, is a masterpiece, which those who would see that wonderful writer dissected with the skill of a Velpeau,— laid bare in his whole intellectual and moral anatomy,— should not fail to study.

Till 1840 Sainte-Beuve had, to use Charles Lamb's phrase, sucked his sustenance as sick people do, through a quill; but in that year he was partially relieved from his dependence on his pen, by being appointed keeper of the Mazarin Library. Hitherto he had lived in the plainest and quietest way in two small rooms on the fourth floor of a house near the School of Medicine, paying for them and his breakfasts about five dollars a month. By "living like a hermit, and working like a horse," he had contrived to live independently, without prostituting his pen to any venal service; and it was his just pride that, however paltry his earnings, he had never borrowed a dollar. In 1848 a petty and false charge of corruption, which cut him to the quick, led him to resign his librarianship, and he accepted a professorship at the University of Liège. His departure, which took place in October, was treated by his enemies as a sign of guilt and fear; and one writer went so far as to declare that he had fled from Paris because he was scared out of his wits by the Revolution. The simple fact was that the political excitement of this year was unfavorable to letters in Paris, and Sainte-Beuve was compelled to exile himself for a season, in order to obtain a livelihood in the only calling that was congenial to his tastes. Of the Revolution of the twenty-fourth of February he thus wrote in his note-book:

"What events! what a dream! I was prepared for much, but not so soon, nor for this. . . . I am tempted to believe in the nullity of every judgment, my own in particular — I who make it a business to judge others, and am so short-sighted. . . . The future will disclose what no one can foresee. There is no use in talking of ordinary wisdom and prudence: they have been utterly at fault. Guizot, the historian philosopher, has turned out more stupid than a Polignac: Utopia and the poet's dream, on the contrary, have become facts and reality. I forgive Lamartine everything: he has been great during these days, and done honor to the poetic nature."

At a later day he changes his tone, and thus playfully satirizes "the good provisional government, which did so many things, and left so many undone":

"The fortunes of France crumbled to pieces in a fortnight, but it was under the invocation of equality and fraternity. As to liberty, it only existed for madmen, and the wise took good care to make no use of it. 'The great folk are terribly scared,' said my portress, but the small fry triumphed: it was their turn. So much had never been said about work before, and so little was never done. People walked about all day, planted liberty-trees at every street-corner, illuminated willy-nilly, and perorated in the clubs and squares until midnight. The Exchange rang with disasters in the morning: in the evening it sparkled with lanterns and fireworks. It was the gayest anarchy for the lower classes of Paris, who had no police and looked after themselves. The street-boys ran about with flags; workmen without work, but paid nevertheless, walked in perpetual procession; the demireps had kicked over the traces, and on the sidewalks the most virtuous fellow-citizenesses were hugged without ceremony: it must be added that they did not resent it too much. The grisettes, having nothing to eat, gave themselves away for nothing or next to nothing, as during the Fronde. The chorus of the Girondists was sung on every open lot, and there was a feast of addresses. Lamartine wrought marvels such as Ulysses might have done, and he was the siren of the hour. Yet they laughed and joked, and the true French wit revived. There was general good humor and amiability in those first days of a most licentious spring sunshine. There was an admixture of bad taste, as there always is in the people of Paris when they grow sentimental. They made grotesque little gardens around the liberty-trees, which they watered assiduously. . . . The small fry adored their provisional government, as they formerly did their good king Louis XII, and more than one simple person said with emotion, 'It must be admitted that we are well governed, *they talk so well!*' "*

Hardly three months had elapsed before the provisional government fell to pieces, an event which Sainte-Beuve thus pungently characterizes:

"The politicians of late years have been playing a game of chess, intent wholly upon the board, but never giving a thought

* "Les Cahiers de Sainte-Beuve."

to the table under the board. But the table was alive, the back of a people which began to move, and in the twinkling of an eye chessboard and men went to the devil."

At Liège Sainte-Beuve gave a special course of lectures on Chateaubriand,— since published in two volumes,— a masterpiece of literary criticism, in which the foibles and inconsistencies of the great egotist who began every other sentence with the personal pronoun I, and whose Memoirs, as George Sand said, are full of *grandes poses et de draperies*, are exposed with merciless skill. The real merits of the flattered writer were still acknowledged; but into the weak parts of his artistic and moral nature the probe was thrust to the very handle. That this literary divinity, before whom so much incense had been burned, should now snuff *frank*-incense,— above all, that Sainte-Beuve, whose praise had once been so enthusiastic, should now dare to pronounce the old idol a false god,— was thought by many a gross outrage. A great outcry was raised against the iconoclast by the critics, and there was no end of the ugly names by which he was called. His defense was that when he praised Chateaubriand so fervidly, he was yet in his youth, and was influenced by the charms of Madame Recamier, in whose *salon* he had heard a part of the "Memoirs" read; whereas now he had become older and wiser, and judged the work in his study without the illusion of wax-lights and flowers, and uninfluenced by the *beaux esprits*, the *crème de la crème* of society, which used to gather about her. The simple fact was, that Sainte-Beuve did not know the whole truth about the veteran man-of-letters until the entire seven volumes of his "Memoirs" were published; and that the critic's inconsistency was merely a sign of his fresh knowledge, and a determination to tell the truth without fear or favor.

In 1850 Sainte-Beuve returned from Belgium to Paris. The next year came the *coup d'état*, and he gave in his adhesion to Napoleon III. The year after he was appointed Professor of Latin at the College of France; but, when he attempted to lecture, was hissed by the students from the hall. The cause of this explosion was an article contributed by Sainte-Beuve to the "Constitutionnel," in which, with the adroitest and most subtle satire, he rallied the disaffected politicians of the day for their opposition to the government. With exquisite mock-gravity he put on his old physician's cap, and made a diagnosis of the political diseases of the time, which he characterized as *le mal du pouvoir perdu, et le mal de la parole perdue*. In conclusion, he says: "For myself, I can have no great pity for people whom no other misfortune has befallen than that of no longer governing me" (*de ne me plus gouverner*). In 1865 he was made Senator of France, in which capacity he distinguished himself by his independence of the appointing Imperial power,— especially by his championship of religious liberty. His defense of Renan, in particular, won back the friends whom he had estranged; and when a deputation from the schools of Paris waited on him and testified their admiration, he was probably one of the most popular literary men of France.

The year 1840 may be termed the turning-point in

Sainte-Beuve's life. Up to that time his judgment had been taken captive by many enthusiasms, and in the hot blood of youth he had become again and again impassioned for ideas which he afterward learned to regard with indifference. His writings thus far had shown that the critical faculty in him was far stronger than the creative; and, at the age of thirty-six, it triumphed over all the other faculties, and he gave himself up to that calling for which Nature had preëminently qualified him. Between 1840 and 1845 appeared his "Literary Portraits" and his "Portraits of Contemporaries," which made his name famous in France, and won for him a place in the Academy, in spite of the opposition of Victor Hugo, who voted against him eleven times. After his return from Belgium to Paris in 1850, he was hesitating about what to do, when De Véron, the editor of the "Constitutionnel," invited him to write a series of weekly literary articles for that journal. At first, the proposal both flattered and frightened him. The "Constitutionnel" numbered its readers by thousands, and how was he, accustomed to the leisurely style of reviews, to talk to such a public,— so many-headed and so various,— of pure literature and criticism? How, especially, was he to interest it in such topics in "those times of political preoccupation and tempest?"

Dr. Véron overcame these objections,— his offer was accepted, and the result was a series of masterly literary portraits, full of grace and fascination, which have no parallel in the literature of the world. What literary man among us has forgotten how they electrified the *blasé* public? What reader of French literature does not recall with a thrill of pleasure tingling through every nerve, the first half-dozen volumes that blazed on us twenty-four years ago? How joyfully we paid down the price for them, as we pounced upon them at the bookstore; or, if another had got the start of us, how we begged, borrowed, or snatched them from the lucky possessor! How we read, and wondered, and felt as if borne along on a sparkling torrent! What a breadth, depth, and minuteness of knowledge,— what a freshness of treatment of old topics,— what sagacity and penetration,— what a command of illustration,— what a familiarity with foreign literatures,— and all the facts and thoughts conveyed in a style so delicate, so brilliant, so even, so strong; touching all themes, not with the blacksmith's hand of iron, but with the surgeon's hand of steel! It is said to be a characteristic of genius to clothe with fresh interest the well-picked bones of a subject; tried by this test, Sainte-Beuve must rank among the Soyers and Savarins of letters. Nothing could be more hackneyed than many of his themes, out of which, apparently, the last drop of interest had been squeezed years ago; yet, in his hands, though drained to the very dregs, they receive a redintegration of essence hardly less miraculous than the conversion of dry bones into living beings.

It was now that the insatiable and restless curiosity of Sainte-Beuve, that tendency to successive enthusiasms and successive repentances, which had been in some degree a source of weakness to him, proved, along with his inexhaustible love of letters, a source of strength. The very exigencies of the press,— the clatter of the engine and the cry of the printer's devil,— the hurry and severe compression from an instant summons that brooked no delay, — had a tendency to improve his style. They proved the flint and steel for eliciting sudden scintillations of originality,— displayed at one time in the picturesque felicity of the phrase, at another in the thought or its illustration. Indeed, both M. Guizot and M. Littré said of the "Causeries" that "they were so much the better that he had not had time to spoil them." His manner, hitherto artificial, oblique, and discursive, is now rapid, direct, and decisive. He is no longer open to the charge of Balzac, that he wrote not French, but rather a new language which might properly be called Sainte-Beuve. He no longer coquets with his themes, but looks them full in the face, and pronounces his literary judgments with the positiveness of deep conviction and the fearlessness of conscious strength. We feel that we are in the hands of a master of his art, while the minute biographic details, the literary allusion, and the historic anecdote invest it with an indescribable charm. The style is so easy and natural that we feel, as we read, that it would be easy to write such essays ourselves; and yet nothing is more certain than that to reproduce their charm would be as hopeless as an attempt to reproduce the delicious egotism of Montaigne, the subtle grace of La Fontaine, the vivacity, wit, and sparkle of Voltaire, or the sly, tickling, temeritous humor of Charles Lamb.

It must not be supposed that, because these papers of

Sainte-Beuve were produced rapidly, they therefore cost but little toil. Alluding to the labor demanded for them, the author said: "I descend on Tuesday into a well, from which I emerge only on Sunday." M. Schérer, his best critic, truly says that they were issued from a Benedictine's cell. When we reflect on the prodigious amount of reading and observation which are condensed into one of these brief papers, we are surprised that Sainte-Beuve was able to complete one of them in the five days of the week in which he was shut up at the forge, and almost invisible even to his most intimate friends. Think what an enormous amount of toil,— what an expenditure of investigation and thought,— is implied in the successful prosecution of such a task for twenty or thirty years! The "Causeries du Lundi" were begun in the "Constitutionnel," and continued in the "Moniteur," from 1849 to 1869,— making, with the "Nouveaux Lundis," and the "Portraits Littéraires" and "Portraits Contemporains," previously written, more than forty volumes of literary, historical, and biographical essays, on the most extraordinary variety of subjects, and all executed with the most conscientious care and accuracy, so as to be as perfect as the author's time and space would permit.

It is easy to write an average literary criticism,— especially of the fulsome, laudatory, or savage, cut-and-thrust kind, which we find in many American journals. For such a purpose, little preparation is required; you have only to cut the leaves of the book to be reviewed, and then smell of the paper-knife. But to discuss the most various and heterogeneous themes with never-failing originality, accuracy, and knowledge,— to give proofs on every page of careful, painstaking research, study, and thought,— to penetrate to the core of every author, and pluck out "the heart of his mystery,"— to live with him in his times, to feel with his feelings, and think his thoughts,— in short, to be completely *en rapport* with him,— above all, to give the results in a style of exquisite clearness, terseness, and beauty,— and, again, to do all this for more than twenty years,— is a task which would seem to require, not one pair of brains and one pair of hands, but the brains and hands of an Academy. The topics of Sainte-Beuve, gathered from the whole realm of literature, seem to be almost expressly chosen to show how vast is his comprehension, and how wide the range of his sympathies. Men and women, orators and philosophers, poets and prose-writers, statesmen and generals, wits and beauties, politicians and economists, freethinkers and theologians, Catholics and Protestants, all in turn flit across his magic page, and in an instant are vividly and accurately photographed.

Nothing is more surprising than this perpetual antithesis in Sainte-Beuve's themes; the delight with which, consciously or unconsciously, he brings into juxtaposition the most incongruous personages. In his page Bayle fraternizes with Pascal, Racine hobnobs with Hugo. On one Monday you listen to the sparkling wit of Voltaire, on another to the grave and weighty wisdom of Guizot. Now you are treated to the terse and exquisite sense of Joubert, and anon to the lachrymose confessions of the Narcissus of France,— the disenchanted, used-up, and self-admiring Lamartine. This week Mirabeau is brought before you with his voice of thunder, his lofty port, and lion-like mane of hair; the next, you are tasting the quintessence of Chamfort's sparkling wit, or listening to the rasping repartees of Madame du Deffand. At one time you are hearkening with delight to the chirrup, now gay and mocking, now sad and tender, of Béranger; at another, you are quailing at the scream of "the eagle of Meaux." To-day, Montaigne charms you with his gossipy self-revelations and shrewd, racy remark; to-morrow you listen to the despotic accent of Napoleon, the resonant, silvery voice of Montalembert, or the musical tones of Fenelon. Sainte-Beuve, seems, in short, to have taken his motto from Horace,—

"Nullius addictus jurare in verba magistri,
Quocunque me rapit tempestas, deferor hospes,"

and he is equally at home with persons of the most opposite schools,— with Renan and Bonald, Comte and Cousin, Chateaubriand and Corneille, Littré and Lacordaire. He can appreciate alike the cold, classic elegance of Boileau, and the fiery fervor of Alfred de Musset; he can relish the worldly wisdom of Chesterfield, in spite of his "morals of a harlot and manners of a dancing-master," and keenly enjoy the epigrammatic point, the chiselled fineness, and statuesque relief of De Maistre's inimitable style, notwithstanding his dogmatism, and though, in his ultramontane zeal, he gives to truth itself the air of paradox and the accent of defiance. Nor is this eagle-eyed critic content to limit his range to the fields of French literature and history; he makes less frequent, but not rare flights into the regions of foreign and of ancient history and poetry. Of this we have examples in his brilliant papers on Cowper, Pope, Gibbon, Goethe, Grimm, Frederic the Great, Franklin, Dante, Galiani, Firdousi, Theocritus, Virgil, and Pliny.

Though the busiest of workers, Sainte-Beuve fully recognized the importance of idleness. He knew perfectly well that all of our best knowledge is acquired in hours which unresting plodders consider lost,— that, as Claude Tillier says, "*Le temps le mieux employé est celui que l'on perd.*" He was well aware that the petty cares, the minute anxieties, the microscopic distractions, the infinite littles which go to make up the sum of human experience, are all helps as well as hindrances to a writer, and like the invisible granules of powder, give the highest polish to character. "I have arrived," he says, "perhaps by way of secretly excusing my own idleness, perhaps by a deeper feeling of the principle that all comes to the same, at the conclusion that whatever I do or do not, working in the study at continuous labor, scattering myself in articles, spreading myself about in society, giving my time away to troublesome callers, to poor people, to *rendezvous*, in the street, no matter to whom or to what, I cease not to do one and the same thing, to read one and the same book, the infinite book of the world and of life, that no one ever finishes, in which the wisest read farthest; I read it then at all the pages which present themselves, in broken fragments, backward, what matters it? I never cease going on. The greater the medley, the more frequent the interruption, the more I get on with this book in which one is never beyond the middle; but the profit is to have had it open before one at all sorts of different pages."

The uniform excellence of Sainte-Beuve's criticisms would be unaccountable, considering their marvellous number and variety, could we not lift the curtain of his study, and see the artist at work. It is doubtful if a critic ever lived who had a loftier ideal, and a profounder horror of the *à peu près*. He never began to write upon any subject until he had fully cleared the ground before him. He ventured no opinion of a book or its author till he had *bottomed* them. Though gifted with an extraordinary aptitude for collecting precisely the kind of material that he needed, as well as for arranging and classifying it, and for perceiving its mutual relations, he devoted to the preparation of one of his "Lundis" the six working-days of a laborious week. Assisted by an intelligent secretary, he began every Monday morning to prepare the article of the coming Monday. During the first three days, his secretary was busy in collecting all books and documents discoverable concerning the matter in hand, and in reading and commenting on them in company with the critic. Meanwhile a rough outline of the article had been dictated, Sainte-Beuve filling in blanks, and making additions with his own hand. On the fourth day Sainte-Beuve ruminated on the article already planned in his brain; and thus on Friday, when he began its actual composition, "his mind had already been disciplined into a state of the most complete readiness, like the fingers of a musician who has been practicing a piece before he executes it in public." On the fifth day the "Lundi" was carefully written, copied, and revised, and sometimes written again. In this way he labored for twelve hours daily, refusing to receive visitors, or to be interrupted in any way, and taking no relaxation till evening. On Saturday the manuscript was ready for the printer, and Sainte-Beuve took it to the office of the "Constitutionnel," and read it to Véron, the editor, who, though not a man of genius, had an instinctive perception of what was likely to please the public. After listening to Véron's suggestions, the author had the article put in type; another revision was then made as minute and searching as the first, and the essay was at last ready for publication. When it finally appeared, the accuracy and aptness of every quotation, and the correctness of every name and date, were as remarkable as the artistic finish and consummate effect of the whole. One of the very latest "Lundis" was a paper on "Jomini," displaying not only the usual acuteness of the critic, but a surprising mastery of the technical difficulties of the theme.

But what, it will be asked, was the secret of Sainte-Beuve's rare excellence as a critic,— what were his qualifications, and what was his method? First, that he was a man of great originality and power, with a rare and strongly marked individuality, is evident at a glance. What were the distinctive traits of this individuality, it is exceedingly difficult to say. We read, and are fascinated by, his books; we analyze his poems, his history, his novel, and his criticisms; we learn, in some degree, the secrets of his art and his processes; but of the man himself, in his essence, in his inmost being, we know almost nothing. The keenest analyst of others, he himself defies analysis. Belonging to no sect or party, political, social, or religious,— having no *assiette*, no *point d'appui*,— he refuses to be classified, ticketed, or labelled; to go into any of our pigeon-holes. "We set our formulas for him like traps," says one of his reviewers, "but he is too wary to be caught in any of them." He eludes all our detective methods, and puzzles and perplexes us like another Proteus.

A circumstance which increases the difficulty of defining and appraising this literary appraiser is the paradoxes in his intellectual and moral character. Among these was "a respect for tradition amounting to reverence, and a readiness to welcome novelties akin to a passion." Profoundly venerating truths hallowed by time, he hailed with joy every new discovery, and bade farewell without pain to the most cherished illusion. Especially did he abhor all cast-iron rules and precedents, all fixed formulas which interfere with the most perfect freedom of judgment. "The time," he declared, "was past for pronouncing decisions in the mere name of literary tradition." It was this dislike of fixity of opinion, of intellectual immobility, which, in part, led him to leave the "Romantic" school of poets, to which he had, early in life, given in his adhesion. His so-called "treachery" to that alliance was owing partly to a perception of their extravagances, and partly to a perception of the fact that to establish schools in literature, to wear their badges and to repeat their watchwords, tends to fetter the judgment and to limit one's intellectual freedom.

In one of his essays he quotes with warm approval a passage from Eckermann's Conversations with Goethe on this point: "What," asks Goethe, "does all this fuss about *classic* and *romantic* mean? All that is necessary is to produce works that are truly good and solid, and they are sure to become classic." So thought Sainte-Beuve; to make a work classic, it was enough, he believed, that it was good,— that it was true to nature and to art, and a genuine contribution to human thought. In a paper entitled "What is a Classic?" he says: "A true classic is an author who has done something to enrich the human mind; who has really added to its wealth; who has caused it to take another step forward; who has discovered some incontestable moral truth, or caught sight in the human heart, where everything seemed known and explored, of some unrecognized but eternal human passion; who has expressed his thought, his observation, or his discovery, in some form, no matter what, which is at once large and grand, delicate and judicious, healthy and charming; who has addressed everybody in a style of his own, which is yet the style of everybody,— a style at once new and antique, and which may readily be current in all ages."

As a critic, Sainte-Beuve was impartial to a fault. It is safe to say there never was a literary judge who was more indefatigable in collecting the materials for his decisions, or who tried more earnestly to keep his mind from all bias, and from every influence which could interfere, in the slightest degree, with the clearness, vividness, and truthfulness of its impressions. His jealousy of himself was carried, at times, to an almost ridiculous extreme. So keenly was he sensible, and so morbidly fearful, of the influence of friendship upon one's opinions, that he sacrificed, it is said, some of his pleasantest intimacies to his love of impartiality. He also, late in life, avoided forming new ties that might possibly hamper his freedom of speech. Not less was he on his guard against any bias arising from personal predilections and prejudices,— from the secret leanings which, it has been said, "haunt every man as his shadow," and warp the mind from absolute straightforwardness and rectitude. Especially strong was his aversion to all metaphysical systems which profess to unfold the essential laws of being and the true idea of the universe. They seemed to him as only so many prison-houses of the human spirit. In striking contrast to the famous maxim of Goethe, he declared that he would willingly take "the *true*, the true only," as his device, leaving "the good and the beautiful" to take care of themselves. To ascertain this truth, he was never weary of re-opening and reëxamining a subject, of studying it in every possible light, and of testing his very latest and most laboriously obtained conclusions by a fresh analysis. He hated ever to admit that the last word had been spoken, that the pleadings were closed, and that the cause was ripe for judgment. "Criticism," he once wrote, "is an *invention*, a perpetual *creation*. One needs to renew, to repeat continually his observation and study of men, even of those he knows best and has portrayed; otherwise he runs the risk of partially forgetting them, and of forming imaginary ideas of them while remembering them. No one has a right to say, '*I understand men.*' All that one can truly say, is, '*I am in a fair way to understand them.*'"

Sainte-Beuve was never ready to tie up his bundle of opinions on any subject, and to lay it away on the shelf, labelled "complete." He believed in keeping all the windows of the mind open, and letting the winds of knowledge blow through all its apartments. Nothing, therefore, was more offensive to him than dogmatism,— an assumption of infallibility of any kind, whether literary or philosophical, papal or protestant. Opinions, however well-grounded in appearance, he looked upon as only "provisional statements,— as formulas, convenient enough, but only proximately correct, for the expression of facts which, in their essence, or in their absolute character, the mind is incapable of grasping." Beginning life, he tells us, as a full-blooded believer of the most advanced form of eighteenth century thought,— passing through the psychological and *doctrinaire* school of the *Globe*,— surrendering himself next to poetical romanticism and the world of Victor Hugo, where he seemed for a time to be engulfed,— coasting the shores of Saint-Simonism and the society of Lamennais,— skirting, not very joyfully, the confines of Methodism and Calvinism (*j'ai dû m'efforcer à l'intéresser*),— he never, he tells us, in this long circuit, gave in his full adhesion to any of these schools; he never gave up his judgment or his will (save momentarily, and by the effect of a charm, to Victor Hugo); he never pledged his belief; but simply gratified his curiosity. It was this curiosity, he adds, the extreme delight he always took in discovering the relative truth of everything and of every system, that led him on in this series of experiments, and it was to him only "a long course of moral physiology."

In all this we have a revelation, at once, both of Sainte-Beuve's strength and of his weakness. "*Rien d'absolu, et une expérience toujours remise en question,*"* is a good motto for a philosopher, if not construed too literally. There is no surer mark of a well-balanced mind than self-distrust,—a dislike for positivism in matters where there can be no positive knowledge,—a horror of absolute conclusions, where only partial data have been obtained, and a complete generalization is impossible. "A wise questioning is, indeed," as one has said, "the half of knowledge"; "a life without cross-examination is no life at all." But "*toute perfection,*" as Voltaire says, "*est près d'une defaut*"; and this philosophic caution, so commendable in moderation, becomes in its excess a glaring defect. Conclusions *have* to be drawn sometimes, if we would be of any service in the world; and it is better now and then to draw them illogically, or from scanty data, than to have no settled convictions. There is a medium between Hildebrand and Hobbes; to avoid being a pope, it is not necessary to be a pyrrhonist. The man who, like Dr. Arnold of Rugby, wakes up every morning with the feeling that nothing is settled,—who like Lord Eldon, cannot admit that two and two make four without shedding tears, or expressing

* See the "Monday-Chat" on Guizot, p. 222.

some doubt or scruple,— may be eminently honest and impartial; but he must lack the most potent of all stimuli to intellectual exertion. Lessing once said: "Did the Almighty, holding Truth in his right hand, and Search-after-Truth in his left, deign to tender me the one I might prefer, in all humility, but without hesitation, I should request Search-after-Truth." But what if the Almighty, with the Search-after-Truth, were to give Lessing an assurance that he would never find Truth,— that it would forever elude his search, being absolutely undiscoverable? Would he *then* enjoy the pursuit,— forever beating the bush, and never catching the bird?

Again, the man who has a morbid aversion to conclusions,— who constantly withholds his decision of practical questions,— is in danger of forming a habit of overlooking the chief value of the facts which come under his notice; and he is lucky if he does not sink into a condition like that of David Hume, in which he amuses himself with his ideas with the indifference of a sultan for his slaves, feeling confident of nothing, yet at the same time distrusting his scepticism, and constantly doubting whether he ought to doubt of that of which he has doubted. One of Sainte-Beuve's keenest and kindliest critics has confessed that here he was at fault. "A little more frankness, a little more trust by Sainte-Beuve in his own instinctive convictions, a little more confidence in his readers and in mankind in general, a little more willingness to take the ordinary risks of authorship in the enunciation of opinions," the critic thinks, and thinks truly, "would have given to his writings a healthier tone and a heartier ring."

Another secret of Sainte-Beuve's excellence as a critic, and, indeed, his principal charm, lies in the psychological method which he introduced. In adopting this method, he was doubtless influenced by his physiological and other scientific studies. Though keenly sensitive to the beauties of style, he yet regarded a book not so much as a product of art, as the writer's mental offspring, as a photograph of the author, a portraiture of his mind and character. The human aspect of the work was of more importance than its cunning workmanship. It was "the precious life-blood of a master-spirit," its "purest efficacy and extract," a kind of incarnation of the author's soul; and hence it was to be judged, not so much with reference to the skill displayed in its execution, as to the intellectual and spiritual life that breathed through it, and the creative ideas that gave it birth. Hence, beyond any other critic, Sainte-Beuve attached peculiar importance to biographical details. While he surpassed all his contemporaries in the difficult art of reproducing the contents of a work of genius, giving, as he often did, the quintessence of a bulky volume in twenty or thirty pages, and reporting the author's exact intellectual stature, he was not content with this; but ascended from the stream to the fountain, detected the spirit of the writer in the coloring of his work, analyzed his genius from its development in words, and from the unconscious self-revelations of the author drew a portrait of the man.

Hence all Sainte-Beuve's criticisms are not merely

studies in literature, but also studies in character. There were not wanting persons, however, who objected to this method; its author, they said, had a good deal of natural taste, but no fixed principles; "Sainte-Beuve was a very good judge, but he had no code." In demurring to this disqualification, Sainte-Beuve was at pains to set forth in several "Causeries" the theory upon which he proceeded. "Literature," he says, "the act of literary production, has never seemed to me distinct from, or at least separable from, the rest of the man and his whole organization. I may relish a work, but it is difficult for me to judge it independently of a knowledge of the man himself; I should be inclined to say, 'As is the tree, so will be the fruit.' The study of literature thus leads me quite naturally to the study of character." He then adds that it is very useful to begin at the beginning, and, when possible, to take into account the author's birthplace and his race. If we know his *race* thoroughly in its physiological character and historical development, we shall have a great deal of light thrown upon the secret and essential quality of the minds formed by it. But most frequently this deep root eludes our research. The great man will be recognized and recovered, to a certainty, in his parents, and especially in his mother, his most direct and certain parent, — also, in his sisters, in his brothers, even in his children. We discover in these relatives some essential lineaments of character which, in the great man himself, are often masked through extreme concentration, or too intimate union with other qualities. The elements of the

man are exhibited in his kindred with less concealment
and less disguise; we profit by an analysis which nature
alone has been at the pains of making.

Take sisters, for example. "This Chateaubriand, of
whom we were speaking," says Sainte-Beuve, "had a sister
who had a certain degree of imagination based on stupidity (*bêtise*), a combination which must have approached to
downright extravagance. Then he had another sister,
who was altogether divine (Lucile, the Amelia of René).
She was endowed with an exquisite sensibility, a kind of
tender melancholy imagination without anything to correct or divert it; she died by her own hand in a fit of
madness. The elements which *he* united and associated,
at least in his talent, were distinctly and disproportionately shared between *them*." Sainte-Beuve adds that he
was not acquainted with the sisters of Lamartine, but he
remembered hearing Royer-Collard speak of them in their
early youth as something charming and melodious, like
"a nest of nightingales." Again, the sister of Beaumarchais had all his humor, wit, and sense of fun, which
she pushed to the extreme limit of propriety, when she
did not go beyond it. "She was the very sister of Fi-
garo, the same stock, and the same sap!"

The next essential point to consider touching the great
author, after the chapter of his studies and his education,
is the first group of friends and contemporaries among
whom he was cast at the moment when his talent unfolded, when it "filled out," so to speak, and assumed its
manhood. These early associations give it an impress
which it never loses, whatever may be its future develop-

ment. By "group" Sainte-Beuve means, not a fortuitous and artificial assemblage of able men, whose aims are the same, but a natural and spontaneous association of young spirits and young talents, not precisely alike or of the same family, but born under the same influence and launched upon the world together; united, in spite of a wide diversity of tastes and vocations, by the feeling of having one work in common to accomplish. Such was the little society of Boileau, La Fontaine, Racine, and Molière, at the opening of the *grand siècle;* such the reunion of Chateaubriand, Fontanes, and Joubert, in the beginning of the Nineteenth Century; such the group of young students and poets at Göttingen, who, in 1770, published between them the "Almanach des Muses,"— Burger, Voss, Kelty, Stolberg, and others; and such the critical circle at Edinburgh, of which Jeffrey was the chief, and from which sprang the famous review.

Sainte-Beuve emphasizes with great earnestness the importance of studying an author in the early stages of his career, his first flight. "There is nothing," he says, "like surprising 'a talent' in its first fire, its first gush,— to breathe it in its morning freshness and early bloom . . . before any acquired or artificial qualities have impaired its originality. There is also a second period, not less decisive, which must be marked, if we would understand the entire man; it is the period when he begins to deteriorate, to decline, to go astray." Again, "it will greatly help us to judge of the reach and elevation of a writer's talent, to observe whom he chooses as his antagonist and rival in early life. The one is the measure of the other; Calpe is equal to Abyla."

Finally, Sainte-Beuve declares that it is impossible to try too many ways to become acquainted with a man. As long as you have not asked yourselves a certain number of questions about an author, and answered them satisfactorily,—if only for your private benefit and *sotto voce*,—you cannot be sure of possessing him entirely. And this is true, though these questions may seem to be altogether foreign to the nature of his writings. For example, what were his religious views? How did the sight of nature affect him? What was he in his dealings with women, and in his feelings about money? Was he rich? Was he poor? What was his regimen? What his daily manner of life? Finally, what was his besetting vice or weakness? for every man has one. There is not one of these questions that is without its value in judging an author or his book, unless it is a treatise on mathematics; and they are especially important if it is a work of pure literature, into which some of the writer's whole nature has entered. The critic who neglects them runs the risk of inventing false beauties and being one-sided in his admiration,—a result which is inevitable when he judges merely as a rhetorician.

All these points are vividly put, striking, and suggestive; and if Sainte-Beuve thus severely catechises *himself* every time he estimates an author, we can partially account for the surprising insight he displays. His method, let us add, is essentially different from that of M. Taine, with which it is liable to be confounded. It is less physiological and less fatalistic; less physiological, because the facts of climate, race, and temperament supply to Sainte-Beuve in his study of an author only one of the data for the solution of the problem, whilst in the judgment of M. Taine they contain the solution of the entire problem; less fatalistic, because after giving the fullest importance to these factors, Sainte-Beuve still, in his final solution, attaches great significance to "what one calls liberty, which supposes in every case a great variety of possible combinations," while M. Taine regards the individual as resulting inevitably from all the elements in question, united as in a chemical combination. But even Sainte-Beuve's method, immeasurably superior as it is to the old, conventional modes of criticism, has its objections. What right, it may be asked, have we, in estimating a book, to go beyond the book itself,—to travel "out of the record," and to consider the character of the writer,—still more that of his parents, grandparents, uncles, aunts, and cousins? Are we obliged to find melodious versification in John Smith's poem, because his sisters sang like nightingales; or wit in Peter Snooks's comedy, because he had a witty sister? Or, conversely, shall we say that an author has no genius because his mother or great-grandmother was a fool? Does it help me to estimate Emerson's lofty platonism or the moonlight chastity of his style, to know that he is descended from Baron Bulkeley, down through six hundred years, and that his ancestors for two centuries were ministers of the gospel?

What matters it, if a book charms, inspires, or instructs us, whether the author smoked or drank stimulants; or borrowed money, or forgot to pay his tailor and his washerwoman; whether he quarrelled with his wife, like Milton, Coleridge, and Shelley,— separated from his wife, like Landor, Bolingbroke, and Bulwer,— was divorced from his wife, like Byron,— or, like Pope, Hume, Gibbon, Lamb, and Macaulay, kept out of the matrimonial noose altogether? To know the vices and weaknesses of a great writer, his oddities and eccentricities, and manner of life; to know that Aristotle was fond of finger-rings; that Julius Cæsar wore a laurel-wreath to hide his baldness; that Petrarch pinched his feet till he crippled them; that Dryden continually ejaculated "**Egad!**" and took huge pinches of snuff; that Pope had a voracious appetite for stewed lampreys, Dr. Parr for hot lobsters with shrimp sauce, and Johnson for a leg of mutton, or for a veal pie with plums; that Shelley was a vegetarian, and that Handel ate enormously, and at tavern always ordered dinner for three; that Goldsmith was vain and foppish, and blazed forth in suits of scarlet, sky-blue satin, or green and gold; that Boswell's scrofulous hero had fits of rage and of penitence, of gloom and laughter,— that he pronounced the letter *u* like *oo*, saying, as he squeezed the lemon-juice into the bowl, "Who's for *poonch?*"— that he always stood in the rain to do penance for disobedience to his father, and had a trick of touching the door-posts as he walked, and of picking up and treasuring pieces of orange-peel; that Buffon always wrote in ruffles, with his hair in curls and scented, and Richardson in a laced suit; that Dr. Robert Hamilton, whose work upon finance fell like a bombshell upon Parliament, would run against

a cow and beg her pardon, or pull off his hat to his own
wife in the streets, and apologize for not having the
pleasure of her acquaintance; that Lord Erskine always
drew on his bright yellow gloves before he rose to speak;
that Byron shaved his brow to make it look higher, and
found his inspiration in green tea, tobacco, and semi-
starvation; that Scott had a Northumbrian *burr* in his
speech; that Charles Lamb stammered out his wit and
wisdom, took too much "egg-flip hot," and found in
tobacco his "evening comfort and his morning curse";
that Schiller could compose only in a room filled with
the scent of rotten apples,— that within the Chateaubriand of *Atala* there was an obscene Chateaubriand that
indulged in the coarsest talk,— to know all these petty
details is pleasant, and gratifies a natural curiosity; they
give picturesqueness and charm to biography; they may
help occasionally to explain the growth and prominence
of some idiosyncrasy, or some characteristic sentiment or
idea; but how a knowledge of them is necessary to a
just estimate of the literary productions of these authors,
it is hard to see. In choosing a public officer, a man to
fill a responsible position, it is right to demand guaran-
tees of character; but what has Art to do with guaran-
tees? Every work is its own warranty; it carries with
it its *raison d'être* in its very qualities. The natural order, it seems to us, is to try a man by his works, and
not the works by the man; and for such a trial the best
qualification is a naturally delicate taste, improved by the
study of the best models, a knowledge of the fixed can-

ons of judgment that have stood the test of time, and a judicial impartiality.

Again, may we not attach too much importance to external influences, however interesting? It is true that, as the oak is identical with the acorn from which it sprang, and as in the egg the embryologist may detect the prophecy and type of the rooster or hen, so every man is, to some extent, what his ancestors have made him. We are all our fathers' sons. But is this all? A human being is something else than a chemical compound; and in the man of genius, however rigidly you may analyze him, there will always be a final residuum,— a mysterious something,— an impalpable element, which will defy your blowpipes and retorts, and elude every device of your laboratory. It is precisely of this most important and essential element, the peculiar gift or turn that causes one brother to be radically unlike another,— which causes a man to be "Peter Corneille instead of Thomas, Gabriel de Mirabeau instead of Mirabeau Tonneau,"— that the facts of race, family, education, and morals, give us no account. It has been affirmed that, had we intellect enough, we could infer a man completely from the sound of his voice or from a piece of his skin; and it is, perhaps, true, that an archangel could construct a man completely, and tell all that he is capable of, from a paring of his nail. The quality and size of the paring would disclose more or less the nature of the tissue with which it was connected,— this, again, would lead to still further revelations, and so on until the whole body was reconstructed, which body could be associated only with such and such intellectual and moral manifestations. But even an archangel would be puzzled to construct a work of pure imagination,— an "Iliad" or an "Æneid,"— from a knowledge of the life, character, and ancestral antecedents of the author. Many of the events in a man's life make no more impression on him than rain-drops on an eagle's wings. He rushes through the world, and is no more colored by them than "the arrowy Rhone" is said to be changed in its passage through the lake of Geneva. Indeed, we need make no other criticism on Sainte-Beuve's method than that which he himself has declared will be provoked by the method of M. Taine in his "English Literature." In that work M. Taine has dwelt with great emphasis on the profound differences wrought in the constitution of minds, in the form and direction of talents, by races, positions, and periods; but "something still eludes him, the most vital part of man eludes him, which is the reason why out of twenty men, or a hundred, or a thousand, apparently subject to almost the same intrinsic or external conditions, not one resembles the other, and *that there is* ONE *among them all who excels through originality.* In fine, he has not reached the spark of genius in its essence, and he does not display it to us in his analysis. He has merely explained and enumerated bit by bit, fibre by fibre, cell by cell, the stuff, the organism, the parenchyma (as you might call it), wherein this soul, this spark, once it has entered in, disports, changes freely (or, as it were freely), and triumphs."

Again, if a writer's book is to be judged by the light

of his personal character, why not apply the same rule to sculpture, painting, and even architecture and landscape gardening? Must we know what Taine calls "the *race*, the *milieu*, and the *moment*" of Raphael before we can properly estimate the Sistine Madonna? Finally, if Sainte-Beuve's theory be true, we cannot weigh the greatest authors, because their lives and ancestry are hidden by an impenetrable veil. How much do we know of Homer (if he is not a myth), or of the Greek tragic poets?—how much of Virgil, Dante, Chaucer, or Shakspeare? All the known facts concerning the author of "Hamlet" are a few obtained from the most frigid of sources, legal documents, and his very existence is plausibly disputed. When these men wrote, those "new terrors of death," the "lues Boswelliana" and the interviewer, were unknown. What more remarkable book of its class, or dearer to the bibliopole, can be named than "The Anatomy of Melancholy"? Yet of that "gulf of learning," Burton, the author, from whom our learned Thebans quietly crib their erudition, and Sterne plagiarized his denunciation of plagiarism, we know only that he was an indefatigable Oxford student, and that he foretold his own decease,—which happened so exactly at the day he predicted, that some of the students said that "rather than that there should be a mistake in the calculation, he sent his soul up to heaven through a slip about his neck." The latest biographer of Dryden tells us that the names and dates and order of his publications make a large portion of his biography. Yet Dryden was Poet-Laureate, and Historiographer-Royal; he was a fellow of the Royal Society, and the literary monarch of the Restoration; and when he died he had a splendid funeral, and was buried in Westminster Abbey.

Finally, a man of genius, when he writes a book, and "all the god comes rushing on his soul," is in an abnormal state; and hence the lives of men-of-letters have often been in glaring contrast to their writings. Montaigne tells us that he always observed supercelestial opinions to be accompanied with subterranean morals; on the other hand, the most latitudinarian professors of epicureanism have often lived like anchorites or trappists. Some of the best sea-songs have been written by men who never snuffed a salt-water breeze; stirring war-songs have been composed by timid men and women who would have shrieked at sight of a mouse; and hymns steeped in the very spirit of devotion have been written by men of doubtful morality, who were never less at home than in a christian church. Charles Lamb was ready to wager that Milton's morning-hymn in paradise was penned at midnight; and we know positively that Thomson, who sang the praises of early rising in the "Seasons," used to lie abed till noon. Dr. Young, the author of the "Night Thoughts," whose Parnassus was a churchyard, who drank of the river Styx instead of Hippocrene, and whose Pegasus was the Pale Horse in Revelations, was a pleasure-hunter, an office-seeker, and a court-sycophant. Sir Richard Steele could discourse eloquently on temperance,— when he was not drunk; Woodworth, in his "Old Oaken Bucket," sang the praises of cold water under the inspiration of brandy. Dr. Johnson, who wrote so well on politeness, interrupted his opponents with "You lie, sir!" "You are a vile Whig, sir!" Burns was a compound of "dirt and deity"; Rousseau, who was always filling people's eyes with tears, betrayed and slandered all his benefactors in turn, and sent his children to the Foundlings' Hospital. Who has forgotten Byron's reply to the unsophisticated gentleman who congratulated him on the delight he must have taken in a visit to Ithaca? "You quite mistake me, sir; I have no poetical humbug about me. . . . Ideas of that sort are confined to *rhyme*." When Moore proposed to Scott to go and see Melrose Abbey, as Sir Walter had described it, by moonlight, "Pooh, pooh," said Scott, "you don't suppose I ever saw it by moonlight!"

The truth is, the pedigree of an author and the details of his life and character are points of interest about which curiosity never tires of lingering, and they may occasionally throw light on vexed passages in his writings; but to say that without these particulars we cannot properly estimate his works, is too extravagant a statement to go unchallenged. As well might it be said that we cannot decide upon the bouquet of a wine without knowing all the particulars of its vintage, or pronounce upon the beauty and perfume of a rose, without analyzing the soil whence it sprang, and knowing all its surroundings and all the processes of its growth. There is a literary beauty which is impersonal, distinct from the author and his organization; and, we believe, therefore, that Wordsworth, narrow as was his critical range in general, was right when he demurred to the intrusion of biographic details into literary criticism, and maintained that a poem or other work of art should be judged by its own merits as a kind of existence that is separate from the mind that originated it, and independently of the author's character or principles as a man. But, whatever we may think of Sainte-Beuve's theories, it is certain that to them is largely due the subtle charm of his criticisms; for had his method been different, he would not have given us those biographic details which are so prized by his readers. "*A little of all, and nothing of the whole, after the French manner*"; this, which was Montaigne's motto, he tells us is also the motto of French criticism, and it seems to have been his own when he wrote his essays,—essays which Taine has happily compared to those "compounded and precious perfumes where twenty choice essences are inhaled at once, and mollified by their mutual harmony." The true way to regard the *Causeries du Lundi* is as studies in literary biography; and, as such, they have no rival. They are, indeed, "miniatures of the most exquisite workmanship," in which every feature and every expression of the subject are caught and painted to the life. Many of them remind us of those pen-and-ink sketches of Leech, in which the whole character of a man is condensed in a single stroke of the pencil.

Their importance is enhanced by the fact that France is the only country in which at this day literary criticism of the highest order flourishes. In France only, among living nations, is literature pursued as an art; nowhere else is literary work performed with such conscientiousness, or with so constant a reference to the loftiest ideals; for nowhere else can be found a public with taste and sympathy sufficient to support an artist by appreciation. The very excellence of French criticism, as of French literature generally, has caused it in some quarters to be underrated. Wherever there is superlative excellence in the embodiment of the beautiful, wherever there is perfection in the forms, the substantial and less obvious merits of a work are almost sure to be overlooked. The French, who, if not the most original, are certainly the acutest and most logical thinkers in the world, are frequently considered frivolous and shallow, simply because they excel all other nations in the difficult art of giving *literary interest* to philosophy; while on the other hand, the ponderous Germans, who, living in clouds of smoke, have a positive genius for making the obscure obscurer, are thought to be fearfully original because they are so fearfully chaotic and clumsy. But we have yet to learn that lead is priceless because it is weighty, or that gold is valueless because it glitters. The Damascus blade is none the less keen because it is polished, nor is the Corinthian column less strong because its shaft is fluted and its capital carved.

Great Britain has produced many men with high intellectual qualifications for criticism; but they have been nearly all self-imprisoned, one-sided, destitute of catholicity; and, instead of holding the scales evenly, they have too often suffered their prejudices, national, political, and religious, to affect the balance. We cannot forget that it was Sir Henry Wotton, an Englishman, who said that "critics are like the brushers of noblemen's clothes"; and that it was Sir Walter Scott, the most charitable of men, who, living at the critical capital of Britain, said that, if great authors are the pillars of literature, critics are the caterpillars. We cannot forget that "Blackwood's Magazine" sneered at Tennyson as "a cockney poet"; that the "Quarterly Review" called Hazlitt a blockhead, killed poor Keats, and scoffed at the author of Jane Eyre; that the "Edinburgh" hooted at Byron, and sealed up the living waters of Wordsworth's poetry from his countrymen for twenty years. All the critics of that generation,—Jeffrey, Gifford, Wilson, Lockhart, and Croker,—were simply intellectual gladiators, engaged to fight to the death for this or that set of doctrines. "As, with a change of a word, Rivarol said of Mirabeau, 'They would do anything for party, even a good action.'" Dr. Johnson, their predecessor, had some solid qualities as a critic, but he lacked comprehensiveness and catholicity, and, above all, that subtle instinct which detects minute beauties,—the delicate taste which discovers the most secret flavors of excellence. His mental eyesight was like his bodily; he saw broad outlines, but not minute details. He weighs Cowley, Dryden and Pope accurately; but the moment he enters the enchanted ground of romantic poetry, he is like a deaf man seated at a symphony of Beethoven. Again, Johnson was too moody, too prejudiced, and too positive, to be a good critic.

Macaulay has some of the finest qualities of a great reviewer; but his intense prejudices, his dogmatism, his utilitarianism, and contempt for high philosophy and religion,—to say nothing of his mannerism, his perpetual brilliancy of style, his exaggeration, and fondness for epigram and paradox,— suffice alone to disqualify him for sitting on the throne of criticism. He sees everything, not in the "dry light" of truth, but distorted and refracted through a false medium of passions and prejudices; and hence his history is only a big, brilliant Whig pamphlet. To him criticism is only a tribunal before which men are brought to be decisively tried by one or two inflexible tests, and then sent to join the sheep on the one hand, or the goats on the other. Albany Fonblanque said of him truly that "he is a great master of color who cannot draw. He fastens upon a feature, and gives it as a man." It is true that Macaulay did not stoop to any baseness. He never threw literary vitriol. But he could do what was nearly as bad; he could, to show his own thews, fall upon a poor fifth-rate poet, and beat him without mercy. Who can forget how he jumped upon "Satan" Montgomery, and pounded and kicked him till there was not a whole bone in his body? Who that has read his late biography, can believe that he could have impartially reviewed a book written by one of those persons whom he always sneeringly terms "Yankees"? Hallam has a more judicial mind; he means to be severely impartial; but, unfortunately, the discriminating faculty in his mind was developed disproportionately to the faculty of admiration. He prefers works artistically correct, fashioned by square, rule, and compass, to those that manifest a vigorous and irregular originality. The rugged, gnarled oak, with the grotesque contortions of its branches, delights him less than the regularity of the clipped and trimmed trees of Versailles. Hence, while he has done heaped justice to the cold, classic literatures of Europe, he has "damned with faint praise" the bold, impassioned writers of the Elizabethan period in England. Matthew Arnold has fine critical abilities; but he has rung the changes upon "sweetness and light" till they have become a cant; and he is so full of crotchets, biases, and pet prejudices, not to say dandyisms and affectations, that we sometimes prefer the Philistines.

Sainte-Beuve was no such "hired master of tongue-fence," no such dispenser of praise or blame, as any of these we have described. The least sentimental, he was also the least cynical of writers; though he had an eagle's eye for faults, yet he was essentially a loving critic. Especially did he delight in cheering on the younger members of the literary guild, and in rescuing neglected authors from oblivion. In summing up his qualities, we know not which most to admire, his geniality, vivacity, and catholicity of nature, his Parisian delicacy and *finesse*, his profound knowledge of men and books, or that calm, penetrating wisdom,— that uncommon common-sense,— which is so conspicuous in all he wrote. Two crowning qualities he had in a degree rarely seen in a critic,— insight and disinterestedness; a faculty of penetrating into the secrets of the most opposite natures, and a power of detecting and appreciating whatever is good in the most opposite schools. Though less enthusiastic than many critics of inferior perspicacity, he was never chary or niggard of deserved praise; and the conscientiousness with which he credits the authors whom he dissects, and whose weaknesses he exposes, with every particle of excellence that can be discovered in their writings, is one of his most salient qualities. Belonging, except in youth, to no Mutual Admiration Society,— to none of those close corporations of literary Ishmaelites that applaud all within and denounce all without the pale,— he weighed all authors fairly in his literary scales, whatever their nationality, sect, or party; and we feel that the estimates he has placed upon them mark, with rare exceptions, their just value. In short, as Wistanley says of Matthew Paris, in speaking of his history, we may say of Sainte-Beuve: "Though he had sharp nails, he had clean hands." This very impartiality was to some writers whom he criticised his most offensive quality; justice was the one thing they had most reason to dread; and hence he tells us that in his long career he had irritated and envenomed more people by his praise than by his blame.

Sainte-Beuve is not properly what one would call an epigrammatic writer; he has fewer striking passages that can be torn from their context without injury, than many writers of less genius; and yet it would not be difficult to cull out from his fifty or more volumes a great number of pithy and pointed sayings,— flowers enough to form a respectable anthology. Even his happiest aphorisms are not usually of the kind that startle and delight at the first reading; they are quiet and suggestive, disclosing more and more meaning in proportion as they are pondered; e. g., "One has always the voice of his mind."— "One is always of his time."—"He is dying of words suppressed (*rentrées*), and not heard."—"It is always one's self that one loves, even in what one admires."—"The first and almost the only question which one always has to ask, in speaking of a woman, is: 'Has she loved, and how has she loved?'"—"Malesherbes is great enough, provided one does not present him to us *drapé*. . . . He had believed in the Promised Land before the passage of the Red Sea."—The history of conversation, like that of all which is essentially relative and transitory, and dependent upon the very impressions of the time, appears to me impossible. . . . Even if the things said could be conveyed in writing, in letters, most of them would be congealed in the process, *for paper cannot smile.* Nothing more faithfully reflects the taste of an age than its prevalent style of conversation. The serious conversation of yesterday would seem a little timid, or superficial, or insipid, tomorrow, were echo to report it fully. The refined and polished conversation of one period will appear heavy to another. . . . It has been said of Collections of Thoughts that they have the inconvenience of appearing commonplace, when they are not pretentious; the same things, when said, made a different impression. The smile and accent gave them currency; but, fixed upon paper, they are quite another thing. *Paper is brutish (bête).*"—"If it be true that there are some books which cultivated and tender unoccupied hearts love to re-read once a year, —love to have flower periodically in the memory, like the lilacs and the hawthorn,—*Édouard** is one of them."

How happily has Sainte-Beuve characterized Pope, *that mens curva in corpore curvo*, to whom Taine has done such injustice:

* By Madame de Duras.

"Pope did not write with his muscles; he merely made use of his mind. . . . If we are fair toward the ex-tinker Bunyan, who, in his fanatical dreams, has given token of strength and of imagination, let us not, on the other hand, crush Pope, that agreeable and clever creature, *that quintessence of soul, that drop of clear spirit in cotton wool.* Do not treat him roughly, and when taking him by the hand, to seat him in our medical and quasi-anatomical arm-chair, let us be careful (as if he still lived) not to make him scream. . . . It is true he was precocious: is that a crime? . . . If such a thing as the literary temperament exist, it never was revealed in a more characteristic and more distinctly defined manner than in the case of Pope. Generally we become classical by the fact and discipline of education: he was so by vocation, so to speak, and by a natural originality."

What can be more just than the following remarks upon Pope's irritability?—"One does not appreciate the beautiful to such a degree of intensity and delicacy, without being terribly shocked at the bad and the ugly. Exquisite enjoyment must be paid for. When one's mind is so open and so susceptible to beauties, even to the extent of shedding tears about them as Pope did, it is equally sensitive to defects, even to the point of being nettled and irritated at them. He who most keenly enjoys the perfume of the rose will be the first to be disgusted with bad odors. Thus no one, perhaps, has been conscious of literary stupidity, and suffered from it in so high a degree, as Pope."

Few English critics have analyzed and described the genius of Gibbon, the historian, so felicitously in as few sentences, as it is characterized in the following passages:

"Culture, coherence, order, method; a fine, cold, acute, constantly exercised and sharpened intelligence; tempered, lasting affections; in other respects, the sacred spark being wanting, a thunder-clap being never heard; these are the traits under which Gibbon presents himself to us at all times, and from his youth up. . . . Gibbon does not give forth a perfect light; he stops on this side of the summit where perchance it shines. He excels in analyzing and deducing the complicated parts of a subject; but he never collects them in a startling point of view and with an outburst of genius. He is more intelligent than elevated. Faithful to his humor, even in the processes of his mind, he *equalizes* all things too much. Shall I indulge in a pleasantry he himself indicates? The gout, when he has it, never attacks him by fits, and it treats him in nearly the same way as it did Fontenelle, following a slow and regular course; in the same way, his History uniformly marches with equal pace, without fits and starts, and without fury. If a great revolution were anywhere to occur in the human mind, he would not feel it; he would not announce it by lighting a beacon on the top of his tower, or by ringing the silver bell. This is the historical complaint which must be brought against his exposition of Christianity. . . . In the portraits of christians, even the greatest of those times, Gibbon contents himself with being always vague; he does not exhibit them in their best parts, and, as a learned ecclesiastic of our day has remarked, 'his work swarms with equivocal portraits.'"

Every reader of Taine, especially of his "English Literature," will recognize the acuteness and justness of the following criticism of his style: "In fact, he likes force even in grace; he does not hate superabundance and excess. . . . He bows down, or he raises up, according to his feelings; he will despise Butler, for his bepraised *Hudibras;* he will magnify Bunyan, the fanatic, for his *Pilgrim's Progress.* When I say magnifies him, I go too far; he describes him and his work, but describes them in such a way that his words set the picture before you so as to make the impression reach the quick and even the skin. . . . In his descriptions or picturesque analyses, his concise, rapid style, advancing in series, in rows and strings of epithets, in thick and reiterated strokes, in sentences, and, as it were, in short, sharp recurring lines, has made a critic of the old school say that he seemed to hear rough and thick hail falling and rattling on the roofs:

'Tum multa in tectis crepitans salit horrida grando.'

This style produces in the long run a certain and inevitable impression on the mind, which at times affects the nerves. Here, the man of science and of vigor has to take care lest he cause some fatigue to the man of taste."

Among the interesting essays in the third volume of the "Causeries" is a notice of M. Droz, who in 1806 published an essay on "The Art of being Happy." After speaking of the work as "a confession, a confidential disclosure," made by "a wise, tranquil, elevated soul, animated by a pure zeal, which has found for itself the secret of happiness, and wishes to communicate it to others," Sainte-Beuve makes the following happy remarks: "But men, with regard to this matter, which touches them so closely, are more rebellious than one thinks; every person wishes to be happy or unhappy in his own way. In order thus to regulate our desires, they must be already very moderate. The men who have ardent desires are only irritated and made impatient by these suggestions of calm wisdom, which recall the slow conversations, the quiet manner of Termosiris and the smiling old men of Fenelon. Ask, then, the poet, who has said that life runs *in purple waves* in his veins, to be pleased to slacken and moderate it, as one might do with waves of milk or honey. At the Cape of Good Hope there is a gigantic bird, the albatross, which as soon as the tempest upheaves the ocean, is happy only while hovering over the vast waste of waters. If that bird chances to reach the border of the trade winds, it immediately turns back, and plunges again into the region of storms. Mirabeau took pleasure in struggling with the tempest; and has not even the noble Vauvenargues said: 'A somewhat daring turn of imagination opens to us oftentimes pathways full of light. Let those believe it who will, that one is made miserable by the embarrassments that attend great undertakings. It is in idleness and meanness of life that virtue suffers, when a timid prudence prevents it from taking flight, and makes it creep in its shackles; but misfortune itself has its charms in great extremities; for the opposition of fortune rouses a courageous spirit, and makes it gather up all its forces, which were before unused.'"

Among the most interesting papers in the "Causeries" are several in which the author has had occasion to speak of the first Napoleon, for whose genius he had the highest admiration. When the great captain first appeared, he remarks, society in travail demanded a savior; civilization, exhausted by frightful struggles, called for one of those rare and powerful men who thoroughly comprehend the condition of affairs, and are strong enough in head and arm to reconstitute the state. Napoleon was one of these men. But though he was able to rescue a nation on the brink of a precipice, and to place it again, so to speak, on its feet, yet his temperament would not allow him to leave it in repose. His excessive genius loved adventure. He loved, before everything else, his chief art, that of war; he delighted in its excitement, its risk, its game, the *gaudia certaminis*. "I am aware," continues Sainte-Beuve, "that one would never dare anything great, that one would never do immortal things, if he did not in a moment risk all to win all; but it is not his having risked all once or twice, that I complain of in Napoleon, but his proclivity to risk always." After the miracles of Austerlitz and of Jena, Napoleon, says his critic, pushed Fortune to extremities, and wanted absolutely to make her yield to him more than she could give. There is a moment when the nature of things revolts, and makes genius itself pay for its abuse of power and success. This was evident at Eylau; and from the summit of that bloody cemetery, under that freezing sky, Napoleon, for the first time warned, might have had a vision of the future. The disastrous future of his Russian expedition was there revealed to him, abridged, in a prophetic vision.

Sainte-Beuve quotes from Thiers the following vivid comparison of the English and the French soldier:

"The English soldier, well-fed, well-dressed, firing with remarkable accuracy, advancing slowly because he is ill fitted for marching and lacks personal ardor, is firm and almost invincible in certain positions in which the nature of the ground seconds his enduring character; but if you force him to march to attack, and to conquer difficulties that can be overcome only by vivacity, by boldness, and by enthusiasm, he is at fault. In a word, he is steady and firm, but not enterprising. As the French soldier, by his ardor, his energy, his promptitude, his readiness to brave everything, was the predestined instrument of the genius of Napoleon, so the steady but slow soldier of England was made for the narrow but sagacious and resolute mind of Arthur Wellesley."

Upon this passage Sainte-Beuve sensibly and pithily remarks, how much in the long run prudence and tenacity have the advantage over genius and power misused and abused. Men who, compared with Napoleon, stand only in the second rank, have been able to win for themselves and their country more solid and lasting successes than he, and to hold them firmly. Such is the advantage which the Cromwells and the Princes of Orange have over him in history, and the same is true of the combined genius of Pitt and Wellington which finally vanquished him.

In a later "Causerie," Sainte-Beuve reviews the Memoirs of the campaigns of Egypt and Syria dictated by Napoleon, and makes some discriminating remarks on the style of Napoleon, which in its temper, he thinks, strongly resembles that of Pascal.

"It is simple and naked. His military style may be compared with the most perfect styles of antiquity on such subjects,—with those of Xenophon and Cæsar. But in the works of these two consummate captains the tone of recital is more silky and subtle, or, at least, lighter and more elegant. The style of Napoleon is more blunt and abrupt, and I would say drier, if from time to time the great traits of his imagination did not shed a light upon his composition. He received a less attic education than those two illustrious ancients, and he knows more of algebra. His brevity has a stamp of positiveness. Generally, the will is revealed in his style. The immortal 'Thoughts' which Pascal left behind him in the form of notes, and which were meant for his eye alone, often recall, by their bluntness, by the despotic accent of which Voltaire accused him, the character of the letters and dictated pieces of Napoleon. . . .

"Napoleon, in dictating, does not think merely; he acts; or, when he recollects, he has so many things to seize at once that he crowds them into the smallest space. Napoleon stopped at the point where thought, style and action are confounded. In his case, the style, properly so called, has not time to detach itself."

In speaking of Napoleon's Egyptian expedition, Sainte-Beuve notices the fact that he had hardly disembarked, when he advanced against Alexandria, and assaulted the city with a mere handful of his troops, and without waiting for his cannon. "'It is a principle of war,' says Napoleon, 'that when one can use the thunderbolt, it should be preferred to cannon.' He opposes this procedure to that of other generals, who in similar circumstances have wasted several days, and lost their opportunity through their anxiety to be too well prepared. But in order thus to use the thunderbolt when cannon are wanting, there is one thing necessary,— it is to be a thunderbolt one's self."

In the third volume of the "Causeries" there is a charming paper on the Duchess of Maine, one of the oddest and most extravagant productions of the reign of Lewis XIV,— of monarchical government pushed to excess. It was said that during her whole life she never went out of her house, and that she had not even put her head out of the window:

"Philosophers, some philosophers at least, have imagined that if man, after his birth and in his first movements, met with no resistance in his contact with things around him, he would be unable to distinguish himself from the external world, and that as by degrees he reached out his arms or attempted to walk, he would believe that the world formed a part of himself,— of his own body. He would come at last to think that everything else was but an appendage and extension of his own personality; he would say, with perfect assurance, '*I am the universe!*' Madame du Maine held this belief; for a long time she realized the dream of the philosophers. She never experienced any resistance to her wishes until the time of the Regency. She early arranged matters so that she could have no such experience by shutting herself up in that little court at Sceaux, where all was hers, and was herself only (*n'était qu'elle*). For any person but herself to have a will or a desire, would have seemed to her an impatience and a revolt. . . . During the foolish conspiracy which she planned, out of spite to the Regent (1718), and into which she urged her timid husband, she saw at last that the world was bigger, more rebellious, and more difficult to move than she had believed. Every other person would have learned some lesson from this, or, at least, would have been disgusted and saddened by it; but the force of nature and of first impressions won the day. . . . She remained persuaded as before, that the order of the world, when it went well, was arranged wholly and only for her. In a word, to resume the former comparison, she was like a person who has fallen one day by a misstep from the first story of her house, without very much damage, but who, on account of that, has not put and never will put her head out of the window."

That Sainte-Beuve had little sympathy with the literary taste of the age,—at least with some of its leading qualities,—is evident from many passages in the "Causeries." Above all, did his delicate and refined taste revolt at the flaring colors, the excessive emphasis, the perpetual attempts to gild copper, and to dazzle with an unnatural and fatiguing brilliancy, which characterize so many of the popular and even eminent writers of our time. The present age he regarded as "a state of self-styled civilization, in which the cry prevails over the smile, in which it is necessary to insist with all one's might upon everything, and in which *even pleasantry often needs a speaking-trumpet!*" Again, he says: "A friend who, after having seen a good deal of the world, has almost entirely withdrawn from it, and who judges from a distance, and as it were from the shore, the swift whirlpool in which we are tossing, lately wrote to me touching certain rough estimates I had made of contemporary works: 'All that you say of our *sublime writers* interests me exceedingly. Sublime they certainly are! What they lack is calmness and freshness, a little pure cold water to cool our burning palates.' . . .

In Sainte-Beuve's "Portraits of Women," from which the last passage has been taken, there are many beautiful and striking reflections, over which the thoughtful reader will linger. In his sketch of Madame Roland he says:

"The perfect moral being, if it ever is formed in us, is formed early; it exists at twenty in all its integrity and in all its grace. Then, if ever, we bear within us our Plutarchian hero, our Alexander. At a later day we too often survive our hero. In proportion as he develops and is displayed more in the eyes of others, he suffers loss. When everybody begins to appreciate him, he is already degenerating. Sometimes (horrible thought!) he has already ceased to exist. Frankness, self-devotion, fidelity, courage, — these still keep the same names, but they hardly merit them. Every soul, as it moves on, suffers all the injuries, all the waste of which it is capable. 'All men,' said the noble and kindly Vauvenargues, 'are born sincere, and die deceitful.' It might have sufficed him, for the expression of his bitter thought, to say that they die *undeceived*. At least, even in the best men, what is called progress in life is far inferior to the primitive ideal which they realized at some moment in youth. . . .

"'How many a Hampden,' says Gray in his *Country Churchyard*, 'sleeps unknown under the sod.' I have tried sometimes to imagine what Cardinal Richelieu would have been, if fate had restricted him to a private life: what an ill-tempered neighbor, or, to speak vulgarly, what a bad *bedfellow* he would have made! Bonaparte, just before '95, — when he is without employment, and when he is going to extinguish Bourrienne or Madame Permon with his strange whiffs,—suggests a similar idea. How rare are the beings who seem equally in their place, equally good and excellent, in private life, and great in public life, like Washington and Madame Roland!"

Sainte-Beuve closes several volumes of the "Causeries" with a series of disconnected "Thoughts," which, he says, are addressed less to the public than to *habitués* and friends. We have room for but one of them: "To gather together, to maintain, and bring to bear at once, at a given instant, the greatest number of related things (*rapports*), to act in mass and in concert, is the great and difficult art, whether one be a commander of an army, an orator, or a writer. There are generals who cannot assemble and manœuvre more than ten thousand men, and there are writers who can handle at most but one or two ideas at once. There are writers who resemble Marshal Soubise in the Seven Years' War: when he had all his troops gathered at his disposal, he knew not what to do with them, and he dispersed them again that he might fight to better advantage. So I know of writers, who, before writing, dismiss half of their ideas, because they can express them only one by one: it is pitiful. It shows that one is embarrassed by his very resources."

Sainte-Beuve wrote no great work; there is no one massive whole on which you can lay your hand and say, here is a full reflection,— the pith and quintessence,— of the man. But if he was not a great man, he was, as a writer has well said, what Mr. Ruskin esteems as something better,— an encourager of greatness. To be great one's self, that eloquent writer tells us, is but to add one great man to the world; whereas to exhibit the greatness of twelve other men, is to enrich the world with twelve great men.

At the beginning of his career Sainte-Beuve had a mannerism which seemed ingrained; he "caressed and refined his style"; but with years it mellowed more and more, and he ended with a simplicity which was the perfection of art. It was the great muse Necessity, he tells us, that, in the first instance, compelled the change; that Necessity which, at certain great moments, impels the dumb to speak and the stammerer to articulate, compelled him in an instant to employ a sharp, clear, rapid form of expression,— to address everybody in everybody's language; and for this he was thankful. Henceforward his rank as the leading critical spirit of the age was assured. Moving in the best Parisian circles,— studying, thinking, observing,— devouring books to an extent that might appal the most omniverous German scholar,— he kept his mind fresh and teeming, and the drafts he made on it seemed never to diminish the capital. Like all great writers, he had the defects of his qualities. He is never dull; he never, as Rivarol said of Condorcet, "writes with ópium on leaves of lead"; but, on the other hand, his style, with all its merits, rarely rises to eloquence, for eloquence demands deep conviction and deep feeling, which Sainte-Beuve did not have. It delights, also, in striking contrasts,— in large masses of light and shadow,— forms of expression which the critical mind, devoted to analysis and to the discovery of delicate shades of affinity or difference, never employs. Sainte-Beuve was not what Dr. Johnson calls "a good hater." With his aversion to magisterial airs and to emphasis, was bound up a certain lack of earnestness, of moral force, which, whether natural, or the result of self-repression, will seem a defect to many positive and aggressive minds. They would be glad if they could say of him as he has said of Montalembert: "*il a la faculté d'indignation. Il a conservé dans sa vivacité première le sentiment du juste et de l'injuste.*" It would be refreshing to them if he would occasionally flame up into a burning wrath, and hurl a thunderbolt or two, or deal a good sledge-hammer blow. Perhaps this lack of anger and scorn was due to his doctrine of "Indifference," which he declared to be a distinguishing quality of the critical genius. Perhaps, had one thus accused him, he would have said that "with some natures earnestness does not show itself in active force, but in the form of serenity and sweetness; that the Greek Pallas-Athene is not seen in the attitude of a wrestler, but in calm self-control and repose." Be this as it may, we must admit that, with all his shortcomings, he was a man of letters to whom, in the words of the "Edinburgh Review," "neither France, nor perhaps Europe, will soon produce a rival,— in short, an epitome of the finest culture of modern times."

It is sad to think that this fine intelligence died an unbeliever. We have seen that at the age of twenty he had already become a fervent disciple of the doctrine of Condillac pushed to its last consequences by Cabanis and Tracy,— believing that thought is a secretion of the brain, and that "*rien de l'homme ne survit à l'homme*"; and though there were brief periods when his scepticism was shaken, and even as late as 1830 he could write to a friend, "I have come, I hope, to believe that there is no true repose here below but in religion, the orthodox Catholic religion, practised with intelligence and submission," yet the subsoil of his nature was materialistic, and the belief in which he died is summed up in the mournful conclusion of his History of Port Royal, in which he declares that he is "only one of the most fugitive of illusions in the bosom of the infinite Illusion" (*une illusion des plus fugitives au sein de l'Illusion infinie*). Let us remember, however, to his credit, while pitying him for this dreary conviction, that he was frank and outspoken in his opinions, neither cloaking his atheism on the one hand, nor flaunting it in the world's face on the other. He had not learned the modern and jesuitical trick of wearing the shield and device of a faith, and shouting the cry of a church, while all the time secretly repudiating or explaining away its doctrines. In a day when "the theologian would fain pass for rationalist, and the freethinker for a person with his own orthodoxies if you only knew them," it is something in a man's favor that, if he holds doctrines that we dislike, he does not sail under a false flag, but can say with Burns:

> "——— ——— I rather would be
> An atheist clean,
> Than under gospel colors hid be,
> Just for a screen."

Sainte-Beuve had his inconsistencies, his positive faults

and his infirmities; but he did not cant against cant, dogmatize against dogmatism, or pretend that only doubters and disbelievers are honest,—that they only sit in the serene regions of "sweetness and light," and are entitled to the name of "advanced thinkers." It is pleasant to know that there were christians, earnest, zealous christians, ultra-orthodox in belief, who could love him in spite of his chilling scepticism, as an incident related by the Paris correspondent of the "Chicago Tribune" shows: One evening Sainte-Beuve was dining in a restaurant, at a table near one where Lacordaire was sitting, and thus spoke of religion to a companion: "My dear sir, it is stronger than me. I cannot believe in God, because I believe only in what I understand." Lacordaire, overhearing the remark, rose abruptly to his full height, and, raising one hand to heaven, exclaimed: "There is Sainte-Beuve, who does not believe in God, because he does not understand him. Nor does he understand why or how the same fire melts butter and hardens eggs; and yet he eats an omelette!" Sainte-Beuve, taken aback by this abrupt apostrophe, made no reply; but, rising in his turn, he took the fiery Dominican by the hand, and "from that moment the two men, who presented so glaring a contrast, physical and intellectual,—the one corpulent, impassioned, credulous, violent, inspired, and almost an apostle; the other small, slender, incredulous, patient, lettered,—formed a sincere and ardent friendship which was broken only by the priest's death."

LEWIS THE FOURTEENTH.

UNDER the imposing title of *Works** there are extant six volumes of the most interesting and the most authentic of the writings of Lewis XIV, which might more justly be entitled Memoirs; they are composed, indeed, of real memoirs of his reign and of his principal actions, which he undertook to write for the instruction of his son. The narrative is often interrupted by very judicious moral and royal reflections. The six or seven years which elapsed after the death of Cardinal Mazarin, and which constituted the first epoch of the reign of Lewis XIV (1661–1668), are there exhibited and described successively and in a continuous detail. The succeeding years, down to 1694, are described in a series of letters which have to do more specially with campaigns and military operations. To these are joined a number of private letters, relating to all the epochs of the reign. The whole forms a mass of documents, notes and precepts emanating directly from the cabinet of Lewis XIV, and which shed the greatest light both upon his acts themselves and upon the mind by which they were planned and performed. One evening, in 1714, the king, being near his end, sent the duke of Noailles to bring from his closet some papers written with his own hand, which he wished to throw into the fire: "he burned at first several which affected the reputation of different

* Les Oeuvres de Louis XIV (6 vols. in 8vo, 1806).

persons; he was going to burn all the rest, notes, memoirs, pieces of his own composition upon war or politics. The duke of Noailles earnestly entreated him to give them to him, and the favor was granted." The originals, deposited by the duke in the king's library, have been preserved there; it was from these manuscripts that the selections were made in 1806 for the six volumes of which I speak, and to which, I know not why, the public has never rendered the justice nor accorded the attention which they deserve. These volumes have been sold for a long time at a low price. It was thus also, but a few years ago, with the nine volumes of Napoleon's authentic *Memoirs*. As for the works of the Great Frederic, they comprise so much miscellany, that one cannot be surprised that the fine historical portions, which form their substance, should have been for a long time lost in the literary jumble which concealed and compromised them. Nothing like this appears in the Memoirs of Lewis XIV, any more than in those of Napoleon; both are pure history, the reflections of men who speak of their art, and of the greatest of arts, that of governing. Our levity is thus shown; the most frivolous of political pamphlets was read by everybody, while many distinguished and serious minds did not trouble themselves even to learn whether there was an opportunity to read these writings attributed to the greatest men, the stamp of whose genius or good sense is visible on every page.

Lewis XIV had only good sense, but he had a good deal. The impression which the reading of his writings makes, and especially of those which date from his youth, is well fitted to redouble our respect for him. The smile which we cannot restrain at certain passages will soon die on the lips and give place to a higher sentiment when we know that all souls require, after all, some springs of action, and that a prince who should doubt himself, a sceptical king, would be the worst of kings. The wheel of history, which turns incessantly, has taken us back to the point of view to which we needed to be taken, in order better to comprehend, perhaps, the qualities of a sovereign and royal nature, and its use in society. Let us spend a few pleasant moments in viewing it in Lewis XIV in its purity and its hereditary exaltation, and before Mirabeau has come.

Lewis XIV in childhood had certain remarkable traits and serious graces which distinguished him from all other children of his age. The wise and sensible Madame de Motteville has traced for us some charming portraits of him in those years; she says that, at a ball which took place at Cardinal Mazarin's,—

"The king had on a suit of black satin, embroidered with gold and silver, in which the black served chiefly to set off the embroidery. Some flesh-colored feathers and some ribbons of the same color completed his attire; but the beautiful features of his face, the mingled sweetness and gravity of his eyes, the whiteness and liveliness of his complexion, with his hair, which was then of a very light, flaxen hue, adorned him still more than his dress. He danced to perfection, and, although he was then but eight years old, one could say of him that he was one of the best-mannered and certainly one of the most beautiful persons in the company."

Again, speaking of his intimacy with the young Prince of Wales (afterward Charles II), who was then in France, she says:

"The king, who was charmingly beautiful, although young, was already tall. He was grave, and in his eyes there was a serious look, which indicated his dignity. He was prudent enough not to say anything, from fear of not speaking well."

About that time the king fell sick of the small-pox, causing his mother to feel the greatest uneasiness. He manifested to her a tender and touching gratitude:

"During that malady the king impressed all who approached him with his sweetness and goodness. He spoke kindly of those who waited on him; he said witty and obliging things to them, and was docile in regard to all that the doctors desired of him. The queen received from him proofs of regard which deeply affected her. . . ."

These first traits it was essential to make known. One of the austerest contemporaries of Lewis XIV, Saint-Simon, who saw and knew him only in the last twenty-two years of his life, amid some penetrating analyses which he has given of his various qualities, observes:

"He was born wise, moderate, secretive, master of his feelings and of his tongue. *Will one believe it? he was born good and just*, and God had given him ability enough to be a good king, and perhaps even a very great king. . . ."

That there was in Lewis XIV a primal soil of goodness, of sweetness, and of humanity, which disappeared too soon amid the idolatries of the supreme rank, Saint-Simon perceives, and testifies even by his astonishment; Madame de Motteville makes us see in it a natural characteristic of the child-king, and more than one word of Lewis XIV, in the sincere pages of his youth, will confirm us in this view of his character.

Gravity and sweetness,— all his contemporaries have agreed in noting these two conspicuous traits, although sweetness gave place more and more to gravity. "I have often remarked with astonishment," says Madame de Motteville again, "that when at his games and amusements, that prince seldom laughed." There is a letter extant in which he asks the duke of Parma (July 5, 1661,) to send him a Harlequin for his Italian troupe; he makes the request in the most serious terms, and without the slightest expression of gaiety. If he was at a ball, or danced, Madame de Sévigné, who watched him anxiously during the trial of Fouquet, applied to him some lines of Tasso, from which it appears that, even at the ballets, he had, like Godfrey de Bouillon, a physiognomy which inspired fear rather than hope. "He was personally kind, civil, and easily accessible to everybody, but had a grave and majestic manner which inspired people with respect and fear, and prevented those whom he esteemed the most from taking liberties, even in private, although he was familiar and sportive with ladies."

The sweetness which mingled with his words is singularly attested and depicted in a fine passage of Bossuet:

"He who would understand how far reason presides in the counsels of that prince, has only to listen when he is pleased to explain their motives. I might call to witness here the wise ministers of foreign courts, who found him as convincing in his conversation as formidable by his arms. The nobleness of his expressions came from that of his sentiments, and the precision of his words is the image of the justness that reigns in his thoughts. While he speaks with so much force, a surprising sweetness opens all hearts to him, and gives, I know not how, a new lustre to the majesty which it tempers."

This would be the best epigraph to place at the head of Lewis the Fourteenth's writings, and it would be found partially justified by their perusal.

When beginning at twenty-three to desire to reign wholly alone, Lewis XIV made it one of his essential occupations and duties, to note his principal acts in writing, to give an account of them, and to use them as a means of teaching his son, who, at a later day, will be able to train himself thereby in the art of reigning. The idea of glory, which is inseparable from Lewis XIV, mingles with these motives, and as posterity will one day be busy with his deeds, and as the passion and genius of different writers will be exercised upon them, he wishes his son to have thus the means of correcting History. if it should make any mistakes.

Lewis XIV, who had little knowledge of letters, and whose early education was very much neglected, had received that far superior instruction which a just and upright mind and a noble heart obtain from the events in which one is early engaged. Mazarin, who in his last years understood him, had given him in conversation some political advice, which the young man apprehended more quickly than would many minds reputed more cultivated and more subtle. Mazarin declared to those who doubted the young king's future, "that they did not know him, and that there was stuff enough in him to make four kings and an honest man."

Lewis has himself revealed the first idea he had of things, and that first inner education which gradually went on in his mind, his first doubts in view of difficulties, his reasons for waiting and delaying; for, "preferring, as he did, a high reputation, if he could acquire it, to all things else, even to life itself;" he understood at the same time, that "his first measures would either lay its foundations, or would cause him to lose forever even the hope of it;" so that the same sole desire of glory, which urged him on, almost equally restrained him. He says:

"I did not cease, nevertheless, to exercise and to make trial of myself in secret and without a confidant, reasoning alone, in my own mind, upon all the events that occurred; full of hope and of joy when I discovered sometimes that my first thoughts were the same as those at which clever and accomplished people arrived, and fully persuaded that I had not been placed and preserved upon the throne with so great a passion for doing well, without being able to find the means."

After Mazarin's death Lewis XIV had no longer any motive for delay:

"I began then to cast my eyes over all the different affairs of the State, not indifferent eyes, but the eyes of a master, deeply concerned at not seeing one which did not invite and urge me to give attention to it, but carefully observing what the times and the condition of things would permit me to do."

Lewis XIV, religious as he is, believes that there are lights which are proportioned to the situations, and particularly to that of a king: "God, who made you king," says he, "will give you the lights which you require, so long as your intentions are good." He believes that a sovereign naturally looks at the subjects presented to him, in a more perfect manner than most men. Such a conviction, we feel, is dangerous; it is going soon to be abused. Nevertheless, limited and understood in a certain sense, this idea is a correct one. "I do not fear to tell you," he writes for his son, "that the higher a station is, the more duties it has which one can neither see nor understand but by occupying it."

Saint-Simon, whom I shall here dare to contradict and refute, has said of Lewis XIV:

"Born with a mind below mediocrity, but with a mind capable of forming, polishing and refining itself, of borrowing from others without imitation and without difficulty, he profited infinitely by having lived all his life with people of the world who had the most talent, and of the most various kinds,—with men and women of every age, of every class, and of every character."

He returns several times to this idea that Lewis XIV had only a mind *below mediocrity*, but was very capable of acquiring knowledge and of improving himself, of appropriating whatever he saw others do. There is one important thing, however, which Lewis had not to borrow from anybody, and which was very original with him; it is that office, that real function of the sovereign, of which no one about him had then an idea, which the troubles of the Fronde had suffered to be debased and to decay in men's minds, and which Mazarin, even at the restoration of the kingly power, had but slightly reinstated in the public reverence. Lewis XIV felt its inspiration, and manifested its character visibly to all. Nature had designated him for this, physically, by a singular mixture of comeliness and majesty. Wherever he had been, he had been at once distinguished and recognized as one recognizes "the queen among the bees." The solid qualities of his mind, his laborious application to affairs, as well as the sentiments of his heart, corresponded with this desire of nature and the part assigned to him by destiny. Later, and speedily too, he will outgrow this character, but, in the beginning, he only realizes it in perfection and with a great fitness.

Saint-Simon, who came at the end of that reign, and at an epoch when the spirit of opposition reappeared, has not sufficiently noted that first moment of entire and pure royal originality in Lewis the Fourteenth's career. His long reign, indeed, began very much to weary the peoples, and they longed everywhere to be released. But the reply which we might make to Saint-Simon, is made by Lewis XIV himself, and in terms worthy of both:

"Hardly do we remark the admirable order of the world, and the regular and useful course of the sun, before some derangement of the seasons, or some apparent disorder in the machine, makes us give it a little more reflection. So long as all goes well in a State, one may forget the infinite blessings which royalty confers, and only envy those which it possesses; man, naturally ambitious and proud, never finds in himself a reason why another should rule him till his own necessity makes him feel it. But of this very necessity, as soon as there is a constant and regular remedy for it, custom renders him insensible. It is the extraordinary accidents which make him consider the blessings that government ordinarily confers upon him, and reflect that, without rule, he would be a prey to the strongest, he would find in the world neither justice nor reason, neither security for his possessions nor remedy for his losses; and it is thus that he comes to love obedience as much as he loves his own life and his own tranquillity."

This is what Lewis XIV writes, what he dictates. Saint-Simon has given us an account of two or three audiences which he had with him, and has vividly described the feeling of respect, of submission, and of grateful joy which he brought away from them. With the rarest qualifications as an observer, he recognized his master as he approached him, and the very detail into which he enters upon this subject is proof of it. The page which I have just cited permits me to believe that, if (supposing an impossibility) a political conversation had taken place between them, Lewis XIV, in a simple style and with an easy good sense, would still have maintained, on all essential points, his sovereign superiority. Let us leave to each the name which properly designates him. Saint-Simon was a great painter and a profound moralist; Lewis XIV was a king. He wished to show to all the earth, and it is he who says it, *that there was still one king in the world.*

In the reforms of every kind which he undertakes simultaneously in the finances, in the administration of justice, in the military regulations, in foreign affairs, Lewis XIV does not betray, however, any immoderate haste. He examines, he hears, he consults; then he decides for himself: "decision demands a master's mind." This last point was always the great claim of Lewis XIV: not to let himself be governed, to have no prime minister. It has been remarked that in this there was more of appearance than of reality, and that soon, for lack of a prime minister, he had some chief deputies, who, by art and flattery, knew how to make him adopt, as if by his own impulse, whatever they desired. But at the beginning, and during the first seven or eight years of his youth, it seems to me that Lewis escapes from this reproach. The peculiar cast of his mind is judicial and ratiocinative; he has a positive mind, which loves public affairs, finds them agreeable because of their utility, and keeps an account of facts in the greatest detail. "No man," he says, "who is ill-informed, can help reasoning badly." And with a conclusion worthy of a moralist, he finely adds: "I believe that no man, who should be well informed and well persuaded of all that is, would ever do otherwise than he ought."

He finds a real pleasure even in application and self-information; he enjoys clearing up what is obscure: "I have already begun," he writes on the evening of Fouquet's arrest, "to taste the pleasure there is in laboring one's self at the finances, having, in the little attention which I have given them this afternoon, noticed some important things into which I saw but little; and one must not suspect that I shall stop." He makes us feel at every moment the kind of charm there is in the exercise of good sense.* He believes that good sense, tested by practice and experience, is the best counsellor and the surest guide; and he is tempted sometimes to regard written counsels (beginning with those he gives to his son), as useless; but he immediately changes his mind, and he thinks that it is profitable to every good mind to be put on its guard in advance, and forearmed against errors. Regretting that he came so late to the study of history, he thinks that "the knowledge of those great events which have occurred in the world in different ages, when digested by a solid and active mind, may serve to strengthen the judgment in all important deliberations." Note well that *solid and active mind*, clothe it with splendor and majesty, and you have the best definition which can be given of him in his youth.

His thoroughly royal soul keeps its equilibrium, even in its grandest flights; its very exaltations have a certain moderation at first. Striving to exalt the sentiments of his son, without puffing him up, he says. "If I can explain my thought to you, it seems to me that we must be at the same time humble on our own account, and proud on account of the office we fill." Some of these first pages exhibit more extensive and more various aptitudes of mind than he knew how to manage.† He would have really clever princes know how to transform and

---

* The poets are not, in general, very reliable witnesses, but their suffrage serves here only to interpret the unanimous opinion. Thus La Fontaine, in an Epistle to Madame de Thianges, has said:

"Chacun attend sa gloire ainsi que sa fortune
  Du suffrage de Saint-Germain.
Le Maître y peut beaucoup; il sert de règle aux autres,
  Comme maître premièrement,
Puis comme ayant un sens meilleur que tous les nôtres."

† "His soul was greater than his mind," says Montesquieu.

to renew themselves according to political conjunctures. To be great, it is not enough for a prince to be born seasonably: "There are several of them in the world, who have obtained the reputation of cleverness simply by the advantage they have had of having been born at a time when the general condition of public affairs was exactly adapted to their turn of mind." He himself aspires to something better; he wishes to be one of those who are intellectually competent for various and even opposite situations. "For, finally, it is not easy to transform one's self at every hour in the way one should," and "the state of the world we live in is subject to revolutions so different, that it is not in our power to maintain long the same policy." In reading this passage, it seems as if Lewis XIV had had a presentiment of the rock on which, at a later day, his pride was going to founder. He was not one of those spirits that welcome the changes of the times, and his final policy was but the exaggeration of his early policy, amid general circumstances which were undergoing incessant modification.

When we read these notes written day by day, these reflections which he made on each event, when we unite with this a perusal of the diplomatic instructions which he addressed at the same time to his ambassadors and agents at the different courts, we cannot help admiring, amid the carousals and fêtes, the industry, solidity, prudence, and tenacity which mark the character of this ambitious young prince. How free is he from levity and from impulsiveness! What secrecy he has,— that royal quality necessary to success as well as to esteem, the absence of which alone throws into the background so many politicians; "for great talkers," he observes, often utter great nonsense." How, on every occasion, he prefers the slower and surer course! But it is in respect to treaties, above all, that he believes one should not pride himself upon his dispatch. He says:

"He who would proceed too fast here, is liable to take very false steps. It matters not at what time, but on what terms, a negotiation is concluded. It is much better to finish matters later than to ruin them by precipitation; and it often happens that we even delay, by our impatience, that which we were too anxious to push forward."

This policy was successful in his case at the peace of Aix-la-Chapelle (1668). The young king thus gives precepts of a premeditated and sure slowness, which seem to belong to Philippe de Commynes, and which properly come from the disciple of Mazarin.

I think I find a remarkable analogy between this way of seeing and doing which characterizes Lewis XIV, and that of the distinguished men of his time. Boileau counselled writers to remand their works twenty times to the anvil, and he advised Racine to compose laboriously easy verses. Lewis XIV gives his son political precepts entirely analogous; he counsels him to reconsider a plan twenty times before executing it; he would have him learn to find slowly in every affair the easy expedient. So also in many a moral reflection, which he intermingles with politics, he shows himself a worthy contemporary of Nicole and of Bourdaloue.

Even in military affairs and in the sieges which he undertakes, he yields to the difficulties which are pointed out to him, "persuaded," he says, "that whatever desire one may have to signalize himself, the surest road to glory is always that which reason shows." I do not say that, in his conduct, he did not swerve many times from that first resolution: for me, it is sufficient to characterize him, that he formed it in the very first heat of his ambition.

Although he is conscious of a leading and dominant ambition, and one so noble, Lewis XIV desires not to listen to it only, but to counterbalance it by others which may have no less reference to the State: "*There should be variety in glory* as well as in everything else, and in that of princes more than in that of private persons; for he who speaks of a great king, speaks of almost all the collected talents of his best subjects." There are talents in which he thinks that a king should not very much excel; it is well and honorable for him to be surpassed in them by others; but he must appreciate them in all. The knowledge of men, the discrimination of minds, and the assignment of every person to the employment for which he is fitted and in which he will be most useful to the public, is properly the great art, and it is, perhaps, the greatest talent, of a sovereign. There are princes who are right in fearing to let themselves be approached too nearly, and to communicate with others; he does not think that he is of the number, and sure as he is of himself, and of never running the risk of being taken by surprise, he succeeds by this easy communication in penetrating more deeply into the minds of those whom he addresses, and in knowing personally the most upright people in his kingdom.

It has been said that Lewis rendered monarchy despotic and Asiatic: such was never his thought. Having observed "that the liberty, the mildness, and, so to speak, the pliancy (*facilité*) of the monarchy, had passed its just bounds during his minority and the troubles of the State, so as to become licentiousness, confusion, and disorder," he believed it his duty to retrench that excess while trying at the same time to preserve the humane and affectionate character of the monarchy, to maintain near him persons of quality in an *honorable familiarity*, and to keep in communication with the people by means of pleasures and shows suited to their genius. In this Lewis XIV but half succeeded; he evidently, in his pomps, did violence to the genius of the French monarchy, and, as he grew old, ceased to be longer in sympathy with the general feeling of the nation.

He thought, and he said expressly to his son, that empires are preserved only as they are acquired, that is to say, by vigor, by vigilance, and by labor. When any injury is done to the body of the State, "it is not enough to repair the mischief, unless one adds some good thing which it had not before." He would have his son, instead of stopping on the way, and looking about him and beneath him, which are less serviceable acts, look higher:

"Think rather of those whom one has the most reason to esteem and to admire in the past ages: who, from a private position or one of very moderate influence, by the mere force of their merit, have come to found great empires, have passed like lightning from one part of the world to another, charmed the whole world by their great qualities, and left during so many ages a long and eternal memory of themselves, which seems, instead of perishing, to extend and strengthen with the daily lapse of time."

It was the unhappiness of the descendants of Lewis XIV not to have meditated enough upon this thought. The condition of hereditary kings was going to become more and more like that of the founders of empires; henceforth to preserve required almost the same genius and the same courage as to create and to acquire. I pass by Lewis XV and the mean indignities of his reign: but one may say that the good, honorable, moderate character of the respectable Bourbons who succeeded, was not equal to the occasions; they did not know how to conform to the wishes and the counsel of their great ancestor. Therefore, the ascendency went to *those who passed like lightning from one part of the world to another.*

Judicious and sensible as Lewis XIV generally was, and disposed as he evidently was to anticipate everything and to weigh everything, he felt that there are moments when, as king, it is necessary to risk a little and to plan a little at a venture, under penalty of lacking wisdom itself. The religious thought which is joined to this in his mind, adds to rather than detracts from whatever is politically remarkable in this royal maxim; and it is in these affairs that we recognize in him the real man of talent in the difficult art of ruling. He says:

"Wisdom advises us in certain junctures to trust much to chance; reason herself counsels us then to follow I know not what impulses or blind instincts, which are above reason, and seem to come from Heaven,—which are known to all men, and are most worthy of consideration by those whom it has itself placed in the first rank. To say when we must distrust them and when abandon ourselves to them, is what nobody can do; neither books, nor rules, nor experiences teach this; owing to a certain justness and a certain boldness of mind, they are found incomparably freer in the person who owes no account of his actions to anybody."

A certain justness and a certain boldness of mind: do you not admire the excellent choice and the happy juncture of these words, and the large and noble manner in which he treats of the simplest things?

I know it may be said that the text of these Memoirs was finally written out by a secretary, and simply from the king's notes; but whoever may have been that secretary, Pellisson or quite a different person, I find nothing in these pages which does not give token, from one end to the other, of the presence and dictation of the master. All there is simple and worthy of him who said: "One observes almost always some difference between the letters which we ourselves take the trouble to write, and those which our cleverest secretaries write for us,— a difference which reveals in the latter *something indescribably less natural, and the uneasiness of a pen which is eternally in fear of doing too much or too little.*" I discover none of this uneasiness, none of this rhetoric or this affected simplicity, in the pages which form the historic Memoirs of Lewis XIV. Everything there is set forth calmly and in order, with a perfect clearness, which coincides with what his contemporaries (Madame de Caylus, Madame de Motteville, Saint-Simon) have told us of the easy nobleness of the king's words: his commonest discourses were never devoid *of a natural and palpable majesty.** The style of Lewis XIV has not the vivid

---

*One day in the youth of Lewis XIV, when the Court was at Lyons, Brienne read to the queen-mother in her room, when she was at her toilet, a draught of some Letters Patent for the removal of the remains of Sainte Madeleine. He had caused these Letters Patent to be polished up by M. d'Audilly, at the request of Du Fresne, his chief deputy, who was well acquainted with the pious writer. While this was going on the king entered, directed the reading to be recommenced, and interrupted: "You make me speak like a saint, and I am not one." Brienne said to him that his chief deputy had caused these Letters to be revised by one of the cleverest men, in style and eloquence, in France. "Who is that clever fool?" said the king. When M. d'Audilly was named, "I am very glad of it," replied the king, "but that is not suited to me at all." He took the Letters, tore them in pieces, and threw them to Brienne: "Write some new ones," said he, "in which I shall speak as a king and not as a Jansenist." It was this *royal note* which Lewis XIV gave afterward to the Perignyses and to the Pellissons, and which they sought to observe in the draughts which he entrusted to them; it is this mark which it is most important to-day to find again and to recognize, without attempting to exalt unreasonably such or such a secretary.

and blunt brevity which characterizes the pages of Napoleon, that which Tacitus calls the *imperatoria brevitas*: that incisive character of the conqueror and of the despot, that short, hurried, abrupt rhythm, under which one feels palpitating the genius of action and the demon of battles, differs completely from the more tranquil, fuller, and in some sort hereditary style of Lewis XIV. When that monarch forgets himself, and is negligent, he uses long sentences, those sentences which have since been the appanage of the younger branch of the race, and of which one does not see the end; this is the manner of Lewis XIV when he dozes. But commonly, in the habitual current of his style, he maintains a proper proportion, the exact and happy medium of the purest of languages. Henry IV, the first Bourbon king, preserved in his style something warlike and Gasconish, which Lewis XIV wholly lacks. The pitiful Lewis XV, who did not want talent, and of whom some piquant sayings are reported, had endless perplexities and tautology in his habitual conversation: it was the Bourbon style after it had begun to soften and weaken. Lewis XIV alone exhibits to us this style in all its true plenitude and perfection, and, as it were, in its just and royal stature.

It has been said of Lewis that nobody told a story better than he: "he told a story, and narrated, better than a man of the world." He did these things with infinite grace, and with noble and delicate turns which only he could give to them. We have a sketch of his way of painting and describing, in his letter written from Montargis to Madame de Maintenon, upon the arrival of the Duchess of Burgundy in France; but of narrative properly so called or of story we have no specimen.

Pellisson, who was in some respects the Fontaines of that time, and whom Lewis XIV drew from the Bastille to attach him to himself and to make him his ordinary rhetorician, has transmitted to us a conversation, or rather a speech, which was taken down at the siege of Lille, on the 23d of August, 1667, from the very lips of the king. It is a speech upon glory, and upon the incentives which filled the soul of the prince at that moment. He had exposed himself in an action two days before, and, as he was censured for it, he gives his reasons for his conduct with an ingenuous solemnity. This speech shows young Lewis to us nakedly, in his first display of ambition: "It seems to me," says he, "that one robs me of my glory when he can win glory without me." That word *glory* returns at every moment to his lips, and as he concludes he becomes aware of it: "But it would ill become me to speak longer of my glory before those who are its witnesses." In this state of exaltation, this beginning of an apotheosis, in which he is thus surprised, we find him, however, more estimable than at a later day; he has some words of sympathy for friends, for the servants who expose and sacrifice themselves before his eyes: "There is no king," says he, "however ill his heart may be constituted, who can see so many brave men throw away their lives in his service, and remain with his arms folded." That is why he decided to go out of the trench, and expose himself unprotected to the fire: "I thought that on an occasion when all the appearances indicated that we should see some fine engagement, and when my presence was everything, I ought to show openly something more than a hidden valor."

Lewis XIV was not much of a soldier, and yet he professed to be one; nothing would better prove his weakness, were it necessary, than this discussion, this extraordinary apology, which he thought it necessary to make because he went one day into the trench, and at another time a little in advance of it.

Should we press him on his vain-glorious side, it would be only too easy to speak flippantly and irreverently of him. From time to time in his own speeches, we see him stop and return to himself, in order to congratulate himself deliberately; he regards himself as the type and figure of the accomplished prince; he sees himself already at full length and postured before posterity. But it is more useful to dwell upon the noble springs of action which he found in that faith and in that royal consciousness, which made him say amid certain political perils: "But, at least, whatever may be the event, I shall always have all the inward gratification which a generous soul must have when it *has satisfied its own conscience.*"

Speaking of these six volumes of Memoirs when they appeared, M. de Chateaubriand judged them very well in these words:

"The Memoirs of Lewis XIV will increase his renown; they do not unveil any baseness, they reveal none of those shameful secrets which the human heart too often conceals in its abysses. Seen more nearly and in his private life, Lewis does not cease to be Lewis the Great; one is charmed to find that so fine a bust has not an *empty head*, and that the soul corresponds to the nobleness of the external man."

It is this sentiment which predominates as we read these Memoirs, and which triumphs over all the criticisms and all the strictures which a just mind has a right to make upon them.

And since we are now considering Lewis XIV as a writer and as one of the models of speech, I will signalize, in concluding, a direct benefit he confers, and which reaches the whole literary class. I pointed out the other day and enumerated the literary persons who grouped themselves about the superintendent Fouquet, and who flourished emulously under his auspices. If we suppose for a moment that Fouquet had remained in power and established himself there, and that Lewis XIV had not disturbed him, we may very easily distinguish the elements and the spirit of the literature which would have prevailed; it would have been a freer literature in every sense than that which flourished under Lewis XIV, and the eighteenth century would have been partially anticipated. We should have had La Fontaine without any restraint, Saint Evremond, Bussy, the Scarrons, the Bachaumonts, the Hesnaults; many epicureans and some libertines would have glided over the foreground. That first literature of the day after the Fronde, and anterior to Boileau and Racine, being unrestrained by the master's eye, would have grown up with more and more freedom under so mild a Macaenas. It was all ready, we see it even now; libertinism and wit would have been its double danger; it showed elements of corruption. The young king came, and he brought along with him, he inspired (*suscita*) his young literature; he applied the proper corrective to the old, and, saving some brilliant exceptions, he impressed upon the mass of the productions of his time a solid, and, finally, a moral character which is also that which reigns in his own writings and in the habit of his thought.*

January 19, 1852.

* In reprinting this study, I have often recollected this saying of La Bruyère: "The character of the French people makes seriousness necessary in the sovereign."

FENELON.

THE present volume* must be added as an indispensable complement to the twenty-two volumes of Fenelon's *Works* and to the eleven volumes of his *Correspondence*, that is to say, to the very beautiful and very fine Paris edition (1820–1829), which the abbe Gosselin and the abbe Caron had in charge. In this new volume are collected some writings that are not without interest, some business and official letters, others of a spiritual and advisory character, and especially some charming friendly and familiar letters: these are quite sufficient to identify Fenelon in every respect. The last part of the volume contains some of La Fontaine's *Fables* translated into Latin prose for the use of the duke of Burgundy. A specimen of these translated Fables had already been published; to-day we have an entire series, extending to the eighth book. The keen relish of Fenelon for La Fontaine is well known. When the poet died he praised him in a pretty Latin piece, in which he celebrated his artless graces, his open and simple nature, his unadorned elegance, and that singular negligence which was permitted to him alone, an inestimable negligence which is far superior to a more polished style. (*Politiori stilo quantum praestitit aurea negligentia!*)

Fenelon and La Fontaine resemble each other in this,

* Lettres et Opuscules inédits de Fénélon, 1850.

that we like them both without knowing why, and even before we have studied them carefully. A kind of perfume emanates from their writings, which insinuates itself into the mind and prepossesses it in their favor; the physiognomy of the man speaks at the very first in behalf of the author; the look and the smile mingle together, and, as we approach them, the heart inclines to them without demanding a very exact account of the reason. An examination of either author will bring to light many defects, many weak or languid passages, but the first impression will continue to be the true one, and it will also be the last. It seems as if La Fontaine alone, of all the French poets, had partially complied with the desire which Fenelon expressed in a letter to La Motte, that gifted man so little like La Fontaine: "I am so much the more impressed by whatever exquisite compositions we have in our language, because it is neither harmonious, varied, free, grand, nor fit for lofty flights, and because our scrupulous versification renders beautiful verse almost impossible in a long work." La Fontaine, however, with such a language as Fenelon described, knew how to be playful in poetry, and to give to the most fastidious readers that sentiment of the exquisite which modern poets so rarely excite. He gratified that other wish of Fenelon: "It is necessary, if I am not deceived, to take only the choicest part of each theme, and to touch only that which one can beautify." And, finally, he seems to have been brought into the world expressly to prove that in French poetry it was not entirely impossible to find what Fenelon furthermore desired: "I would like something indescribable, which is an ease to which it is very difficult to attain." Take our celebrated authors, and you will find in them nobleness, energy, eloquence, elegance, passages that are sublime; but the indescribable ease which communicates itself to all the sentiments, to all the thoughts, and which captivates the reader, that ease mingled with persuasion, you will rarely find, save in Fenelon and La Fontaine.

The reputation of both went on increasing to the eighteenth century, whilst that of many of their illustrious contemporaries seemed to diminish, and was unjustly contested. I would not pretend that one has not been sometimes surfeited with these two men of renown, so diversely amiable, but not dissimilar in classes so different, and that those who have praised them have not indulged in that exaggeration and declamation which were so disagreeable to them. For example, Fenelon has been very much praised for a toleration in doctrinal matters, and almost for a laxity, which certainly did not characterize him. The philosophers have treated him as if he was one of their number, and he has found favor even with the very persons who would destroy that which he adored. But shall I say it?— in spite of all the objections which may be justly made to this false philosophical view which men have wanted to take of Fenelon, there was an instinct which never wholly deceived those who treated him with this peculiar favor; for, if Fenelon was not tolerant in matters of doctrine, he was so personally and in his natural character, and he knew how to give to everything a tone, a graceful turn, an unction which made men accept even the harshest prescriptions.

I find some of these which have such an appearance in the volume I have just read, showing that Fenelon was by no means a bishop according to the too easy ordination of La Harpe, D'Alembert, and Voltaire. A number of the new letters (and they are not otherwise the most interesting) are addressed to M. de Bernières, then governor of Hainault and afterward of Flanders. This M. de Bernières, who, if I am not deceived, sprang from a family closely allied to Port Royal, was a good man, of good mind, and lived in perfect sympathy with the archbishop of Cambray. In March, 1700, Fenelon wrote a letter asking him to unite with himself in making regulations for the observance of the church laws during the coming Lent: "It has seemed to me," says the prelate, "that the rule would never be re-established, if it were not promptly renewed after ten years of continual dispensation. Peace has been established for more than two years; the winter is mild; the season is very far advanced, and people must have more vegetables than in other years; the high prices are lessening daily. Should we let the people still eat eggs, a kind of prescription would be established against the law, as has happened with milk, butter, and cheese. . . ." Here, then, we have Fenelon as bishop, in good earnest, strict in the pettiest details, and treating them as important. But close by him we recognize, even in these very details, the Fenelon of tradition, the popular Fenelon. M. de Bernières, during that same Lent of 1700, requested that the army might have certain dispensations from the rule, and Fenelon hastened to grant them to the soldiers; but "it does not seem, sir," he adds, "that I should grant to the officers, paid by the king, a dispensation which I refuse to the poorest of the people." This sentiment of equity, especially with regard to the humble, this happiness of the people, also evidently prepossesses him in other passages; but they would teach us nothing new, and I pass to the other letters of the collection. There are some letters addressed to Madame de Maintenon. Fenelon, it is well known, was one of her chief favorites, whom she had most frequently consulted, before she had the weakness to abandon him. Saint-Simon, in his *Memoirs*, has given so lively an account of Fenelon's introduction to the court, of that initiation into the little private world of Madame de Maintenon, and the dukes of Beauvilliers and Chevreuse, of the rapid good fortune of the happy prelate, which was soon followed by so many vicissitudes and disgraces, the shipwreck of hopes which is to-day a touching part of his glory, that we can only refer the reader to that great painter, and it would be profanation to meddle with his pictures, even when one believes that some of the lines are too bold or too free. Saint-Simon was endowed with a double genius, which is rarely possessed to the same extent: he had received from nature that gift of penetration and almost of intuition, the gift of reading minds and hearts through physiognomies and faces, and of discerning there the secret play of motives and intentions; he carried into that piercing observation of the numberless masks and actors that crowded around him an inspiration, an ardor of curiosity, which seemed at times insatiable and almost cruel; the eager anatomist is not more prompt to open the still palpitating breast, and to search there in all directions that he may disclose the hidden disease. To this first gift of instinctive and irresistible penetration Saint-Simon joined another, which is not often found in the same degree of potency, and whose daring exercise made him unique in his line; that which he had plucked out, as it were, with that ravenous curiosity, he portrayed with the same fire, with the same ardor, and almost the same fury of description (*de pinceau*). La Bruyère, also, has the faculty of penetrating and sagacious observation; he notices, he lays bare everything and every man about him; he reads with subtlety their secrets on all the foreheads around him; then, returning home, he leisurely, fondly, cunningly, slowly tráces his portraits, recommences them, retouches them, polishes them, adds to them lineament after lineament, till he finds them to be perfect resemblances. But it is not so with Saint-Simon, who after those days at Versailles or at Marly, which I call debauches of observation (so many things had he gathered together, that were wholly diverse and unlike), returns home excited, and there, pen in hand, and at full speed, without resting, without re-reading his composition, and very late in the night, puts down all alive upon paper, in their plenitude and their natural confusion, and at the same time with an incomparable clearness of outline, the thousand characters he has met with, the thousand originals he has seized flying, whom he bears along all palpitating still, and of whom the majority become, by his manipulation, immortal victims.

Fenelon also came very near being one of his victims; for, all the while that Saint-Simon recognizes his charming and delightful qualities, he perpetually insists upon a hidden vein of ambition, which, possessed to the degree that he supposes, would have made Fenelon quite a different man from what one loves to believe he really was. In this respect we believe that the picture of the great painter, to be truthful, must be slightly modified, and that his fancy took too great a flight. He did not penetrate and dwell at leisure in all parts of that amiable soul. Saint-Simon, through the dukes of Beauvilliers and Chevreuse,

knew Fenelon as well as one can know a man by means
of his most intimate friends. He had seen very little of
him personally, and he tells us so: "I knew him only by
sight, being too young when he was exiled." A simple
sight, however, was enough for such a painter, and he
caught and reproduced the charm with marvellous skill.
He says:

"That prelate was a tall, lean man, well made, pale, with a
great nose, eyes from which fire and spirit (*esprit*) streamed forth
like a torrent, and a physiognomy wholly unlike any other I have
ever seen, and which could never be forgotten even if you had seen
it but once. All expressions were united in it, and the most dissimilar ones harmonized. It had gravity and courtesy, seriousness
and gaiety; it spoke equally of the doctor, the bishop, and the great
lord, but the qualities which were most conspicuous in it, as well as
in his whole person, were delicacy, wit, gracefulness, propriety, and,
above all, nobleness. It required an effort to cease to look at him."

When one has once painted a man of this description,
and has shown him gifted with this power of attraction,
one can never afterward be accused of having calumniated
him, even though he may have failed to appreciate some
of his qualities. Moreover, it is with Saint-Simon that
one may advantageously combat and correct Saint-Simon
himself. Let any one read what he says so admirably
of the duke of Burgundy, that cherished pupil of Fenelon,
whom the prelate did not cease to guide when far away
from him, even during his exile at Cambray, by means
of the dukes of Beauvilliers and Chevreuse. That young
prince, whom Saint-Simon represents to us as so haughty,
so fiery, so terribly passionate at first, and of whom, so
contemptuous to everybody, he could say: "From the
upper heavens he looked down upon men as atoms only,
with whom he had no resemblance, whatever they might

be; hardly did his brothers appear to him as intermediate beings between him and the human race;" that same prince, on a certain day, is changed, transformed, and becomes a wholly different man, pious, humane, charitable as well as enlightened, attentive to his duties, fully conscious of his responsibility as future king; and that heir of Lewis XIV dares to utter, even in the *salon* at Marly, that saying which is capable of making palaces crumble, that "a king is made for his subjects, and not the subjects for the king." Well, this prince, thus described by Saint-Simon, and whose death draws from him,— from him the inexorable observer,— accents of touching eloquence and tears, had been thus transformed,— by whom? Let us leave out of the account the effect due to all which you may please to regard as mysterious and invisible in these inner operations, even to what is called Grace; let us leave out the part played by the venerable duke de Beauvilliers, an excellent governor; and to whom, among human agencies, shall we ascribe a larger share in the result than to Fenelon, who, near and afar, never ceased directly to influence his pupil, to inculcate upon him, to instill into his mind this maxim for a *father of his country*, that "a king is made for the people," and all that follows from it?

At the present time, we know more, in certain respects, about this matter than Saint-Simon did: we have the confidential letters which Fenelon addressed, during the whole time, to the prince, the memoranda which he wrote for him, the plans of reform, pieces which were then all kept secret, but to-day are made public, and which, while allowing us to leave to human ambition the place which we must always give to every man's faults, even amid his virtues, show these last to have been, at least, of the first rank, and place the patriotic and generous soul of Fenelon henceforth in the clearest light.

Bossuet, also, in concert with the duke of Montausier, trained a pupil, the first Dauphin, father of that same duke of Burgundy; it was for that royal and unworthy pupil that he wrote so many admirable compositions, beginning with the *Discourse upon Universal History*, which posterity will forever enjoy. But, looking at the matter more closely, what a difference in care and anxiety! The first Dauphin was, no doubt, a poorer subject for education; he had a gentleness that amounted to apathy. The duke of Burgundy, with strong passions and even vices, had at least some force, and betrayed the sacred fire in him. "Lively and sensitive natures," Fenelon finely says, "are capable of terrible excesses; but they have also great resources, and often come back after long wanderings . . . whilst one has no hold upon indolent natures." Meanwhile do you see that Bossuet, in order to overcome the indolence of his pupil, and to rouse his sensibilities, did nearly the same thing that Fenelon did, in the second case, to subdue and humanize the violent passions of his pupil? The first great man did his duty with amplitude and majesty, as he was wont, and he went beyond it. The second multiplied his attentions and solicitudes, his ingenious and vigilant cares, his insinuating and persuasive addresses, as if his heart were bound up in his pupil's; he had all the tenderness of a mother.

To return to the present volume, I said, then, that we do not find in it any of the letters which Fenelon, when he first came to the Court, addressed to Madame de Maintenon, while she was still under the spell. The tone of Fenelon's *Spiritual Letters* is generally delicate, refined, easy, and very agreeable to soft and feminine minds, but a little tame, and infected with some of the jargon of quietistic spirituality; it savors too strongly of the neighborhood of Madame Guyon. Fenelon is also too lavish in them of expressions designedly infantile and mincing, such as Saint François de Sales addressed to his ideal devotee, *Philothée*. Speaking of certain familiarities and certain endearments which, as he thought, the Heavenly Father grants to souls that have become young and simple again, Fenelon will say, for example: "It is necessary to be a child, O my God, and to play upon your knees, in order to deserve them." Some theologians have sought to quarrel with these expressions and others like them, on doctrinal grounds; a severe good taste suffices to proscribe them. And it is here that the sound and manly method which Bossuet carried into every subject manifests its complete superiority.

In speaking thus of Fenelon's Letters, I am aware of the exceptions which it is proper to make: there are some which are very fine in every respect and some very weighty ones, such as that to a lady of quality *upon the education of her daughter*, and the *Letters upon Religion*, which are supposed to have been addressed to the duke of Orleans (the future Regent), and which are commonly placed at the end of the treatise *On the Existence of God*. But I am speaking of the *Spiritual Letters* properly so called, and I have no fear that those who shall have read a good number of them will contradict me.

Madame de Maintenon, when receiving Fenelon's letters, and while enjoying their infinite delicacy, estimated them, nevertheless, with that excellent judgment and that good sense which she applied to everything that was not beyond her comprehension and the horizon of her mind. She had doubts about certain expressions that were somewhat lively and bold, with the details of which I must here dispense. In order to satisfy her mind, she consulted another spiritual guide, a man of sense, the bishop of Chartres (Godet des Marais), and Fenelon had to justify and explain himself. In the explanation which we read in this volume, and with which he tries to reduce these mystic and slightly strange expressions to their just value, I am struck by a habitual turn of language which has been already noticed, and which is a characteristic trait of Fenelon. In the very act of upholding these expressions, or at least, while justifying them by means of respectable authorities, he concludes each paragraph by saying, by repeating in all forms: "A prophet (or a saint) had already said, before me, something equivalent or stronger; I only repeat the same thing, and rather less strongly; but *meanwhile I submit.*" This refrain of submission, perpetually recurring at the end of a justification which he seems to offer as victorious, produces at length a singular effect, and at last puts out of patience even those who are in the slightest degree theologians. I call that an irritating meekness, and the impression one experiences tends to confirm the remark which Joubert had already made: "The disposition of Fenelon had something in it that was sweeter than sweetness itself, more patient than patience." This, again, is a fault.

That which is not one, most certainly, is the general character of his piety, the piety of which he has personal experience, and whose spirit he breathes. He would have it joyous, buoyant, sweet-tempered; he banishes from it all sadness and asperity: "Piety," said he, "has nothing in it that is weak, or sad, or constrained; it enlarges the heart; it is artless and lovely; it becomes all things to all, to win them all." He reduces almost all piety to love, that is to say, to charity. This sweetness of his, own however, is neither weakness nor compliance. In the little which is given us here of his counsels to Madame de Maintenon, he shows that he knows how to put his finger upon the essential faults, upon that self-love which would take the lead in anything, that enslavement to respectability, that ambition to appear perfect in the eyes of good people, in fine all the essential qualities of that prudent and glorious nature. There is, besides, in the mass of Fenelon's *Spiritual Letters*, a certain variety by which he adapts himself to different persons, and there must certainly have been a similar variety in his conversation. The *Conversations* which Ramsay has transmitted to us, in which Fenelon sets forth the reasons which, as he thinks, should victoriously lead every deist to the Catholic faith, have a breadth, a simple beauty, a copious and luminous eloquence, which leave nothing to desire. Just as the conversation of Pascal and M. de Saci, which has been preserved for us, is one of the most beautiful proofs of the genius of Pascal, so these *Conversations* transmitted by Ramsay give us the highest idea of Fenelon's manner, and surpass in breadth of tone even the majority of his letters.

The most interesting part of the volume now published is composed of a series of familiar letters addressed by Fenelon to one of his friends, a meritorious military man, the chevalier Destouches. Every eminent person that passed through Cambray (and nearly the whole army passed through it at each campaign, during those wars in the last years of Lewis XIV), saw Fenelon, and was entertained by him; and owing to that peculiar attraction of his, more than one lasting intimacy was contracted by him with these passing acquaintances. That which he had with the chevalier Destouches was one of the closest and tenderest. Destouches, then forty-three years old, was serving with distinction in the artillery; he was an intellectual, cultivated man, and keenly relished Virgil. With all that, he was dissipated, abandoned to pleasure, to that of the table, which was not his only fault; and we are obliged to confess that his acquaintance with Fenelon never led to his thorough conversion, since it is he who is supposed to have been the father of D'Alembert, whom he might have had by Madame de Tencin in 1717. Be this as it may, Fenelon loved him, and this one word redeemed all. The amiable prelate told him so in all ways, while scolding him and chiding him, and even while plainly seeing that he was meeting with little success. He wrote to him one day (April, 1714):

"If you were to go and show my letter to some grave and severe censor, he would be sure to say: 'Why does that old bishop (Fenelon was then sixty-three years old) love so deeply a man who is profane?' That is a great scandal, I confess; but how shall I reform? The truth is, I find two men in you; you are double like Sosia, without any duplicity for purposes of trickery; on one side, you are bad for yourself; on the other, you are true, upright, noble, everything to your friends. I conclude with a protest drawn from your friend Pliny the Younger: *Neque enim amore decipior.*"

That is to say: "Affection does not blind me; it is true I love to excess, but I still judge my friends, and with the more penetration the more I love."

This correspondence of Fenelon with the chevalier Destouches shows us the prelate even in those saddest years (1711-1714) recreating himself at times with innocent jesting, like Laelius and Scipio, after having removed his girdle. He seems to have proposed a wager in this correspondence; he seems to have said to his somewhat libertine friend: "You like Virgil; you frequently quote him; well, I send you back to Horace; I wish, to beat you, no other auxiliary than he, and I pledge myself to instill into you almost all the counsels that are suited to your case, or, at least, all the counsels that are useful in life, by disguising them in verses of Horace." Horace, indeed, reappears in every line of these letters, and it is as often he that speaks as Fenelon. These letters give a perfect idea of what that conversation, the most charming and the most refined, must have been in the sweet hours of gaiety and enjoyment; they are the table-talk and the "after-dinners" of Fenelon, the liveliest things in a subdued tone. We perceive in them the habits of thought and feeling, and the precise accent of that fine nature, as if we were present. Destouches had sent some Latin epitaphs to the prelate: "The epitaphs," replies Fenelon, "have much significance, every line is an epigram; they are historic and curious. Those who made them had much wit; but they wanted to have it; one should have it only inadvertently, and without thinking of it. They are composed in the spirit of Tacitus, which searches for what is bad." Further on, after having quoted some strophes of Horace upon peace, Fenelon chances to recall a stanza of Malherbe: "That is the ancient style," he says, "which is simple, graceful, exquisite, here is the modern, *which has its beauty*." How well that is said! how well is the proportion, the gradation from the modern to the ancient, preserved, and how decidedly does one feel that he prefers the ancient! Serious and touching thoughts sometimes intersperse these plays of the mind. The year 1811 was big with interest to Fenelon. The first Dauphin died on the fourteenth of April, and the duke of Burgundy became the next heir, and, according to all appearance, was very near to the throne. One would have said that in the background of his exile at Cambray Fenelon enjoyed the full radiance of the Court, and that he already reigned by the side of his royal pupil. Consulted in writing upon every political or ecclesiastical matter, often secretly heard as arbiter in the Jansenist disputes, become again a doctor and an oracle, he played already the chief *rôle* in his turn. But suddenly misfortunes begin to befall him; the duchess of Burgundy dies on the twelfth of February, 1712; the duke of Burgundy follows her on the eighteenth, six days afterward, at the age of twenty-nine; and all the hopes, all the tendernesses, shall we dare say the secret aspirations, of the prelate, vanish. We see traces of his profound grief even in this jesting correspondence; but how simple and true the words are, and how utterly they reject every malicious thought! Learning of the death of the princess, which so little preceded that of his pupil, Fenelon wrote to Destouches (February 18):

"The sad news that has reached us from your region, Monsieur, robs me of all the joy which was the soul of our intercourse: *Quis desiderio sit pudor.* . . . Truly the loss is very great to the Court and to the whole kingdom. One must be greatly pained for those who lament her with so just a grief. (*What a delicate way of indicating his fears with regard to the duke of Burgundy!*) You see how frail life is. Four days; they are not sure! Everybody puts on a wise look, as if he were immortal; the world is but a crowd of living people, who are feeble, false, and ready to rot; the most shining fortune is but a pleasing dream."

These are not the loud accents of Bossuet, the broad flaps of his wing, as he cries from the top of the pulpit: *Madame is dying! Madame is dead!* But, with less *éclat* and thunder, is not this as eloquent and as penetrating?

On hearing of the death of the duke of Burgundy, Fenelon has but a word; it is brief and heart-felt; it is what it should be: "God knows I suffer; but I have not fallen sick, and that is a good deal for me. Your heart, which makes itself felt by mine, soothes it. I should have been deeply pained to see you here; think of your bad health; *it seems to me that all that I love is going to die.*" To write thus to the chevalier Destouches amid such grief, was to honor him very highly.

The mundane rebound of this cruel loss was keenly felt by Fenelon. The day before, he was the man of the future reign and of the highest expectations; to-day, he is nothing, his dream has dissolved, and, if he could forget this for an instant, the world is immediately at his side to tell him of it. An eminent man, a friend of Destouches, had offered his daughter to one of Fenelon's nephews; the day after the death of the duke of Burgundy, this man retracts and withdraws his promise. Fenelon is not astonished at this; he casts no blame upon that father so anxious for the safe marriage of his daughter; he praises him, and even thanks him for the blamelessness of his conduct. He writes to Destouches:

"With regard to your friend, I conjure you to cherish no ill will toward him on account of his change; his wrong-doing consists at most in having expected too much from a frail and uncertain support; it is upon such uncertain hopes that the worldly wise are wont to hazard certain schemes. He who cannot pardon men for such things must become misanthropic: we must, for ourselves, avoid such rocks in life, and we must readily pardon them in the case of our neighbor."

Admirable and serene, or, at least, tranquil disposition, which peeps out in more than one place in this correspondence! Fenelon knew the world and men profoundly, he has no illusions in regard to them. Was a tender heart like his to have, then, nothing more to learn in the way of disgusts and bitternesses? But he is not, for all this, misanthropic, and if he ever were so, he would have a way of being so which would not resemble anybody's else. He writes to Destouches:

"I am very glad, my dear good fellow, that you are pleased with one of my letters which has been shown to you. You are right in saying and believing that I ask little of men in general; I try to do much for them, and to expect nothing in return. I find a decided advantage in these terms; on these terms I defy them to disappoint me. It is only upon a very small number of true friends that I count, and I do it not from motives of interest, but from pure esteem; not from a desire to derive any advantage from them, but to do them justice in not distrusting their affection. I would like to oblige the whole human race, especially virtuous people; but there is scarcely anybody to whom I would like to be under obligation. Is it through haughtiness and pride that I think thus? Nothing could be more foolish and more unbecoming; but I have learned to know men as I have grown old, and I believe that it is the best way to do without them without pretending to superior wisdom." "I have pitied men," he says again, "although they are seldom good."

This rarity of good men, which appears to him to be the *shame of the human race*, led him to love his chosen friends all the more: "The comparison only makes us too highly prize those persons who are true, gentle, trustworthy, reasonable, susceptible of friendship, and superior to all self-interest." Once only is he caught betraying a curious mind; it is concerning prince Eugene, in whom he thinks he perceives a truly great man. He confesses that it would be curious to know and to observe him:

"His military deeds are great; but what I esteem most in him is qualities in which what is called fortune has no part I am assured that he is true, free from ostentation and from pride, ready to hear without prejudice, and to reply in precise terms. He steals moments for reading, he loves merit, he adapts himself to all nationalities, he inspires confidence; that is the man whom you are going to see. I also would like well to see him in our Low Coûntries; I confess I have some curiosity concerning him, although I have little left for the human race."

The death of the duke of Beauvilliers (August 31, 1714,) finished breaking the last close ties that attached Fenelon to the future: "True friends," he wrote on that occasion to Destouches, "make all the sweetness and all the bitterness of life." It was to Destouches also that he wrote that admirable letter, already cited by M. de Bausset, upon the desirability "of all good friends having an understanding to die together on the same day," and he cites thereupon Philemon and Baucis; so true is it that there is a real affinity, and not one of which we have dreamed, between the soul of Fenelon and that of La Fontaine.

This is enough to indicate the interest of these new letters. Some further details might be found there of Fenelon's last year. The peace which had just been signed imposed new duties upon him. He writes to Destouches:

"That which ends your labors, begins mine; the peace which restores your liberty, takes mine away; I have to visit seven hundred and sixty-four villages. You will not be surprised that I wish to do my duty,— you, whom I have seen so scrupulous about yours, in spite of your misfortunes and your wound."

Six weeks before his death, in one of his pastoral visits, his carriage had upset, and he had come near being killed; he tells the story very pleasantly:

"A very long absence has delayed the reply I owe you. It is true, dear man, that I was in the greatest danger of being killed;

I have still to learn how I was saved; never was one happier in losing three horses. All my people cried out to me: '*All is lost! save yourself!*' I did not hear them; the glass windows were raised. I was reading a book, having my glasses upon my nose, my pencil in hand, and my legs in a bear-skin sack; such nearly was the position of Archimedes, when he perished at the capture of Syracuse. The comparison is idle, but the accident was frightful."

He enters into the detail of the accident: a mill-wheel, which suddenly began turning at the end of a bridge without railings, one of the horses frightened and jumping headlong, etc. Even to the last, in spite of his mental sorrows, and though he had been heart-sick ever since the loss of his cherished pupil, Fenelon could smile, and that without great effort. He has that light-hearted gaiety which is neither dissipation nor a lie, and which, in him, is but the natural expression of a chaste, even, temperate soul; he has that joy of which he has said so well that "frugality, health and innocence are its true sources." In his last letter of December 1, 1714 (that is to say, a month before falling ill with his final sickness), he jested still with Destouches upon the *pretty* repasts in which the chevalier indulged, at the risk of repenting of them: "It is at Cambray," he says, "that one is sober, healthy, light-hearted, content and gay by rule." The general tone of these friendly letters is marked by these very words. In reading this familiar correspondence, I find again, as in everything of Fenelon's, a certain blending of the gay, the concise, the lively, the smooth, the easy, the insinuating and the enchanting.

Among the pleasantries we meet with in these letters, there are some which relate to the dispute about the Ancients and the Moderns which was then raging in the Academy, and which was rekindled anew at the very time when peace was made in Europe. La Motte, a friend of the chevalier Destouches, had just translated, or travestied, Homer's *Iliad*, and he sent it to Fenelon, to ask his opinion of it. Fenelon on this occasion was a little weak. Invoked as judge and as arbiter between the two parties, he evaded. He thought that in these matters which do not concern the safety of the State, one may be more accommodating than in others, and incline toward politeness. He replies to La Motte with compliments and praises, without wishing to decide upon the substantial merits of the work; he gets out of the difficulty by means of a verse from Virgil, which leaves the contest undecided between two shepherds: *Et vitula tu dignus, et hic.* . . . The contest undecided between La Motte and Homer! And it is Fenelon, the translator, the continuer of the *Odyssey*, the father of *Telemachus*, who speaks thus! Is it really possible to carry toleration to this point? Evidently Fenelon had not that irritability of good sense and of reason which makes one say *No* vehemently, that straightforward and prompt faculty, and even a little blunt too, which Despréaux manifested in literature, and Bossuet in theology. We find here, again, a weak side.

To each one his glory and its shadows. We may catch Fenelon at fault on several points. Bossuet, in theology, pushed him rudely. I find him equally refuted, and forcibly rebuked, in respect to his *Dialogues upon Eloquence* and some bold assertions concerning the ancient orators, by a well-informed man, a severe and by no means contemptible mind, that is equally opposed to Rollin and to Gibert. But what matter, to-day, a few inaccuracies? Fenelon had the spirit of piety, and he had the spirit of antiquity. He unites in himself these two spirits, or rather he possesses and holds them each in its sphere, without contention, without a struggle, without placing them in conflict, without letting anything apprise us of the discord, and that is a great charm. With him the contest between Christianity and Greece does not exist, and Telemachus is the only monument of that happy and almost impassible harmony.

Telemachus (how can one avoid saying a word of it in speaking of Fenelon?) is not purely ancient in its style. A reproduction of the purely ancient style to-day, would be more or less of a copy and an imitation. We have had, within a short time, some striking samples of that style, elaborated and reproduced with feeling and skill. *Telemachus* is something different, something much more natural and more original in its very imitation. It is the *antique* recovered naturally and without effort by a modern genius, by a christian heart, which, nourished by the Homeric language, remembers it freely, and draws from it as from the fountain; but he insensibly remoulds and transforms it, as he recollects it. This beauty, thus diverted, softened and not changed, runs in Fenelon's work, in a full channel, and overflows like a copious and flowing stream, a stream ever sacred, which adapts itself to its new declivities and its new banks. There is but one thing to be done, in order to appreciate *Telemachus* properly; forget, if you can, that you read it too much in your childhood. I had that happiness last year; I had, as it were, forgotten *Telemachus*, and I have been able to read it again with the freshness of a novelty.

As a literary man, Fenelon has been greatly praised, and many attempts have been made to characterize him; but nowhere, in my judgment, has he been described with a happier delicacy of expression or with a more striking truthfulness than in the following passage, which has reference to his style as well as to his person: "It is not transports which he makes us experience, but a succession of peaceful and ineffable sentiments; there was in his discourse an indefinable tranquil harmony, an indefinable pleasing slowness, an indefinable prolongation of charms, which no language can describe." It is Chactas who says that in *Les Natchez*. It is very singular that such a speech should be found on the lips of an American savage, but it is none the less beautiful and perfect for that, and worthy of being inscribed at the end of Fenelon's pages.

April 1, 1850.

BOSSUET.

THE glory of Bossuet has become one of the religions of France; we recognize it, we proclaim it, we honor ourselves by paying to it daily a new tribute, by finding new reasons for its existence and for its increase; we no longer discuss it. It is the privilege of true greatness to become more conspicuous in proportion as one draws away from it, and to command attention at a distance. What is singular, however, in this fortune and in this kind of apotheosis of Bossuet, is that he becomes thus greater and greater to us, while, for all that, we do not necessarily admit that he was right. in some of the most important controversies in which he was engaged You love Fenelon, you cherish his graces, his noble and fine insinuation, his chaste elegances; you could easily pardon him what are called his errors; and Bossuet has combated those errors, not only forcibly, but furiously, with a kind of roughness. No matter! the loud voice of the adversary transports you in spite of yourself, and compels you to bow your head, without regard to your secret affection for him whom he beats down. So with the long and obstinate pitched battles which have been fought upon the Gallican question. Are you a Gallican, or are you not? According to your belief, you applaud or you heave a sigh at this part of his career, but his illustrious course none the less, as a whole, maintains in your eyes its elevation and its majesty. I shall dare to say the same thing of the war without truce which Bossuet waged against Protestantism in all its forms. Every enlightened Protestant, while reserving the historic points, will acknowledge with respect that he has never encountered two such adversaries. In politics also, though one may not be very partial to the sacred theory and to divine right, as Bossuet revives and establishes it, one would be almost sorry if that doctrine had not found so plain, so manly, so sincere a spokesman, and one, too, so naturally convinced of its truth. A God, a Christ, a bishop, a king,— here, in its entirety, is the luminous sphere in which the thought of Bossuet expands and reigns; this is his ideal of the world. So, that there was in antiquity a people set apart, who, under the inspiration and leadership of Moses, kept clear and distinct the idea of a creative and ever-present God, directly governing the world, while all the surrounding peoples strayed away from that idea, which was obscure to them, into the mists of fancy, or smothered it under the phantoms of the imagination and drowned it in the exuberant luxury of nature,— this simple idea of order, of authority, of unity, of the continual government of Providence, Bossuet among the moderns has grasped more completely than any other person, and he applies it on all occasions without effort, and, as it were, by an invincible deduction. Bossuet's is the Hebrew genius extended, fecundated by Christianity, and open to all the acquisitions of the understanding, but retaining some degree of sovereign interdiction, and closing its vast horizon precisely where its light ceases. In gesture and tone he reminds one of Moses; in his speech there are mingled some of the expressions of the Prophet-

King,— bursts of intense and sublime pathos; it is a voice preëminently eloquent,— the simplest, the strongest, the bluntest, the most familiar,— one that thunders with a peculiar suddenness. Even when he rolls along with an unbending current and an imperious flood, his eloquence carries with it treasures of an eternal human morality. It is in all these qualities that we regard him as unparalleled, and whatever the use he makes of his speech, he remains the model of the highest eloquence and of the most beautiful language.

These truths are no longer novel: how many times have we heard them! The two works we announce do no more than set forth and develop them, each in its own way. M. de Lamartine has traced in the first pages of his study a portrait of Bossuet thus grandly conceived. M. Poujoulat, in a series of Letters addressed to a foreign politician, tries to show that Bossuet is not only great in the celebrated works of his which one commonly reads, but that he is the same man and the same genius in his entire habit of thought, and in the mass of his productions. A conscientious writer, accustomed to historical labors, to those which touch upon the history of religion in particular, M. Poujoulat writes with a pen that is as grave as the thought.* He states that he has re-read in the country the works of Bossuet, and that he has taken pleasure, after each reading, in gathering his reflections in the form of letters to a friend: one may profitably run over with him the series of Sermons and Theological Treatises, which all contain such real beauties. His work inspires esteem. To comment on Bossuet is, in

Lettres sur Bossuet à un Homme d'État, par M. Poujoulat, 1854. *Portrait de Bossuet*, par M. de Lamartine, 1854.

the long run, a difficult and even dangerous task; the citations which one makes speak for themselves, and light up certain pages to such an extent as to dim everything that adjoins them. M. Poujoulat has very happily escaped this danger by a great fidelity in exposition, and by a sincerity of belief which has permitted him to enter into the discussion of principles. Discussion, perhaps, is a good deal to say; it is not necessary, at least, to understand it in a historic or philosophic sense; it is evident that upon a multitude of points which give occasion for it, M. Poujoulat writes with all the confidence and all the security of French convictions, which do not sufficiently suspect the nature and the force of the objections put forth by a more independent and more extensive critical science. But morally he regains his superiority; he labors constantly to render his commentary useful by applying it to our own times, to ourselves, to the vices of society, and to the disease of our hearts: "Bossuet is especially the man of the age we live in," he thinks; and he gives the reasons for this opinion, which are rather honorable desires on his part, than facts manifest to all.

It would be easy here to bring him into conflict with M. de Lamartine, who, all the while that he admires Bossuet, is of a contrary opinion; but I may be permitted rather to turn aside some time from the commentators and the painters, that I may go straight to the master. Upon Bossuet there is a work still to be done, a work which will exhaust all that may be positively and precisely known of him. M. de Bausset, forty years ago, gave an agreeable History of Bossuet, rich even in details, and which, in certain respects, will not be improved; but, in many passages there is room for further researches, and for the investigations which distinguished men of letters and academicians then willingly spared themselves. To these investigations and researches, at once pious and indefatigable, a scholar of our day, M. Floquet, has devoted himself for several years, and the *History of Bossuet* which will result from them, will soon appear. This will be a solid and final basis for the study and admiration of the great man. Meanwhile I have under my eyes an exceedingly commendable work of a young man of merit, who died a short time ago. The abbe Victor Vaillant, having to give in to the Paris Faculty of Lettres, in 1851, his thesis as doctor, chose for his theme, *A Study on the Sermons of Bossuet according to the manuscripts*. He showed that those sermons, so well appreciated by the Abbe Maury at the first moment of their publication (1772), had not been given to the public then, nor reprinted since, with all the exactness which might have been demanded. Criticising the first editor, Dom Déforis, with an extreme severity, repeated and in part imitated by that of M. Cousin toward the first editors of Pascal's *Thoughts*, the Abbe Vaillant applied himself afterward to something more useful, that is to say, to discovering the chronological order of Bossuet's Sermons and Panegyrics; looking into the matter closely, he succeeded in determining the dates of a good number of them, at least approximatively. From to-day, then, we may study Bossuet confidently, in his first manner; we are able, as in the case of the great Corneille, to follow the progress and the march of that genius which went on magnifying and perfecting itself, but which had no decline or decay. I will try to give an idea of that first manner by some examples.

Bossuet, born at Dijon on the twenty-seventh of September, 1627, of a good and ancient plebeian family of magistrates and parliamentarians, was reared there in the midst of books and in the family library. His father, who had entered the Parliament of Metz, lately created, as dean of the councillors, left his children in the care of a brother who was a councillor in the Parliament of Dijon. Young Bossuet, who remained in his uncle's house, was educated at the Jesuit College of the city. He distinguished himself early by a surprising capacity of memory and of understanding; he knew Virgil by heart, as, a little later, he knew Homer. "One comprehends less easily," says M. de Lamartine, "how *he was infatuated all his life* with the Latin poet Horace, an exquisite but refined genius, the cords of whose lyre are only the softest fibres of the heart; an indolent voluptuary," etc. M. de Lamartine, who has so well perceived the leading qualities of Bossuet's eloquence and talent, has studied his life a little too lightly, and has here supposed a difficulty which does not exist; in fact, there is no mention anywhere of that *inexplicable predilection* of Bossuet for Horace, *the least divine of all the poets*. M. de Lamartine must have inadvertently read Horace instead of *Homer*, and he has taken occasion to treat Homer, *the friend of good sense*, almost as badly as he formerly treated La Fontaine.* It was Fenelon (and not Bossuet), who read and relished Horace, more than any other poet, who knew him by heart, who quoted him incessantly, who, in his correspond-

* M. de Lamartine, let us say it once for all, is so careless in regard to such matters of fact, he possesses in so high a degree the gift of inaccuracy, that he has been able, in enumerating the friends of Bossuet, in his final article (*Constitutionnel*, April 25, 1851), to write freely: "Pellisson, *precursor of Boileau!* La Bruyère, *precursor of Molière!!!*" One pardons him all that on account of his swan's pen.

ence, during his last years, with M. Destouches, made a kind of pleasant wager that he would beat, refute and incessantly correct his friend with well-chosen quotations from the Satires or the Epistles. Once more, Horace has nothing in particular to do with Bossuet, and there is no occasion to implicate him on his account. The great pagan preference of Bossuet (if one may use such an expression) was naturally for Homer, and next for Virgil: Horace, according to his judgment and taste, came far behind them. But the book which soon preëminently gave direction to the genius and calling of Bossuet, and which became his rule in everything, was the Bible; it is said that the first time he read it, he was completely illuminated and transported. He had found in it the source whence his own genius was going to flow, like one of the four rivers in Genesis.

Bossuet was early destined to the church: tonsured when eight years old, he was hardly thirteen when he was made a canon of the cathedral at Metz. His childhood and his youth were so regular and pure, and pointed so directly to the church as his destination, that Lamartine says: "There is no trace of a fault to be seen in his childhood, or of an act of levity in his youth; he seemed to escape the frailties of nature without a struggle, and to have no other passion than love for the beautiful and the good (and the true). One would have said that he himself respected in advance the future authority of his name, of his ministry, and that he was anxious that there should not be a human spot to wipe away from the man of God, when he should leave the world to enter upon the duties of the tabernacle." Why does M. de Lamartine, who discovers on his way these charming views and these glimpses of a superior biographer, let them escape, through his negligence, and almost immediately spoil them?

Bossuet came to Paris for the first time in September, 1642. It is said that on the very day of his arrival he saw the entry of the dying cardinal, who was returning to Paris after his avenging journey to the South, and was carried in a movable room covered with a scarlet cloth. To have seen, but for a day, Richelieu all-powerful in his purple, and to have seen, soon after, the Fronde, civil war and anarchy let loose, was for Bossuet an abridged course of political philosophy, from which he drew the true lesson: better, surely, one master than a thousand masters, and better still that the master should be the King himself, and not the minister.

Entering upon a course of philosophy at the college of Navarre, he shone there in the theses and public performances; he was a prodigy and a school angel before becoming the eagle we admire. It is known that, having been extolled at the *hôtel de Rambouillet* by the marquis de Feuquières, who had known his father at Metz, and who continued his good will to the son, the young Bossuet was conducted there one evening, to preach an improvised sermon. In consenting to these singular exercises, and to these tournaments where his person and his gifts were challenged, and though treated as an intellectual virtuoso in the *salons* of the *hôtel de Rambouillet* and the *hôtel de Nevers*, Bossuet did not apparently subject himself to the slightest charge of vanity, and there is no example of a precocious genius which has been so praised and so caressed by the world, which has remained so perfectly exempt from all self-love and from all coquetry.

He went often to Metz, to rest in study and in an austerer life from the successes and triumphs at Paris. He became there successively subdeacon, deacon, archdeacon, and priest (1652). He remained there wholly for about six years, in order that he might diligently discharge the duties of archdeacon and canon; he preached there the first sermons we have from him, and his first panegyrics. He there made his first controversial attacks upon the Protestants, who abounded in that province. In a word, Bossuet conducted himself like a young militant priest, who, instead of accepting at first an agreeable post at the centre and in the capital, loves better to inure and harden himself by carrying the arms of eloquence where duty and danger lie, to the frontiers.

One of the oldest sermons of Bossuet, and one of those which he preached in his youth at Metz, has been signalized by the abbe Vaillant: it is the sermon for the ninth Sunday after Pentecost. In this sermon Bossuet wishes to show at once the goodness and the rigor of God, the tenderness and the severity of Jesus. He begins by exhibiting Jesus as compassionate, and weeping over Jerusalem, at the moment when he reënters the city which is going to betray him; then he will show him irritated and implacable, avenging himself, or letting his Father avenge him, upon the walls and upon the children of that same Jerusalem. This sermon,— preached "as God inspired me," says Bossuet in concluding it,— has in it something youthful, vivid, and bold, and, in passages, something hazardous and almost strange. He begins grandly and with a noble similitude: "As one sees that brave soldiers, in certain remote places, where the various chances of war may have thrown them, do not neglect to march at the appointed times to the rendezvous of their brigades appointed by the general; so, the Savior Jesus, when he saw that his hour was come, resolved to quit all the other countries of Palestine through which he had gone preaching the word of life; and knowing well that it was the will of his Father that he should return to Jerusalem, in order to undergo there, a few days after, the anguish of the last suffering, he turned his steps toward that treacherous city, that he might celebrate there that Passover, which has been made forever memorable by the institution of his holy mysteries and by the shedding of his blood." And it is then, while Jesus is descending the Mount of Olives, that he represents him as touched to the quick in his heart with a tender compassion, and weeping over the ungrateful city whose ruin he sees beforehand; then suddenly, without transition, and with an abrupt sally, which may seem to indicate a still juvenile erudition, Bossuet attacks the heresy of the *Marcionites*, who, not knowing how to reconcile goodness and justice in one God, divided the divine nature, and made two Gods: one, purely idle and useless, after the manner of the Epicureans, "a God under whose rule sins rejoice," whom one has since called the *God of honest people;* and over against that God, indulgent to excess, they framed another, purely vengeful, purely wicked and cruel: and pushing the conclusion to the limit, they also imagined two Christs in the image of the two Fathers. After having addressed the heretic Marcion to his face (in the words of Tertullian), "Thou dost not stray so far from the truth, Marcion, . . ." he enters upon his theme, and shows that this compassion and this justice both subsist, but must not be separated; he proceeds in the same discourse to portray the Savior compassionate and the Savior inexorable, the pitying heart and then the angry heart of Jesus: "Hear, first of all, the sweet and benignant voice of that Lamb without spot, and afterward you shall hear the terrible roarings of that victorious Lion born of the tribe of Judah: that is the subject of this discourse."

In this exordium we see a singular fire, an ingenious and exuberant imagination, a slightly subtle erudition, which attacks at the outset a strange heresy; as Chateaubriand said, we see "the foam on the bit of the young courser."

The first head of the discourse in which the orator glorifies the goodness of Jesus, so consistent with his true nature, is characterized by leaps and flights, by vivid and impetuous terms, by significant words which force home the thought; a little archaism mingles with the style: "And touching that (compassion) I recollect," says the orator, "a little saying of Saint Peter's, in which he very well describes the Savior to Cornelius: 'Jesus of Nazareth,' says he, 'a man approved of God, who went about doing good, and healing all that were oppressed.' *Pertransit benefaciendo*. . . . O God! how beautiful these words, and how eminently worthy of my Savior!" He then unfolds the beauty of these words in a paraphrase or strophe full of joyousness. He calls to mind Pliny the Younger glorifying his Trajan who traveled over the world less by his footsteps than by his victories: "And what does this mean, think you,— to travel over provinces by victories? Is it not to carry carnage and pillage everywhere? Ah! in how much more lovely a way did my Savior travel over Judea! He travelled over it less by his steps than by his kindnesses. He went about in all directions, healing the sick, consoling the wretched, instructing the ignorant. It was not simply the places at which he tarried that found themselves the better for his presence: as many as were his steps, so many were the traces of his bounty. He made the places through which he passed remarkable by the profusion of his blessings. In that little village there are no blind men or cripples; no doubt, said one, the kind-hearted Jesus has gone that way." In all this part of the sermon there is a youthfulness, a freshness of tenderness and of compassion which is charming, and it has a flavor of his early genius.

When he portrays to us Jesus desiring to clothe himself with a flesh similar to ours, and when he sets forth the motives for this according to the Scriptures, with what distinctness and saliency he does it! He represents that Savior who seeks out misery and distress, as refusing to assume the angelic nature which would have exempted him from this, — *leaping (sautant)* upon, in some sense, and striving to pursue, to *apprehend* the miserable human nature, clinging to it and running after it although it flies from him, although it is reluctant to be assumed by him; desiring for himself a real flesh, real human blood, with the qualities and weaknesses of ours, and that for what reason? *In order to be compassionate.* Although in all this Bossuet only makes use of the terms of the Apostle, and perhaps of those of Chrysostom, he employs them with a delight, a luxury, a gust for reduplication, which denote vivacious youth: "He has *apprehended* the divine nature, says the apostle; it flew away, it did not wish for the Savior; what did he do? He ran after it with headlong speed, leaping over mountains, that is to say, the angelic ranks. He ran like a giant with great and immeasurable steps, passing in a moment from Heaven to earth. There he overtook that fugitive nature; he seized it, *he apprehended it, body and soul.*" Let us study the youthful eloquence of Bossuet, even in his perils of taste, as one studies the youthful poetry of the great Corneille.

I know that one must be very circumspect when he describes the liberties of youth in Bossuet's style, for he is one of those speakers who have never lacked daring; I do not believe, however, that I am deceived when detecting the superabundance of that age in certain passages. After having, in the first part of the discourse, unfolded, and, as it were, exhausted all the tenderness and compassion of Jesus-Christ made in the image of man,— after having exclaimed: "He has pitied us, *that good brother*, as his companions in fortune, having had to pass through the same miseries as we," Bossuet, in the second part of his discourse, portrays him returning and, finally, becoming angry on account of the hardness of heart which he finds in man: "But as there is no stream whose course is so tranquil, that one may not cause it, by resistance, to acquire the rapidity of a torrent; so the Savior, irritated by all those obstacles which the blind Jews opposed to his goodness, seems to lay aside in a moment all that pacific disposition." Then, by a sudden contrast, Bossuet strives and, as he says, employs all the rest of his discourse, to portray to his hearers the yet smoking ruins of Jerusalem. He delights to set forth the prophecy and the menace as it issued at first from the mouth of Moses; it is couched (*couchée*) in Deuteronomy. He enumerates the circumstances of its utterance, he comments on it, follows it step by step, all the while accompanying it with his eagle cries; and when he has led the Romans and *the Emperor Titus* before Jerusalem, when he is very sure that it is invested, that it is surrounded with walls by the besiegers, that it is more like a prison than a city, and that not a single person who is shut up in it like a famished wolf, can escape to seek for sustenance,—"Behold, behold, christians," he cries in triumph, "the prophecy of my Gospel fulfilled in every particular. Behold thyself besieged by thy enemies, as my master foretold thee forty years before: 'O Jerusalem, behold thou art shut in on all sides, *they have compassed thee round, they have surrounded thee with ramparts and forts!*' These are the words of my text; and is there a single word which does not seem to have been put there to describe that circumvallation, not with lines, but with walls? After that period, what words could paint to you their raging hunger, their fury, and their despair?" Here, again, it seems to me, that young Bossuet indulges in a little excess; and just as in the first part he had gone so far, with regard to the God-made man, as to speak of the qualities of the blood and of the *temperature of the body*, he proceeds in this second part to dwell on the horrors of the famine and the foul details of the contagion. He will use terms still more frightful when he wishes to declare the final sentence, the dispersion of the Jewish nation through the world, and to expose to us *its members drawn and quartered*. It is true he immediately adds: "This comparison excites your horror"; yet he pushes it to the end, without any fear of the consequences. I see in this a proof that he is young still; he has some cruelty, not in the heart, but in his talent.*

* So with the Count de Maistre in that famous passage upon the executioner. This passage of Bossuet resembles and recalls it.

The reader will have remarked how easily he appropriates that of which he speaks and upon which he relies: *my* Gospel, *my* text, *my* twenty-eighth chapter of Deuteronomy, *my* master, *my* pontiff, etc. He loves these sovereign forms; he lays his hand upon things, and while he is speaking he cannot help performing the office of God his master. It is not self-love or arrogance in Bossuet; it is only that his own personality is absorbed and confounded in the public personality of the Levite and the priest. He is at these moments but the man of the Most-High.

A passage in this discourse gives us its date: upon the occasion of the civil disorders which break out in besieged Jerusalem, and which cause these insane people, on returning from the fight against the common enemy, to come to blows with each other, Bossuet has a reflection upon his country: "But perhaps you do not observe that God has let fall the same scourges upon our own heads. France, alas! our common country, so long agitated by a foreign war, completes its distresses with intestine divisions. Again, among the Jews, both parties combined to repulse the common enemy, and were far from wishing to strengthen themselves by its assistance, or to have any understanding with it; the least suspicion of such a thing would have been punished by death without mercy. But we, on the contrary . . . ah! friends, let us not finish, let us spare our shame a little." *But we, on the contrary . . .* this is an allusion to the party which favored the Spaniards, to the prince of Condé, who had become their ally and general. When Bossuet, at a later day, in his Funeral Oration over the prince, shall speak with so much repugnance of civil discords, and *of those things concerning which he wished he could be forever silent*, he will repeat a real and lively sentiment which had already drawn from him a cry both of pain and alarm.

The language of this sermon as of all the discourses of these years, is a little more antique than that of Bossuet when he had become the orator of Lewis XIV; one notes in it some phrases of an earlier age: "But still let us pretend to be christians, if it be, nevertheless, that we spare nothing, etc., (*si est-ce néanmoins* que nous n'épargnons rien, etc.) It is declared that the example of the ruin of Jerusalem, and of that divine vengeance, so public, so indubitable, must serve as a memorial for ages upon ages (*mémorial ès siècles des siècles*.)" Elsewhere it is rather in the employment of certain roughly concise words, and in the almost Latin turn of expression, that one perceives the contemporary of Pascal: " For, finally, do not persuade yourselves that God may let you rebel (*rebeller*) against him for ages: his compassion is infinite, but its effects have their limits prescribed by his wisdom: that wisdom which has counted the stars, which has bounded this universe by a definite roundness (*qui aborné cet univers dans une rondeur finie*), which has prescribed bounds to the waves of the sea, has marked the height to which it has resolved to let iniquities mount." One would believe he was reading a passage in Pascal's *Thoughts*.

I have still much to say upon that first period of Bossuet, at Metz as well as at Paris. How was it with his person in his youth, when he pronounced these discourses, already so powerful, with a precocious authority which was radiant with a visible inspiration, and which was embellished, so to speak, with a certain degree of artlessness (*naïveté*)? M. de Bausset has asked and has answered this question, so far as he could, in very general terms: "Nature," says he, "endowed him with the noblest of figures; the fire of his mind shone forth in his looks; the traits of his genius penetrated all his discourses. It is enough to look at the portrait of Bossuet, painted in his old age by the celebrated Rigaud, to form an idea of what he must have been in his youth." He cites a little farther on the testimony of the abbé Ledieu, who reports that "Bossuet's look was pleasant and piercing; that his voice appeared always to proceed from a passionate soul; that his gestures in oratorical action were modest, quiet, and natural." These delineations, a little tame and after the manner of Daguesseau, have not been satisfactory, we imagine, to M. de Lamartine, who, with that second sight which is granted to poets, knew how to see Bossuet distinctly as he was when young, Bossuet at the age of Eliacim, even before he had entered the pulpit, and when he was simply ascending the steps of the altar. The author of *Jocelyn* says:

"He (Bossuet) was not nine years old when his hair was cut in a circlet at the top of his head. At thirteen he was nominated canon of Metz. . . . That tonsure and that vesture were as becoming to his physiognomy as to his general appearance. One recognized the priest in the youth. His frame, which was greatly to increase, was tall for his age; it had the delicacy and suppleness of the man who is not destined to bear any other burden than thought; who glides composedly, with quiet steps, amid the columns of basilicas, and whom habitual genuflection and prostration soften under the majesty of God. His hair was of *a brown tint* and *silken;* one or two locks rose in an involuntary tuft at the top of the forehead like the diadem of Moses, or like the horns of the prophetic ram; *these hairs thus standing*, whose motion one notices again even in his portraits taken at an advanced age, gave *du vent* and inspiration to his hair. His eyes were black and penetrating, but mild. *His look was a continual and serene gleam;* the light did not dart forth in flashes, *it ran from them with a radiance which allured the eye without dazzling it.* His lofty and flat forehead revealed *through a fine skin the interlaced veins of the temples.* His nose, almost straight, slender, delicately sculptured, between the Greek softness and the Roman energy, was neither turned up with impudence, nor depressed by the heaviness of the senses. His mouth opened wide between delicate lips; *his lips quivered often without utterance, as if with the wind of an internal speech* which modesty repressed before older men. A half smile, full of grace and of mute after-thought, was their most frequent expression. One saw in them a naturally sincere disposition, never rudeness or disdain. To sum up generally, in that physiognomy the charm of the character so completely hid from view the force of the understanding, and suavity so harmoniously tempered the virility of the entire expression, that one detected the genius only by *the exquisite delicacy of the muscles and nerves of the thought,* and the effect on the beholder was attraction rather than admiration."

Here is a primitive Bossuet very much softened and mellowed, and, it seems to me, a Bossuet who is made, very much at one's fancy, to resemble Jocelyn and Fenelon, in order that it may be said afterward: "The soul of that great man was evidently of one temper, and the genius of another. Nature had made him tender; theological dogmas had made him hard." I do not believe in this contradiction in Bossuet, the most undivided and the least contested nature that we know. But what I am not less sure of is, that the illustrious biographer treats literary history here absolutely as history is treated in a historic romance; wherever facts are wanting, or the dramatic interest demands it, the character is carelessly invented. Without refusing the praise which certain ingenious and delicate touches of this portrait merit, I will permit myself to ask more seriously: Is it proper, is it becoming, thus to paint Bossuet as a youth, to flatter (*caresser*) thus with the brush, as one would a Greek dancing woman, or a beautiful child of the English aristocracy, him who never ceased to grow under the shadow of the temple,—that serious young man who gave promise simply of the great man, all genius and all eloquence? What! do you not feel it?—there is here a moral contradiction. In a sermon delivered in his youth, upon the occasion of one's taking the veil, Bossuet, speaking of the modesty of the virgins, and contrasting it with the freedoms of many christian girls in the world, said: "Who could recite all the artifices they employ to attract the looks of men? and what are those looks, and can I speak of them in this pulpit? No: it is enough to tell you that the looks which please them are not indifferent looks; they are *those passionate, eager looks, which drink in deep draughts from their faces all the poison they have prepared for men's hearts;* these are the looks they love." An orator, I know, is not a virgin; the first condition of the orator, even the sacred orator, is to be bold and daring; but what boldness was Bossuet's! I can say that, with his manly and virile modesty, he would have blushed, even in youth, at being viewed in that way in order to be painted. Far, far from his taste these fondlings and these physiological feats of a brush which amuses itself with carmine and with veins! Go rather and see in the Louvre his bust by Coysevox: a noble head, a fine bearing, pride without arrogance, a lofty and full forehead, the seat of thought and majesty; the mouth singularly agreeable in expression, delicate, speaking even when it is in repose; the profile straight and preëminently notable: in the whole a look of fire, of intelligence, and of goodness, the figure which is the worthiest of the man, just as he was formed to address his fellows, and to look at the heavens. Take away the wrinkles from that face, give it the bloom of life, throw over it the veil of youth, imagine a young and adolescent Bossuet, but be sparing of your descriptions of him, for fear you may fall short of the severity of the subject and of the respect which is due to it.

May 29, 1854.

II.

I DESIGN in this paper only to continue my view of Bossuet in his early career, not before he was renowned (for that was early), but before he became glorious. The reverence we have for him does not need to become superstitious, and there is no reason why we should not acknowledge the perils and the striking inequalities of a youthful manner of speech which will soon attain of itself to the plenitude of its eloquence. It is a long distance from the *Panegyric of Saint Gorgon*, which he preached at Metz during the years of his stay there, to the *Panegyric of Saint Paul*, which signalized the first years of his preaching at Paris, and which is already in the style of the greatest of our sacred orators. In the *Panegyric of Saint Gorgon*, the subject was evidently at fault; little more was known of that martyr than his suffering, and the orator found himself compelled to fall back upon the frightful details of the physical torments which had to be undergone by the person whom he was to extol: "The tyrant made the holy martyr sleep upon an iron gridiron, already red with the fierce heat, which instantly contracted his bared nerves. . . . What a horrible spectacle!" And he describes the affair, not dispensing with any circumstance. We have two discourses of Bossuet upon the same subject, or, at least, one entire discourse and the outline or sketch of another which he delivered also: it was a tribute paid to a parish of the town which was under the patronage of the saint. Bossuet is not one of those ingenious men of talent who have the art of treating commonplace subjects excellently, and of introducing into them foreign materials; but let the subject which is presented to him be vast, lofty, majestic, and he is at ease, and, the higher the theme, the more is he equal to its demands. When he quitted Metz to establish himself in Paris, Bossuet showed immediately the effect of the change in his eloquence, and in reading his subsequent productions, we feel as if we were passing from one climate to another. "In following the discourses of Bossuet in their chronological order," the abbe Vaillant very well says, "we see the old words fall successively as the leaves of the woods fall." The superannuated or trivial expressions, the offensive images, the slips of taste, which are still less the fault of Bossuet's youth than of all that epoch of transition which preceded the great reign, disappear and leave in use only that new, familiar, unexpected speech, which will never recoil, as he said of Saint Paul, from *the glorious meannesses of Christianity*, but will learn also magnificently to consecrate its combats, its spiritual government, and its triumphs. Called often from the year 1662 to preach before the Court, having to speak in churches or before large bodies in Paris, Bossuet acquired there at once the language in use, while still preserving and developing his own; he had completely despoiled the provinces; there, during six years of exercise and discipline, he had been trained; the Court polished him only so far as it was necessary. He was a finished orator at the age of thirty-four. During eight or nine years (1660-1669), he was the great fashionable preacher, as well as the most renowned.

Two opinions resulted from the publication of the Sermons of Bossuet for the first time, in 1772; I have already indicated that of the abbe Maury, who placed these Sermons above everything else of that kind which the French pulpit had produced; the other opinion, which was that of La Harpe, and which I have known to be shared in by other sensible men, was less enthusiastic, and showed more sensitiveness to the inequalities and discordances of tone. It would be possible to justify both of these opinions, with the understanding that the first should triumph in the end, and that the genius of Bossuet, there as elsewhere, should keep the first rank. It is very true that, read continuously, without any notice of the age of the writer, and of the place and circumstances of their composition, some of these discourses of Bossuet may offend or surprise some minds that love to dwell upon the more uniform and more exact continuity of Bourdaloue and Massillon. For example, one opens the volumes, and he finds at the very beginning, one after the other, four sermons or plans of sermons upon All Saints' Day. The first, of which we have only a sketch, and which is little more than a mass of texts and notes, was preached at Metz; the second, which we have complete, was also preached there. This second discourse is fatiguing, slightly subtle, and has too much theological display. Wishing to give an idea of the felicity and glory of the saints in the life to come, wishing to unfold the designs of God in the discipline of his elect, and to show how he takes them, manages them, prepares them, and only succeeds at the very last in perfecting them, the orator, who seeks to give a rational explanation of this procedure, institutes a lofty dissertation rather than preaches a sermon: he must have had little influence that time on the minds of his auditory, and they could not have followed him far. Not that there are not great thoughts, beautiful and grand comparisons, and also the ever true and ever touching complaints about human life, — so agitated and so wretched in itself, that it was necessary, he says, that God should use some address and some artifice in regard to it, to conceal its miseries from us. "And yet, O blindness of the human mind! it is this life which seduces,— this life, which is only trouble and agitation, which amounts to nothing, which draws just so much nearer to its end as the moments of its duration are multiplied, and which will fail us suddenly like a false friend, when it shall seem to promise us the most repose. Of what are we thinking?" But, in spite of these and many other noteworthy traits, this second sermon for All Saints is, I repeat it, fatiguing and a little obscure; and if one would see again the great orator in Bossuet, he must pass to the third: or rather in a well-advised reading of that part of Bossuet's works, one should omit, suppress both the first sermon and the fourth, which are only incomplete sketches,— not stop at the second, which is difficult,— and then one will freshly enjoy all the moral and serene beauty of that third sermon preached in 1669 in the royal chapel, and in which Bossuet, refuting Montaigne, finishing and consummating Plato, demonstrates and almost renders evident to the least prepared minds, the conditions of the only true, durable, and eternal happiness. And here observe that he does not do as in the discourse at Metz, where he thought much more of dividing, of investigating his subject than of lighting it up; he reasons no longer for himself alone, he thinks of his auditors, he does not lose sight of them for an instant: "O breadth, O depth, O boundless length and inaccessible height (of the celestial happiness)! will it be possible for me to comprehend you in a single discourse? Let us go together, my brethren, let us enter that abyss of glory and of majesty. Let us cast ourselves with confidence upon that ocean. . . ." When he would make us comprehend that true happiness for an intelligent being lies in the perception and possession of truth, he sees clearly that he will be asked: "What is truth?" and he is going to try to answer it: "Gross and carnal mortals, we understand everything corporeally; we wish always for material images and forms. Shall I not be able to-day to open those internal and spiritual eyes, which are concealed in the depths of your soul, to turn them aside a moment from the vague and changing images which the senses present, and accustom them to bear the sight of pure truth? Let us try, let us endeavor, let us see. . . ." The second *point* is altogether moral in character, and very beautiful. In order to give a vivid idea of the genuine pleasures which the blessed enjoy, the orator says to himself as well as to his hearers: "Let us philosophize a little, before all things else, upon the nature of the world's joys." He then tries to make us realize, by what is lacking to our joys, what must enter into those of a better state: "For it is an error to believe that we must welcome joy equally, from whatever quarter it originates in, whatever hand offers it to us. Of all the passions, the fullest of illusion is joy." Let us ask ourselves always: Whence comes it, and what is the occasion of it? Where does it lead us, and in what state does it leave us? If it passes away so quickly, it is not the true. The happiness of a being (a great principle, according to Bossuet,) must never be distinguished from the perfection of that being; true happiness, worthy of the name, is the state in which the being is living most in accordance with its nature, in which it is most truly itself, in the plenitude and in the satisfaction of its inner desires. Montaigne (he names him in the pulpit), in vain holds faith in check, degrades human nature, and compares it to that of the brutes, by giving it often the lower place: "But tell me, subtle philosopher, you who laugh so archly at the man who imagines that he is something, will you count it for nothing to know God? To know a primal nature, to adore his eternity, to admire his omnipotence, to praise his wisdom, to commit one's self to his providence,— is that nothing which distinguishes us from the brutes?" He presses him, he pushes him; the witty sceptic has never seen the flash of a sword so near his eyes: "Well then! let the elements demand back from us all that they have lent us, provided that God may also demand back of us that soul which he made in his own likeness. Perish all the thoughts which we have given to mortal things; but let that which was born of God be immortal like Himself. Therefore, sensual man, you who renounce the future life because you fear its just punishments, do not longer hope for nothingness; no, no, hope for it no longer: wish for it, or not wish for it, your eternity is assured to you."

As for the happiness itself, of which he would give us a just idea, the purely spiritual and internal happiness of the soul in the other life, he sums it up in an expression which concludes a happy development of the subject, and he defines it: "Reason always attentive and always contented." Take *reason* in its liveliest and most luminous sense, the pure flame disengaged from the senses.

By these examples, which I might multiply, we see clearly the march and the rapid progress of the genius of Bossuet. Like all inventors, he has had, at first, some perils to overcome, has had to grope about, and he has done it impetuously. I recollect that formerly M. Ampire, in his lectures at the College of France, wishing to characterize those three great epochs of Pulpit Eloquence among us, the time of its creation and puissant establishment by Bossuet, the time of its full growth under Bourdaloue, and finally the epoch of its extreme expansion and autumnal fertility under Massillon, connected with it the ancient names, now become symbols, which consecrate the three great periods of the tragic stage in Greece. Of these names there are two at least which may be recalled here without incongruity; there is something of the greatness and of the majesty of Æschylus, as well as of Corneille, in Bossuet, just as there may be visible something of Euripides, as well as of Racine, in Massillon.

Bossuet's is a talent anterior in origin and formation to that of Lewis XIV, but on the score of its completion and perfection it owed much to that young king. Attempts have been made more than once to rob Lewis XIV of his peculiar useful influence and propitious ascendency over what one has called his age: for some time, however, that unjust and illiberal contest seemed to have been given up, when a great writer of our days, M. Cousin, suddenly renewed it, and desired once more to despoil Lewis XIV of his highest glory in order to carry it back altogether to the preceding epoch. M. Cousin has a very convenient way of exaggerating and aggrandizing the objects of his admiration: he degrades or depresses their surroundings. It is thus that, to exalt Corneille, in whom he sees Æschylus, Sophocles, all the Greek tragic poets united, he sacrifices and diminishes Racine; it is thus, that in order to celebrate better the epoch of Lewis XIII and the Regency which followed, he depresses the reign of Lewis XIV; that, in order to glorify the Poussins and the Sueurs, of whom he speaks, perhaps, with more enthusiasm and applause than direct knowledge and real, felt gust, he blasphemes and denies the merit of the admirable Flemish painting; he says of Raphael that he does not touch the feelings, that he only plays around the heart, *Circum præcordia ludit.* In a word, M. Cousin is voluntarily a man of foregone conclusions, of preconceived ideas, or, rather still, he is the man of his temperament and of his own nature. He clings resolutely to what he prefers, as his starting-point; his personal tastes carry his judgment completely captive. He is wedded, on all occasions, to his own peculiar opinions, and never adopts just ones till he has been opposed on all sides with contradictions and checks, and obliged to limit and moderate his assertions. Regarding the present question, he has gone so far as to maintain that this Lewis XIV, who troubles him, was not entirely himself, and somehow did not begin to rule and to reign, till after the influence of M. de Lyonne and of Colbert, two pupils of Richelieu and of Mazarin, had been exhausted; so you have the great reign thrown back ten or fifteen years, and the minority of the monarch strangely prolonged by an unexpected exercise of authority.* M.

* It is in the preface to the volume entitled *Madame de Longueville* that M. Cousin has said: "The influence of Lewis XIV made itself felt very late. He did not take the reins of government till 1661, and at first he followed his time, he did not rule; he did not appear to be really himself till he was

Poujoulat, taking these assertions very seriously, and without ever permitting himself to smile at them, has combated them successfully. Bossuet, it seems to me, presents us with one of the greatest and most striking examples of the kind of blessings which the age of Lewis XIV owed to the young star of its king, from the very first day. Honored by the queen, Anne of Austria, becoming latterly her favorite preacher, Bossuet had at the outset some of those abounding and ingenious subtleties which characterized the taste of the time. Thus, preaching before the queen-mother in 1658 or 1659 the *Panegyric on Saint Theresa*, influenced, perhaps, by the Spanish saint's refinements of style, and developing at pleasure a passage of Tertullian which declares that Jesus, before dying, wished *to satiate himself with the luxury of patience,* Bossuet will not fear to add: " Would you not say, christians, that, according to the sentiment of that Father, the whole life of the Savior was *a festival of which all the meats were torments?* a strange festival in the opinion of the age, but one which Jesus deemed

no longer led by Lyonne and Colbert, the last disciples of Richelieu and of Mazarin. It was then that, governing almost alone, and superior to his surroundings, he everywhere impressed his taste," etc. etc. The idea of making M. de Lyonne reign and govern in place of Lewis XIV is one of the strangest of all. What! because M. de Mignet, in publishing the *Negotiations relative to the Spanish Succession*, has shown by a series of dispatches that M. de Lyonne was a very clever Secretary of State and Foreign Minister, you, for this reason, make him out to be a man who delays the real accession of Lewis XIV, and who, in your mind, provisionally dethrones him! Never has one more grossly abused the privilege of extracting information from Statepapers than in making them aid such a conclusion. But the sight of all posthumous and unedited papers causes M. Cousin a kind of dazzlement. Lewis XIV, in his Memoirs, speaking of M. de Lyonne at the time of his death, contents himself with saying: "In 1671 a minister died who held the office of Secretary of State, having the department of Foreign Affairs He was a man of capacity, but not without faults; nevertheless he performed that duty well, which was a very important one. I spent some time in thinking whom I should appoint to that place." It is thus that the king expresses himself worthy of his taste! His death sufficed for our safety; but his death did not suffice for *that marvellous appetite* which he had for suffering for us." Here is much of the *bel esprit* which still clings to the style of speech fashionable under the Regency. But when he was called to speak before the young king, he speedily learned to correct such fancies and to repress them. Lewis XIV, when he heard Bossuet for the first time, greatly relished his preaching, and did a charming thing for him, quite worthy of a young prince whose mother was still living: he had a letter written to Bossuet's father at Metz, *congratulating him upon having such a son.* He who does not appreciate this delicate act, is no better fitted to appreciate the kind of influence which that young prince could have on the vast imagination and reasonable mind of Bossuet. The language of Lewis XIV was always accurate, just as the same quality, according to another, characterized his talent for rapid observation. There was in him or about him something which warned men not to exaggerate, not to force things. Bossuet, when speaking in his presence, felt that, with respect to a certain refined taste, he was confronted by a standard. I desire to say nothing that is not incontestable: Lewis XIV, when very young, did Bossuet a service by giving him proportion and all his precision. For his inspiration and his originality the great orator continued to be indebted only to himself and the spirit which replenished him.

There is a fact which may be verified: in this series of Bossuet's Sermons, which have been arranged, not in the chronological order in which he composed them, but in the order of the christian year, beginning with All Saints' Day and ending with Pentecost, if you would put your finger unmistakably upon one of the finest and most faultless, take any one you please of those of which you read, *Preached before the King.*

I cannot help expressing another thought. Oh! when M. Cousin speaks so freely of Lewis XIV, of Lewis XIII, and of Richelieu, giving the palm so confidently to that which he prefers and which he thinks resembles him, I am astonished that he has never once asked himself this question: "What would my own talent have gained or lost, that talent which is daily compared with that of the writers of the great age,— what would have been gained or lost by that admirable talent" (I forget that it is he that is speaking), "if I had had to write or to discourse, were it only for some years, in the very presence of Lewis XIV, that is to say, that calm, sober, and august royal good sense? And would not what I should have thus gained or lost, in inspiration or eloquence, have been precisely that which was excessive in it, and also that which it lacked in gravity, in proportion, in propriety, in perfect accuracy, and, consequently, in true authority?" For there was in Lewis XIV, and in the atmosphere about him, something which enforced the cultivation of these qualities and virtues by all who came within the sphere of the great reign, and in this sense he may be said to have conferred them upon them.

There is no doubt that, if Bossuet had continued in the sermonizing career which he followed from 1661 to 1669, he would not have kept the sceptre, and that Bourdaloue would have come, in the general estimation, only after and a little below him. And yet, perhaps, that solid, forcible, and continuous evenness of style, with less audacity and splendor, was better adapted to the average mass of hearers. I merely mention this idea which I believe to be true, and which does not altogether agree with that which a sovereignly inexact biographer has expressed: "These two rivals in eloquence," says M. de Lamartine, speaking of Bossuet and Bourdaloue, "were *passionately* compared. *To the shame of the time*, the number of Bourdaloue's admirers surpassed in a short time that of the enthusiastic admirers of Bossuet. The reason of this preference of a cold argumentation to a sublime eloquence lies in the nature of human things. The men of middling stature have more resemblance to their age than the titanic men (*l'hommes démesurées*) have to their contemporaries. The orators who deal in argument are more easily comprehended by the multitude than the orators who are fired with enthusiasm; one must have wings to follow the lyric orator. . . ." This theory, invented expressly to give the greatest glory to the *lyric orators* and the *titanic men*, is here at fault. M. de Bausset has remarked, on the contrary, as a kind of singularity, that it never entered any man's head at that time to consider Bossuet and Bourdaloue as subjects for a comparison, and to weigh in the balance their respective merits and genius, as was so often done in the case of Corneille and Racine; or, at least, if they were compared, it was very seldom. *To the honor*, and not to *the shame of the time*, the public taste and sentiment took notice of the difference. Bossuet, in his higher sphere as bishop, remained the oracle, the Doctor, a modern Father of the Church, the great orator, who appeared on funereal and majestic occasions; who sometimes reappeared in the pulpit at the monarch's request, or to solemnize the Assemblies of the Clergy, leaving on each occasion an overpowering and ineffaceable recollection of his eloquence. Meanwhile Bourdaloue continued to be for the age the usual preacher *par excellence*, the one who gave a continual Course of Lectures on moral and practical Christianity, and who distributed the daily bread in its most wholesome form to all the faithful. Bossuet has said somewhere, in one of his sermons: " Were it not better suited to the dignity of this pulpit to regard the maxims of the Gospel as indubitable than to prove them by reasoning, how easily might I make you see," etc. There, where Bossuet would have suffered by stooping and subjecting himself to too long a course of proof and to a continuous argumentation, Bourdaloue, who had not the same impatient genius, was an apostolic workman who was more efficient in the long run, and better adapted to his work by his constancy. The age in which both appeared had the wisdom to make this distinction, and to appreciate each of them without opposing one to the other; and to-day those who glory in this opposition, and who so easily crush Bourdaloue with Bossuet, the man of talent with the man of genius, because they think they are conscious themselves of belonging to the family of geniuses, too easily forget that this christian eloquence was designed to edify and to nourish still more than to please or to subdue.

Here it is just to say that in these Sermons or discourses preached by Bossuet from 1661 to 1669 and later,— in almost all of them, there are admirable passages, which move us readers of to-day, to whatever class we may belong, very differently from the sermons of Bourdaloue. In the *Panegyric on Saint Paul*, at the very beginning, what a probing of the subject to the core, in its inmost, deepest, most supernatural part! Paul is *the stronger the weaker he feels himself to be;* it is his weakness which makes his strength. It is the artless Apostle, endowed with a hidden wisdom, with an incomprehensible wisdom, that shocks and scandalizes, and he will give him no disguise or artifice:

"He will go to that polished Greece, the mother of philosophers and orators, and, in spite of the resistance of the people, he will establish there more churches than Plato gained disciples by that eloquence which was thought divine. He will preach Jesus in Athens, and the most learned of its senators will pass from the Areopagus into the school of that barbarian. He will push his conquests still farther; he will humble at the feet of the Savior the majesty of the Roman fasces in the person of a proconsul, and he will make the judges before whom he is cited tremble on their tribunals. Rome even shall hear his voice, and one day that mistress city shall feel herself much more honored by a letter written with the stylus of Paul, than by so many famous harangues which she has heard from her Cicero.

"What is the reason of this, Christians? It is that Paul has means of persuasion which Greece does not teach, and which Rome has not learned! A supernatural power, which is pleased to exalt that which the haughty despise, has permeated and mingled with the august simplicity of his words. Hence it happens that we admire in his admirable Epistles a certain more than human virtue which persuades in opposition to rules, or rather which does not so much persuade as it captivates men's understandings; which does not tickle the ears, but which directs its blows right at the heart. Just as we see a great river, after running into a plain, retain still the violent and impetuous force which it acquired in the mountains where it had its origin, so the celestial virtue which is contained in the writings of Saint Paul, preserves even in that simplicity of style all the vigor which it brings from the Heaven whence it descends."

There is nothing to be said after such beauties.

Let us take now quite a different kind of sermon, preached afterward at the Court, that upon *Ambition* (1666), that upon *Honor* (1666), and that upon *The Love of Pleasure* (1662); beauties of the same kind appear everywhere. Upon ambition and honor, he says in the face of Lewis XIV everything which could prevent the idolatry of which he is soon to be the object, if it were possible to prevent it. He seeks by the example of a Nero or a Nebuchadnezzar, for "something which may awaken in the human heart that terrible thought of seeing nothing above it. It is there that covetousness," he says, "goes daily subtleizing, and *turning back, so to speak, upon itself.* Thence come unknown vices. . . ." And of that man, little in himself, and ashamed of his littleness, who labors to increase, to multiply himself, who imagines that he embodies all that he amasses and acquires, he says: "So many times a count, so many times a lord, possessor of so much riches, master of so many persons, member of so many councils, and so of the rest: however, let him multiply himself as many times as he pleases, it needs but a single death to humble him. Amid this infinite increase which our vanity imagines, we never think of measuring ourselves by our coffins, which, nevertheless, are the only exact measure." It is the peculiarity of Bossuet thus to have at the first glance all the great ideas which are the fixed limits and the necessary bounds of things, and which take no note of the shifting intervals where the eternal infancy of man sports and forgets itself.

That it may not be said that I seek in Bossuet only for lessons for the great and the powerful, I will add that in this same sermon upon *Honor*, in which he enumerates and considers the different kinds of vanities, he does not forget the men of letters, the poets, men who in their way contend for renown and empire: "These, who pride themselves on their intellectual gifts, the learned, the men of letters, the wits, think they are more rational than those I have named. In truth, Christians, they are worthy of being distinguished from the rest, and they form one of the world's finest ornaments. But who can endure them when, as soon as they are conscious of a little talent, they weary all ears with their facts and their sayings, and because they know how to arrange words, to measure a verse, or to round a period, think they have a right to be heard forever, and to decide everything authoritatively? *O rectitude of life, O purity of morals, O moderation of the passions*, rich and true ornaments of the rational nature, when shall we learn to prize you? . . ." Eternal Poetry, the source, support, and superior rule of true talents, behold yourself recognized incidentally in a sermon of Bossuet at the very moment when Despréaux was trying to recognize you in his way, in his Satires. But from how much higher a region does the spring run, and in how much more stable a region does it originate, in Bossuet than in the Horaces and the Despréaux!

As a literary peculiarity, it is to be noted that in these Sermons of Bossuet there are some very fine passages which one finds repeated even two or three times in different discourses. From these passages I shall cite a complete moral dissertation upon the inconstancy of human affairs, and the freaks of fortune, which sports on every occasion with all the wisest and most prudent precautions: "Use the utmost possible precaution, never will you keep pace with its caprices; when you think you are fortified on one side, disgrace will come upon another; make all the other parts secure, and the edifice will fail at the foundations; if the foundation is solid, a thunderbolt will come from the sky and overturn the whole structure from top to bottom." This eloquent commonplace reappears in the third sermon on *All Saints' Day*, which I have noticed, in the sermon on the *Love of Pleasure*, and, with some variation, in that on *Ambition*: "O man, do not deceive thyself, the future teems with events too strange, and loss and ruin affect the fortunes of men in too many ways, to allow of their being completely prevented. You dam up the water on one side, it works through on the other, it bubbles up even from underground. . . ." After all, Bossuet is an orator: however little he cultivates his art, he possesses it, and, like a Demosthenes, knows all about its practice; this fine passage, which looks so abrupt and sudden, he well knows to be fine; he keeps it in reserve, to be repeated on occasion. We observe also, even in his sermons delivered at the great epoch, some expressions, not obsolete, but peculiarly energetic, which are not in current use: "Our *delightful* age (*delicieux*) which cannot endure the hardship of the Cross"; for our age which is *fond of delights* (*ami des délices*). "That is to wish in some sense, *to desert* the Court, in order to combat ambition." *Deserter*, that is to say, *devaster*, *rendre déserte* (*solitudinem facere*). "There is this difference between the reason and the senses, that the senses make their impression first; their operation is prompt, their attack blunt and *surprising*." *Surprenante* is used here in a proper and physical sense, and not in the figurative sense of astonishing or exciting wonder. But pardon me for dwelling on these academic details in the presence of Bossuet.

In the first years of his residence at Paris, he pronounced the first of his peculiar Funeral Orations. We have those which he delivered on the death of father

Bourgoing, the head of the Oratory (1662), and on the death of Nicholas Cornet, grand-master of Navarre, and the cherished master of Bossuet in particular (1663). There are beauties in these two discourses; a fine passage upon the establishment of the Oratory, is often quoted from the Funeral Oration on father Bourgoing. In the Funeral Oration upon M. Nicholas Cornet, the questions of grace and free-will which then agitated the church under the names of Jansenism and Molinism, are admirably defined, and Bossuet, by the free way in which he handles them, shows how far he is disconnected from parties, and how far he soars above them. The Gallican arbiter, in these perilous matters, is found. However, that which strikes us in these two Funeral Orations, especially in the last, is a remarkable lack of harmony between the style and the subject. We who do not belong to the house of Navarre, cannot be so enthusiastic about that glory of Nicholas Cornet, or sympathize with the apostrophe to his great *Manes*. Bossuet requires large and lofty themes; meanwhile till they come to him, he magnifies and heightens those which he handles; but some disproportion appears. He was thundering a little in the void at those moments, or rather in too narrow a place; his voice was too strong for its organ.

He was to be more at ease, and to feel more at liberty, in celebrating the queen, Anne of Austria, whose Funeral Oration he pronounced some years after; but, singular thing! that discourse in which Bossuet must have poured out the gratitude of his heart, and already displayed his historical riches, has never been printed.

Finally the death of the queen of England came to offer him (1669) the grandest and most majestic of themes.

He needed the fall and the restoration of thrones, the revolution of empires, all the varied fortunes assembled in a single life, and weighing upon the same head; the eagle needed the vast depth of the heavens, and, below, all the abysses and storms of the ocean. But let us note also a service which Lewis XIV and his reign rendered to Bossuet: he would have had these great themes equally amid the disastrous epochs and through the Frondes and civil discords, but they would have come to him scattered, in some way, and without bounds: Lewis XIV and his reign gave him a frame in which these vast subjects were limited and fixed without being contracted. In the august yet well-defined epoch in which he spoke, Bossuet, without losing any of his breadth or any of the audacities of his talent of far-seeing observation, found everywhere about him that support (*point d'appui*), that security, and that encouragement or warning, of which talent and even genius have need. Bossuet, no doubt, put his trust, before all things else, in Heaven; but, as an orator, he redoubled his authority, his calm strength, by feeling that under him, and at the moment when he pressed it with his foot, the earth of France did not tremble.

I am stopping only at the threshold of Bossuet: other publications, I hope, will furnish me with new opportunities, and will provoke me to follow him in some of his other works. I could have spoken with more detail of M. Poujoulat's book; the author would have desired it, and certainly he merited as much for his useful and conscientious labor. But he will pardon me for not entering with him into discussions which would be secondary: I commend the general spirit of his book, and I approve of its general execution, too warmly to be willing to enter upon a formal criticism of particular parts of it. On this occasion then, in the presence of so great a subject, and at the foot of the statue, let it suffice me to have made with a timid chisel what I call a first *blow*.

June 3, 1854.

MASSILLON.

WE lack a history of the life and works of Massillon; it would be a happy theme. We have already many anecdotes, which it would be necessary, however, to verify and arrange in order; continuous researches would infallibly yield some results. A large number of Massillon's letters were abstracted at the time of his death; would it be possible to recover them? It would be necessary to prepare a history of his principal sermons, and to fix their dates, with the memorable circumstances connected with them. A complete Study on Massillon, would naturally become a study of eloquence itself in the last half of the reign of Lewis XIV; we should there follow that beautiful stream of sacred eloquence during all its magnificent course; we should mark its changes as it flows along from the point where it becomes less rapid, less impetuous, less resounding, where it loses the austere grandeur or the incomparable majesty given to it by its banks, and where, in a landscape richer in appearance, vaster in extent, but less sharply defined, it broadens and insensibly mingles with other waters as at the approaches of the mouth.

The name and the labors of Massillon correspond to these two periods, I may say to that of the greatest magnificence and to that of the later profusion. Jean-Baptiste Massillon, born at Hyères in Provence on the twenty-fourth of June, 1663, son of a notary of the place, showed early those graces of mind and person, those natural gifts of speech and of persuasion which have distinguished so many eminent men born in those districts, and which seem an interrupted heritage of ancient Greece. He began his studies at Marseilles with the Priests of the Oratory. It is related that when a child, after hearing a sermon, nothing pleased him more than to gather his schoolfellows about him and repeat to them or reconstruct the sermon which they had just heard. He entered the congregation of the Oratory at Aix on the tenth of October, 1681, and went, the next year, to study theology at Arles; then he became a professor in the colleges of Pézenas and Montbrison. Everything about him gave evidence of superior talents and showed that he was destined to be distinguished, and it has never been well explained, why, about this time, he wrote to the head of the Oratory of Saint-Martha, that "his talents and inclination unfitted him for the pulpit, and he believed that he was better qualified for a Chair of Philosophy or of Theology." It was no doubt but a passing distaste which made him speak thus. Here comes in, or slips in, a delicate question, touching which we have only obscure answers. Was young Massillon led astray by his passions? One of his biographers (Audin) has given some details on this subject which he says he had from an authentic source; according to them Massillon, in his early youth, would have been embroiled with his superiors through some errors of conduct, if he had not been quick to seek a reconciliation. I have found in the manuscript notes of the Troyes Library a charge of the same kind, but coming from a purely Jansenist source.* There was nothing, however,

* Chaudon, in a letter to the learned bibliographer Barbier, says the same thing (*Bulletin du Bibliophile*, 1839, p. 617).

in this which was not simple and natural: Massillon, young, beautiful, endowed with sensibility and tenderness, resembling Racine somewhat in his genius and affections, might easily have had, in those lively years, some slips, some falls or relapses, of which he immediately repented, and it is to these first irregularities, perhaps, and to his efforts to triumph over them, that we must attribute his retreat to the penitential abbey of Septfonts. When he was asked at a later day where he had obtained his profound knowledge of the world and of the different passions, he had a right to reply: "From my own heart."

Whilst he was professor of theology at Vienna, he was ordained as priest in 1692; he made trial of the pulpit, delivered the funeral oration of Henri de Villars, archbishop of the diocese, and went to Lyons and delivered that of the archbishop M. de Villeroy, who died in 1693. These first successes seemed rather to frighten than to embolden him: his departure from the abbey of Septfonts did not take place till some time afterward. His stay at that abbey, which was one of the most austere and reformed after the pattern of La Trappe, became one of Massillon's most pleasing recollections: he had there tasted the honey of solitude in all its sweetness. He thought seriously of burying himself there, of taking there the vow of silence. Toward the end of his life, he loved to transport himself there in imagination, and he sometimes regretfully remembered that cell where he had passed one or two happy seasons in the fervor of a mystic peace.*

* This sojourn of Massillon at Septfonts, at least as a novitiate, has been denied (Account by M. Godfrey, preceding the *Select Works* of Massillon, 1868). This should be noted by the future biographer. The abbe Bayle, a recent biographer of Massillon, appears not at all to doubt the fact itself of that retreat to Septfonts.

The Father of La Tour, having become *supérieur général* of the Oratory, made him enter the congregation, and employed him at Lyons, then at Paris at the Saint-Magloire seminary, where he made him one of the directors. It was there that Massillon began to take his proper rank by his Lectures, the most substantial, or, at least, the severest of his works. His calling as a speaker was henceforth too manifest for him to think of avoiding it. He went, in 1698, to preach the Lent Sermons at Montpelier, and finally he was called, in 1669, to preach at Lent in Paris, in the church of the Oratory, on Saint-Honoré street. He was then nearly thirty years old.

His success was great, and moved the town. Lewis XIV wished that same year (1699) to hear the orator at Court, and Massillon preached there at the Advent. Massillon preached a second time at Court in 1701, and this time it was at Lent; he preached there again at Lent in 1704.* These first sermons of father Massillon (as one called him then), his *Avent*, his *Grand Carême*, form the most considerable and the finest portion of his oratorical work. The *Petit Carême*, which is more celebrated, and which he preached in 1718 before Lewis XV, then a child, belongs already to another epoch and is slightly different in style. After having at first greatly praised this *Petit Carême*, and preferred it to all the rest, while it was a novelty, the public has since been a little too much inclined to sacrifice it to the oldest works of Massillon. This is a

* The father Bougerel, in his accurate Account of Massillon (*Mémoires pour servir à l'Histoire de plusieurs Hommes Illustres de Provence*), speaks only of the Carême of 1704, preached by Massillon at the Court, and says nothing of the Carême of 1701. All these points need clearing up. The abbe Bayle has already cleared up some of them in his *Vie de Massillon* (1867); the abbe Blampignon, in his edition of the works of the great sermonizer, promises us the rest.

point to be examined by itself. Whatever may be the truth of the matter, Massillon manifested all his force and all his beauty as a sacred orator during that first epoch from 1669 to 1704, when the two centuries met: he showed that the great reign lasted always, and that even in that final autumn the succession of masterpieces still continued.

Massillon's discourses have this peculiarity in a literary point of view, that they were never printed during his life-time; the only one of his discourses which he published himself, and regarding which he saw himself criticized, was his funeral oration on the prince of Conti in 1709. With the exception of this piece, Massillon's entire works, including his *Petit Carême*, were presented to the public for the first time only after his death, and then through the efforts of his nephew, in 1745. I am deceived: an attempt had been made in his life-time to publish an imperfect edition of his works, gathered from notes (there was no stenography then); it was by this imperfect and unauthentic edition that the critics were obliged to judge him. When the edition prepared by Massillon's nephew appeared, which was an exact transcript of the manuscript, it won universal approval, and satisfied a great desire of christians and people of taste. It is said that it netted the nephew ten thousand crowns. It is certain that Massillon, during the years of his retirement and when at leisure as bishop, had carefully revised his sermons, had retouched, and perhaps partially rewritten them. The Jansenists accused him of having changed the doctrinal statements in some passages; it is probable that he contented himself with simply making them more consistent and accurate, leaving their primitive form and spirit unaltered. A writer of our day, who has spoken of Massillon with a rare partiality,* has pointed out in this very edition of 1745, which has become the pattern for all the others, some phrases, which it is difficult not to regard as typographical errors, and he has expressed a desire that the text may be again compared with the manuscript. Meanwhile, saving some spots which disappear in the richness of the tissue, and, as it were, in the folds of the stuff, we possess a Massillon sufficiently complete and sufficiently finished for us to enjoy it fully and confidently.

When Massillon appeared, Bourdaloue was ending his career; Bossuet, as a preacher of Sermons, had closed his at the very moment when Bourdaloue began. Thus these great lights had not to rival nor to eclipse each other, but came in peaceful succession like a series of fruitful seasons or like the hours of a splendid day. The innovation of Massillon, coming after Bourdaloue, was the introduction of pathos and a livelier perception of human passions into the economy of the religious discourse, and a slight softening of the sacred word without weakening it. That is the effect which a majority of his Advent Sermons and those of his *Grand Carême* will have upon any one who is able to read them in a proper frame of mind. Let any one (to give himself their full impression) form an idea of the plan, the auditory, and the orator: "Does it not seem to you," said those who had heard him, some years afterward, "does it not seem to you that you see him still in one of our pulpits, with that artless look, that modest bearing, those eyes meekly dropped, that careless gesture, that affectionate tone, that

* M. de Saci, in an article in the *Journal des Débats*, May 4, 1852.

appearance of a man deeply moved,— illuminating the minds of his hearers, and stirring their hearts with the tenderest emotions? He did not thunder in the pulpit, he did not frighten his hearers by the violence of his outbursts and the explosion of his voice; no, but by his sweet persuasion, he poured into them, as if naturally, the sentiments which melt the heart and which manifest themselves by tears and silence. There were no artificial, far-fetched, unreal flowers; no, the flowers sprang up under his feet without his seeking for them, almost without his perceiving them; they were so simple, so natural, that they seemed to escape from him against his will, and to count for nothing in his animated eloquence. The hearer was not aware of them, except by the enchantment which ravished him from himself.*"

Massillon in the pulpit had scarcely any gestures: that dropping of the eye as he began, which he kept dropped habitually, till he afterward, at rare intervals, raised it, and cast it over the auditory, constituted in his case the finest of gestures; he had, says the abbé Maury, *an eloquent eye*. In his exordiums, which were always happy, there was something that arrested the attention, as on the day when he pronounced the funeral oration of Lewis XIV, when, after having silently run his eye over all those magnificent funeral trappings, he began with these words: "God alone is great, my brethren! . . ." or as on that day also, when preaching for the first time before that same Lewis, on All Saints' Day, and taking for his text: *Blessed are those who weep!* he began thus:

*This lively and ingenious description may be found in the reply of M. Languet, archbishop of Lens, to the Discourse on the reception of the Duke of Nivernais, who succeeded Massillon at the French Academy (session of February 4, 1743).

"Sire,

"If the world should speak in place of Jesus Christ, it would not, doubtless, address to your majesty the same language.

"'Blessed is the prince,' it would say to you, 'who has never fought without being victorious; who has seen so many Powers armed against him, only to give them a glorious peace (*the peace of Ryswick*), and who has always been superior both to danger and to victory!

"'Blessed is the prince who, during the course of a long and flourishing reign, enjoys at leisure the fruits of his glory, the love of his people, the respect of his enemies, the admiration of the world . . . !'

"Thus would the world speak; but, sire, Jesus Christ does not speak like the world.

"'Blessed,' he says to you, 'is not he who is the admiration of his age, but he who is chiefly occupied with the age to come, and who lives in contempt of himself and of all that passes. . . .'

"'Blessed is not he whose reign and deeds are destined to be immortalized by history in the memories of men, but he whose tears shall have effaced the history of his sins from the memory of God himself,' etc. etc."

We see the double development of the subject, and with what delicate and majestic art Massillon, who appeared for the first time before Lewis XIV, and who came preceded by a reputation for austerity, contrived to mingle compliment and homage in the same lesson.

A very acute critic has said of him: "The plan of Massillon's Sermons is mean, but their bas-reliefs are superb." I know, also, that professional men, who have made a profound study of these pulpit orators, put Bourdaloue very much above Massillon in respect to the entire arrangement and plan of a discourse. Nevertheless, the plans of Massillon's Sermons do not appear to me particularly mean; they are very simple, and this, perhaps, is what is most fitting in such compositions; the principal and the most effective excellence consists in the fullness of the practical exposition. But Massillon has this art of exposition in the highest degree; one might almost say that it is just there nearly that all his talent lies. To take a text of Scripture, and expound it morally according to our actual needs, to unfold it and draw it out in all its meanings by translating it for us into a language which is ours, and which is suited to all the peculiarities of our habits and of our feelings, to give us lively pictures, which, without being portraits, shall yet not be vague commonplaces, and to reconcile nicety and delicacy of style with the use of general and noble terms,— it is in this that Massillon excels. He seems to have been born expressly to justify the saying of Cicero: "*summa autem laus eloquentiæ est, amplificare rem ornando.* . . . The height and perfection of eloquence is to amplify a subject by adorning and decorating it." He is an unrivalled master of that kind of amplification which Quintilian has defined "a certain heaping up of thoughts and expressions which conspire to produce the same impression: for, although neither the thoughts nor the expressions form a gradual climax, yet the object is found to be magnified and, as it were, heightened by the very assemblage,"— only take away from this definition the painful and disagreeable effect of that word *heaping* (*congeries*). Every exposition in Massillon, every oratorical strophe, is composed of a series of thoughts and phrases, commonly very short, that reproduce themselves, springing one out of the other, calling to each other, succeeding each other, having no sharp points, no imagery that is either too bold or too commonplace, and moving along with rhythm and melody as parts of one and the same whole. It is a group in motion; it is a natural, harmonious concert. Buffon, who regarded Massillon as the first of our prose-writers, seems to have had him in mind, when, in his Discourse upon Style, he said: "In order to write well, it is necessary, then, to be fully possessed of one's subject; it is necessary to reflect upon it enough to see clearly the order of one's thoughts, and to connect them together in a continuous chain, each link of which represents an idea: and when one takes his pen, he should conduct it along this first outline, without permitting it to stray from it, without pressing it too unequally, without giving it any other movement than that which may be determined by the space it is to run over. It is in this that severity of style consists." In Massillon this natural manner had no appearance of severity, but rather an appearance of abundance and overflow, like that of a stream running down a gentle declivity, the accumulated waters of which fall by their own weight. Massillon, more than any other orator, has resources for the fruitful development of moral themes; and the utmost grace and ease of diction spontaneously unite in his style, so that his long and full period is composed of a series of members and of reduplications united by a kind of insensible tie, like a large, full wave which is composed of a series of little waves.

Massillon the orator, if we could have heard him, would certainly have ravished, penetrated, melted us; read to-day, he does not produce the same effects, and considered as a writer, he is not admired by all in the same degree. It is not given to all minds to feel and to relish equally the peculiar beauties and excellences of Massillon. To like Massillon, to enjoy him sincerely and without weariness, is a quality and almost a peculiarity of certain minds, which may serve to define them. He will love Massillon, who loves what is just and noble better than what is new, who prefers elegant simplicity to a slightly rough grandeur; who, in the intellectual order, is pleased before all things with rich fertility and culture, with ornate sobriety, with ingenious amplification, with a certain calmness and a certain repose even in motion, and who is never weary of those eternal commonplaces of morality which humanity will never exhaust. Massillon will please him who has a certain sensitive chord in his heart, and who prefers Racine to all the other poets; in whose ear there is a certain vague instinct of harmony and of sweetness which makes him love certain words even in a superabundance. He will please those who have none of the impatience of a taste too superb or too delicate, nor the quick fevers of an ardent admiration; who have no thirst for surprise or discovery, who love to sail upon smooth rivers, who prefer to the impetuous Rhone, to the Eridanus as the poet has pictured it, or even to the Rhine in its rugged majesty, the tranquil course of the French river, of the royal Seine washing the more and more widening banks of a flourishing Normandy.

Such is the impression which Massillon has made upon me, as I have read and studied him to-day in his ever-beautiful, but regular and calm pages. Let us never forget, when reading them, that he is wanting who animated them by his temperate action and by his personality, he whose voice had all the tones of the soul, and of whom the great actor, Baron, said, after hearing him: "There is an orator! we are but comedians." Let us never forget that in that eloquence, so copious and so redoubled, each of his hearers, on account of the very diversity of expressions upon each point, found the shade of language which suited him, the echo which responded to his own heart; that that which seems to us to-day foreseen and monotonous, because our eyes, as in a great alley or a long avenue, runs in an instant from one end of the page to the other, had then an increasing and a surer effect from the very continuity, when the whole, from the height of the pulpit, was gathered together, and slowly suspended, growing larger as it was unrolled, and thus, as was said of the ancient eloquence, fell at last like snow.

Action, it is very necessary to bear in mind, can never be the same in preaching as in the other kinds of discourse; it cannot, without inconvenience or eccentricity, pass certain limits which it is well to know always how to attain without going beyond them. In a Lent sermon upon *Trifling Faults*, I find an example of that manner which Massillon employed so well to associate his hearers with his descriptions, and to interest them in that which might appear to be only a general enumeration. He attempts to show that there are no trifling faults, that he who despises small ones will little by little fall into great ones; he then turns to his hearer, he takes him to task; he reminds each one of his own recollections: "Do you remember how you fell . . ?" And here comes one of those developments of which I have spoken, and in which the whole art of Massillon is revealed: "One may sometimes," says Voltaire, "heap up metaphors, one upon another; but then it is necessary that they should be well distinguished, and that your object should always be seen represented under different images." He cites an example from Massillon; he might also have properly cited the following:

"Do you remember how you fell? . . . Go back to the first beginning of your irregularities, and you will find it in the most trivial failings; a pleasant sentiment thoughtlessly rejected; a dangerous place too often frequented; a doubtful liberty too often taken; practices of piety omitted; the source of moral disorders is almost imperceptible; the stream which sprang from it has inundated all the soil of your heart; it was at first the little cloud which Elias saw, and which has since covered the whole sky of your soul; it was that small stone which Daniel saw descend from the mountain, and which, since become an enormous mass, has overthrown and broken God's image in you; it was a little grain of mustard seed, which has since grown like a great tree, and produced so much deadly fruit; it was a little leaven," etc.

In the whole course of this exposition, it is impossible to stop and put a *period* at any place; there is but a single and unique thought, which runs out into manifold branches, and assumes various colors. Massillon, in our literature, is the author who has reached the highest perfection in this kind of harmonious period.

But he does not stop here; so far he has only begun to interrogate his hearer; he is going to press him more and more, to circumvent him, to try to attack him at all points till he has found the one that is vulnerable; and he comes gradually to a more striking enumeration and almost a description of them:

"Great God! you who saw in their origin the irregularities of the sinners who hear me, and who since have observed their entire progress, you know that the shame of that christian girl began only with slight compliances; and with vain designs of an honorable friendship; that the infidelities of that woman bound by an honorable tie were at first but little desires to please, and a secret joy in having succeeded; you know that a vain itching to know everything and to decide upon everything, readings dangerous to faith, and not sufficiently dreaded, and a secret desire of intellectual distinction, led that incredulous person little by little to free-thinking and irreligion; you know that that man is sunk in debauchery and hardness of heart only because he stifled at first a thousand feelings of remorse regarding certain doubtful acts, and invented false maxims to quiet his soul; you know, finally, that that unfaithful soul, after an open declaration of conversion," etc.

Such expositions, skillfully introduced at the propitious moment, which, in some sense, hovered over the whole auditory, which moved about over all heads like a vast extended mirror, in a distinct facet of which each person could recognize his own image, and say to himself that the sacred orator had revealed his character; such expositions, which, read to-day, impress us a little like commonplaces, were then, and on the spot, appropriate pictures, and great moving springs of action. After he had thus made the secret wound of every hearer quiver, by touching it incidentally, after he must have seemed almost to come to personalities with each one, Massillon rose to a *résumé* full of richness and grandeur; he hastened to cover over the whole with a great flood of eloquence, and to throw upon it a piece taken from the curtain of the Temple: "No, my dear hearer," said he directly, while magnificently giving to all these lapses and all these present miseries consecrated biblical names,—

"No, crimes are never the first sinful experiences of the heart: David was indiscreet and idle before he was an adulterer; Solomon permitted himself to be enervated by the delights of royalty before he appeared in the high places among foreign women; Judas loved money before setting a price on his master; Peter was presumptuous before he renounced him; Magdalen, no doubt, was anxious to please before becoming the sinner (*pécheresse*) of Jerusalem. . . . Vice has its progressive steps as well as Virtue; as the day instructs the day, so, says the Prophet, the night gives fatal lessons to the night. . . ."

Here an echo is awakened, and returns to us those verses of Hippolytus in Racine:

"Quelques crimes toujours précèdent les grands crimes;
Ainsi que la vertu, le crime a ses degrés. . . ."

It has been often remarked that Massillon recollects Racine, and that he takes pleasure sometimes in paraphrasing him. In the *Petit Carême*, the royal child to whom it is addressed, that precious remnant of all his family,—that miraculous child who has escaped from so many wrecks and ruins,—recalls at every moment the Joas of *Athalie*. Massillon needed not to wait for that similarity of situations, in order to recollect Racine. If Bourdaloue was the most perfect orator, according to the severe Boileau, Massillon is not less the orator who was to arise on the morrow from the creation of *Esther* and of *Athalie;* he received at the beginning of his career, the baptism, as it were, of that noble, tender, majestic, abundant, and mellowed language. "He has the same diction in prose as Racine in poetry," said Madame de Maintenon, after having heard him at Saint-Cyr.

One has even noted in Massillon some accents more tender and melancholy than one is wont to hear in the age of Lewis XIV, and which seem like a confused sigh announcing the new times; in the sermon upon *Afflictions*, for example.* We read there, at the beginning, some very touching words upon the universal suffering, apparent or concealed, which is the lot of all conditions, of all stations, of all souls. Is it Massillon, is it a more christian Bernardin de Saint-Pierre, is it Chateaubriand making father Aubry speak to the dying Atala, but in a purer language which Fontanes must have retouched,— which of the three is it, one might ask, that has written

* M. de Saci, to whom we owe this remark, is astonished that no one has ever pointed out that sermon as one of Massillon's most beautiful and best. Fréron, a man of sense (or Desfontaines) had already distinguished and cited it, from its very earliest publication. (*Jugements sur quelques Ouvrages nouveaux*, tome V, p. 287.)

this beautiful and sweet page of melodious morality, this human plaint which is like a song?—

"There is no perfect happiness on earth, because this is not the time for pleasures, but for pains: elevation has its constraints and its disquietudes; obscurity, its humiliations and its contempts; the world, its cares and its caprices; retreat, its sorrows and its *ennuis;* marriage, its antipathies and its frenzies; friendship, its losses or its treacheries; piety itself, its antipathies and its disgusts; finally, by an inevitable destiny of the children of Adam, every person finds his own ways sown with briars and thorns. The condition which is seemingly the happiest, has its secret bitternesses which corrupt all its felicity: the throne, alike with the humblest place, is the seat of chagrins; proud palaces, as well as the roof of the poor man and the laborer, conceal cruel cares; and for fear that our exile should be too pleasant for us, we always feel here, in a thousand ways, that something is wanting to our happiness."

The great effects of Massillon's eloquence are well known: the most celebrated is that which signalized his sermon on *The Small Number of the Elect*, at the moment when, after having for a long time prepared and wrought up his auditory, he suddenly interrogated it and summoned it to respond, by saying: "If Jesus-Christ were to appear in this temple, in the midst of this assembly, the most august in the world, in order to judge us, to make the terrible separation," etc.* That assembly, *the most*

---

* The following is the entire passage to which Sainte-Beuve refers. Speaking of the small number of the elect, he says: "Let me suppose that this was the last hour of us all; that the heavens were opening over our heads; that time had ended, and eternity begun; that Jesus-Christ in all his glory, that man of sorrows in all his glory, had appeared on the tribunal, and that we were assembled here to receive our final decree of life or death eternal! Let me ask, impressed with terror like you, and not separating my lot from yours, but putting myself in the same situation in which we must all one day appear before God, our judge; let me ask, if Jesus-Christ should now appear to make the terrible separation of the just from the unjust, do you think the greatest number would be saved? Do you think the number of the elect would even be equal to that of the sinners? Do you think, if all our works were examined with justice, he would find ten just persons in this assembly? Monsters of ingratitude! would he find one?"—[TR.

august in the world, was the one in the chapel at Versailles; but it was not there that Massillon first preached that sermon: it was at Paris, in Saint Eustachius's church, that the unexpected, irresistible effect was produced. It is said that the same agitation was produced in the chapel at Versailles,* and it is told that Massillon himself, by his gesture, by his *downcast attitude*, by his silence for some moments, associated himself with the terror of his auditory, and with a sincerity which was here confounded with the proprieties of the occasion, found a way, even in his triumph, to perform an act of profound christian humiliation.

Lewis XIV, who uttered some just but too rare sayings, said to Massillon one day, on going out after one of his sermons; "My Father, I have heard several great orators, and I have been very much pleased with them; as for you, every time that I have heard you, I have been very much displeased with myself." Examples have been mentioned of sudden conversions caused by Massillon's eloquence. A courtier went to the opera, and finding his carriage arrested by the crowd of persons who were going to the church where Massillon was to preach, he said to himself that one show was as good as another, and entered the church: he went out of it pricked in the heart. But it is particularly related that Rollin, then principal of Beauvais college, having one day taken his schoolboys to hear a sermon by Massillon upon the sanctity and fervor of the early christians, the children went away so affected by it, that on the following days they subjected themselves to austerities and mortifications which it became necessary to moderate.

* On this point we have tradition only, with its vagueness and uncertainty. It would be a precious thing if we could find some testimony that was wholly contemporary.

Massillon had in his gifts a power of unction stronger, if I may say it, than his character. He himself, after having thus conquered the simple-minded or the rebellious, after having publicly humbled the pride of men and dissolved their incredulity, had not all the force requisite to rally and confirm the new believers in the mysteries of faith. Here is the weak side, where he inclines toward his century, and no longer belongs altogether to the age of great men. People came to him; they found him an honest man,' an enlightened, affectionate brother, yet a little weak. That golden mouth, which had filled the temple, that beautiful sonorous vase, which gave forth sounds both so human and so divine, was not destined to be a column to bear heavy burdens.

In the interval between his *Grand Carême* and his *Petit Carême* and without detriment to his other sermons, which he did not stop preaching, Massillon delivered some funeral discourses. In this department of sacred oratory, he is eminent, but not great; his faults are here conspicuous. His historic portraits are deficient in vigor; he understands morality better than history. I have before me his funeral oration on the prince of Conti, published in 1709, with notes which a contemporary who took part in the ceremony, and who notices the difference between the printed and the spoken discourses, wrote in the margin in his own hand.* The criticisms made by this reader (of whose name I am ignorant), though a little minute sometimes, are generally very just; he points out inaccuracies and unauthorized expressions in the discourse, as well as awkward phrases and repetitions (the word

* These manuscript notes are found in the copy belonging to the Imperial Library.

goût, for example, repeated to satiety); he shows the weakness and lack of precision in the plan, especially toward the end; he recognizes also and praises the beautiful portions, the lively picture of the prince of Conti on the day of Neerwinden, and especially the spirited portraiture of the graces, the affability, and the habitual charm which caused him to be adored in civil life. We see, by these notes, that the prince of Conti wrote down with his own hand the last conversations which he had with the great Condé at Chantilly upon the war and upon other subjects. What has become of these precious Memoranda? In fine, just as in war Conti was but the chief pupil of his immortal uncle, Massillon, in the funeral oration, is but the brilliant disciple of Bossuet and of those who have celebrated the Condés and the Turennes.

The oration which he pronounced at the funeral of Lewis XIV, the admirable beginning of which I have cited, has some fine passages, but is equally faulty as a whole: Massillon, in praising, did not know how to seize upon the great features, like Bossuet; he mingles truths and qualifications which shade them, where a brilliant coloring, a large and sustained treatment, is demanded. He has contradictions, in which his sincerity and his philosophical beginning, contending with the obligation to praise, are not easily reconciled; as when, for example, he liberally praises Lewis XIV for his revocation of the Edict of Nantes, and at the same time wishes to brand Saint Bartholomew and maintain to a certain point the principle of toleration: in this passage Massillon tries to reconcile two impossible ideas, and he is foiled; he produces only a contradictory and uncertain result. He has, nevertheless, some agreeable and truthful passages, as that, for example, which depicts the grave familiarity and dignified affability of Lewis XIV.

"From that fund of wisdom proceeded the majesty displayed in his whole person; in his most private life he was never seen for a moment to forget the gravity and the proprieties of royal dignity; never did a king sustain better than he the majestic character of sovereignty. What dignity when the ministers of kings came to the foot of his throne! what precision in his words! what majesty in his answers! We collect them as the maxims of wisdom, jealously regretting that his silence should have too often robbed us of the treasures which were ours, and, if I may be permitted to say it, that he should have been too sparing of his words to his subjects, who for him, were prodigal of their blood and their tenderness.

"Meanwhile, as you know, that majesty had no fierceness, but a charming address, when it was willing to be approached; an art of timing its favors, which touched men more than the favors themselves; a politeness of speech which knew always how to say that which men loved most to hear. We went away from him enraptured, and we lamented the loss of those moments which his solitude and his occupations rendered daily more rare."

Here one believes that he is listening to the Massillon to whom Lewis XIV addressed some of those words that were so just, so flattering, and so perfect, and who, a passionate lover of the noble and the good language, regretted that he did not draw oftener from that lofty source; that he did not, by listening to the king, hear oftener the man in France who spoke with the most propriety and politeness. Such a shade of regret expressed in the pulpit by the sacred orator, appears to me to indicate already a complete transition to another age; the Fenelons and the Massillons were the first, indeed, who inclined in that direction, and who wished for a more popular and more familiar royalty.

September 26, 1853.

II.

To ANY ONE who spoke to him of his Sermons preached at Court, Massillon replied: "When one approaches that avenue at Versailles, he feels an enervating atmosphere." None of this enervation appears in any of the early discourses of Massillon (1699–1715). If we overcome, in reading them, the inevitable monotony which belongs to this species of composition, if we enter into the spirit of it, we perceive that we are reading a series of masterpieces. It is always on the moral side, it is through the heart and passions, that Massillon impresses the hearer, and strives to restore his reverence for faith and doctrine. Coming at an age when corruption flourished most rankly, and when it was covered only by a thin veil in the monarch's presence, he well understood the nature of the incredulity which he had to combat, and, on that account, it is curious to see what class of arguments he deems fittest to oppose to it.

The duchess of Orleans, mother of the Regent, wrote in July, 1669: "Nothing is rarer in France" (it should have been said, at Court) "than christian faith; there is no longer any vice here of which one is ashamed; and, if the king were to punish all those who become guilty of the greatest vices, he would no longer have about him nobles, princes, or servants; there would not be even a house in France which would not be in mourning." In speaking thus, Madame did not exaggerate; the Regency of her son soon after proved it. But it was before that auditory which was hardly restrained by Lewis XIV, that Massillon had to preach his Advent and his Lent Sermons, and that he entered, on certain days, upon these vast subjects: *Of Doubts about Religion; Of the Reality of a Future Life.* Before these young debauchees, in whom the spirit of the eighteenth century is already fermenting, he asserts the principle that "the great difficulty with dissoluteness is, that it leads to a desire for unbelief"; that it is the interest which the passions have in never attaining to a future life, where light and condemnation await them, that inclines and obliges the mind to disbelieve in it. He repeats this truth in a hundred striking ways: "Men begin with the passions; doubts come afterward." He does not try to dissemble the fact that these doubts were already, in the fashionable world, the commonest talk of his time. Will he proceed to discuss them, to examine their nature, to enter into the fundamental proofs of religion? No, he knows too well the peculiar character of these doubts, and of those who frame them, or rather who have learned them, and repeat them when they are already vulgar and hackneyed. Whom has he before him? Are they genuine unbelievers, men who, in a sullen and melancholy solitude, during a period of reflection that was full of darkness and of gloom, themselves originated the objections, and then the answers, and who have arrived laboriously at what they believe to be certain results? "No, my brethren," boldly cries Massillon, "it is not with the incredulous that we have here to do, it is with cowardly men who have not strength to take a side; who know only how to live voluptuously, without morality, often without decency, and who, without being impious, yet live without religion, because religion demands order, rationality, elevation, firmness, noble sentiments, and they are incapable of them." It was with this penetrating exordium that Massillon struck at the root of the incredulity of his age, at that which was the peculiarity of the men of pleasure, which was far more a matter of gentility and of pretension than of doctrine, and which might be called libertinism in reality. Right along with this he sketched the portrait of the veritable and pure unbeliever, in doctrine and in theory, the portrait of Spinosa, whom he strangely blackens, and makes out a *monster*, but characterizes, nevertheless, by some of his fundamental traits: "That impious man," he says, "lived concealed, retired, tranquil; he made his gloomy productions his only occupation, and needed nobody else to confirm him in his opinions. But those who sought for him with so much eagerness, who wished to see him, to hear him, to consult him, these frivolous and dissolute persons were madmen who wished to become impious." The rumor spread, indeed, that Spinosa had formerly been summoned to Paris for consultation. There had been journeys to Holland, expressly to see him. He began to be visited by pilgrims and amateurs in unbelief.. Massillon rallies them, these persons who reject all authority in matters of belief, for having needed the authority and the testimony of an obscure man, before they dared to doubt. Upon all these points Massillon is at once a consummate moralist and a provident indicator; he perceives very clearly where, in his time, lies the peril in respect to faith, and by what moral breach it is likely to escape from men's hearts. Corruption and licentiousness are the plague which is attacking the head of the social body, and which is going to infect souls at the core. The Regency preceded the Encyclopædia.

A century after Massillon things had greatly changed: it was no longer the mere corruption of morals which confronted the christian orator as his principal enemy, it was deliberate, fixed unbelief, which had found its way even among honest people. Spinoza, little read, little comprehended, had remained in the shade; but other persons, less incredulous and more eloquent, had openly traced their furrow under the sun, and propagated their germs in all ways: many souls, willingly or unwillingly, had received them; do what he would, every person in his day felt more or less the effects of having come into the world after Voltaire and Rousseau. Again, just a century after Massillon, an orator whom I shall not pretend even to compare with him in talent, but who has with much honor maintained the succession of sacred eloquence, the abbe Frayssinous, was obliged, in his open Lectures under the Empire and afterward, to discuss before honest people, mostly young, no longer desiring to doubt, but rather desiring to believe, the controverted points of doctrine and historic tradition, and he did it with an amount of learning and argument appropriate to that new state of things.

The Sermons of Massillon are not works suited to analysis: we cannot curtail them at pleasure, or cut at will into those fine integral moral discussions, so broad in their scope,— into those vast interior descriptions, where no link in the chain is forgotten; we can only offer, at best, some considerable passages and some bits. What admirable views upon the passions, upon pleasure and its disgusts (sermon on *The Prodigal Son*); upon ambition and its lusts (sermon *On the Employment of Time*); upon envy and its crooked ways (sermon *On the Forgiveness of Offenses*); upon the miseries even of a happy criminal affection, of a passionate attachment felt and reciprocated (sermon on *The Woman who Sinned — La Pécheresse*). "What fears lest the secret should be discovered! what bounds to keep in regard to propriety and reputation! what eyes to avoid! what spies to deceive! what deceptions to fear regarding the fidelity of those whom one has chosen for the ministers and confidants of her passion! what rebuffs to endure from him, perhaps, to whom she has sacrificed her honor and her liberty, and of whom she would not dare to complain! To all this add those cruel moments when the passion, becoming less lively, leaves us leisure to fall back upon ourselves, and to feel all the unworthiness of our condition; those moments when the heart, created for more solid pleasures, is wearied of its own idols, and finds its punishment in its disgusts and in its own inconstancy. Profane world! if this is the felicity of which you so often boast to us, confine it to your adorers! . . ." What eternal truths upon the subject of *Death*, truths still new to-day, and which will ever be so! for that idea of death, which men forget incessantly, and which they try to turn aside, rules them, whatever they may do. Frail creatures, beings of a day, in spite of the lofty progress of which they boast, in spite of the increasing resources which they have at command, death is there, which baffles them to-day as on the morrow after Adam, and which seizes them amid their ambitious schemes, whether accomplished or only projected, amid their rivalries, amid their hopes of revenge and of reprisal upon fortune: "We hasten to profit by each other's remains; we resemble those foolish soldiers who, in the thick of the fight, and at the very time when their companions are everywhere falling by their side under the steel and the fire of the enemy, eagerly encumber themselves with his clothes. . . ." But this comes only after a great and inexhaustible flow of eloquence upon the flight and perpetual renewal of things, one of the most beautiful examples of human speech. As he left the pulpit after these luminous outbursts, oh! how well Massillon knew that he had been eloquent! and when one told him so, he replied: "The devil told me so before you!" At times he appears to suffer from these eulogiums. Of what advantage is it to him to be praised for having read, almost like a prophet, the hearts and the secret propensities of those who hear him, if the propensities resist him, if the hearts remain the same, and do not in any respect reform? "And of what use is it for us to please you, if we do not change you? How are we benefited by our eloquence, if you are always sinners?" Boldly accepting the eulogium, and deriving from it an occasion for self-humiliation, he says: "God no longer withdraws from his Prophets in the midst of the cities, but he takes away from them, if I may dare so to speak, the force and the virtue of their ministry; he strikes these holy clouds with aridity and with dryness; he raises up among you those *who render the truth beautiful to you, but who do not render it lovely; who please, but who do not convert you:* he lets the holy terrors of his doctrine be weakened on our lips; he no longer draws the treasures of his compassion from those extraordinary men formerly raised up in the days of our fathers, who renovated cities and kingdoms, who captivated the great and the people, who changed the palaces of kings into houses of penitence." And alluding to some humble missionaries, who, during the same period, produced much fruit in the country-places, he said: "We discourse, and they convert."

I have mentioned some of the sudden conversions which, according to tradition, were produced by the eloquence of Massillon: and yet without denying the two or three cases which are cited, I see that Massillon had little faith in this kind of conversions by the thunderbolt, "these sudden miracles which, in a twinkling of the eye, change the face of things,—which plant, which pluck up, which destroy, which build up at the first onset. An illusion, my dear hearer," he continued; "conversion is usually a slow, tardy miracle, the fruit of cares, of troubles, of frights, and of bitter inquietudes."

I encounter a difficulty here, and almost a rock, which I shall neither attempt to conceal nor to elude. Massillon deserves to be treated without that tenderness which resembles timidity and a shameful fear. I will say then that at the time of his greatest successes, and when his preaching was most admired and most persuasive, the life of Massillon was odiously criminated. D'Alembert, who is yet wholly friendly to him, says that envy used that means to dissuade Lewis XIV from raising him to the bishopric. Chamfort, in an anecdote devoid of all authenticity, went so far as even to name the person of the other sex with whom, he pretends, he was *occupé* in a mundane way.* The contemporaries of Massillon have named more positively another person of quality among those who were under his guidance.† The collection of

---

* The person whom Chamfort designates is no other than the amiable Madame de Simiane, granddaughter of Madame de Sévigné. M. Aubenas has said a word on this subject, page 505 of the *Histoire de Madame de Sévigné et de sa Famille* (1842).

† The Marchioness de L'Hôpital, wife and soon widow of the great geometer, author of the *Analyse des Infiniment Petits*. "He had married," says Fontenelle, "Marie Charlotte de Romilley de La Chesnelaye, a young lady of an old noble family of Brittany, from whom he had great wealth. Their union was so complete that he shared with her his genius for mathe-

satiric songs called *Recueil de Maurepas* (Imperial Library) contains, in four or five places, coarse couplets insulting to Massillon; and it concerns us, not to discuss, but to repulse, and that by the mouth of Massillon himself, these slanderous accusations, which would not fail to come out sooner or later, and which would be produced with an air of discovery and of triumph.

After his first successes, that happened to Massillon which happens to every eloquent and celebrated preacher; he was sought for, people ran after him, they forced him often to quit that retreat of the Saint Honoré house, where he lived humble, studious, and occupied with meditations on Eternity. Was there a moment when Massillon was not sufficiently on his guard against the malicious and perfidious world that surrounded him, and which demanded only a pretext for railing at him? Did he permit himself to be too much entangled with those requests for guidance which came to him from all sides, and which some half-mundane women also emulously addressed to him? He naturally loved good company; did he suffer himself to be, apparently, a little too much captivated by it? Did he go and pass his autumnal vacations, after 1704, at the estates and chateaux to which he was invited? It is possible that at the time when he became celebrated he had committed some imprudence of that kind, and the jesters, being unable to deprive his powerful speech of its unction and its charm, tried to deprive him of his authority. He seems, in several of his sermons, to have reflected on this, and to have replied to it: let one read, as he thinks

matics." It was that learned person of whom Massillon was spiritual adviser, and he went and passed his vacations at her home in Saint-Mesme in 1704, a little while after the marquis's death: which gave occasion for all the tittle-tattle, jokes, and songs.

of this, the sermon *On the World's Injustice toward Good People*, and that especially *On Slander:* "The shafts of slander," says he, "are never more keen, more brilliant, more applauded by the world, than when they are directed against the ministers of the holy altars: the world, so indulgent to itself, seems never to have kept any severity except for them, and it has for them eyes more censorious, and a language more envenomed, than for the rest of men." He characterizes in vivid and precise terms all the results of the slander, which at first was trivial and insignificant, "this *nothing*, which is going to become real by passing through different mouths." We almost recognize here that *Vaudeville* of which Boileau speaks:

"Agréable indiscret, qui, conduit par le chant,
Passe de bouche en bouche, et s'accroit en marchant."*

But that which was at first but a simple pleasantry, but a malicious conjecture, is going soon to become a serious affair, *a formal and public defamation*, the subject of all conversations. "It is a scandal which will survive you," cries Massillon; "the scandalous histories of Courts never die with their heroes; lascivious writers have caused the disorders of the Courts that have preceded us, to pass even into our satires; and there will be found among our licentious authors those who will inform the coming ages of the public rumors, the scandalous events, and the vices of ours." These words might be written as an epigraph and a sentiment at the head of the whole collection by Maurepas. As for Massillon, to cut short a question which cannot be one, and a justification to which it is unnecessary to descend, it is sufficient to repeat with him: "A corrupt

---

* This also recalls the portrait of calumny drawn by Beaumarchais: "At first a slight rumor skimming lightly over the earth like a swallow," etc. (Barbier de Seville, Acte II, Scène 8.)

priest is never such by halves," and to pass on, without further delay, to the admirable fruits which he never ceases to draw from his genius and his heart,— to the masterpieces of his second period; these are the victorious and sovereign refutations.

The *Petit Carême*, which was preached in 1718 by Massillon, already nominated bishop, before Lewis XV, yet a child, in the private chapel of the Tuileries, has been since youth in all memories. It is said that Voltaire, at one time, had it always on his table by the side of *Athalie*. That *Petit Carême*, generally speaking, was composed for people who profited very little by it, but the fault cannot be charged upon Massillon. That marvellous little work, which it is said he was but six weeks in writing, is composed of six sermons, in which, while dwarfing himself at times, and placing himself within reach of the child-king whom he was trying to instruct, Massillon addresses oftener the great personages who hear him, and, while enchanting them, lectures them upon their vices, their excesses and hardness of heart, their duties, and the christian obligations which are imposed upon greatness. I know of nothing more beautiful or more true than the sermon for the third Sunday in Lent, which treats of the passions and their effects, of incurable satiety, of that vast and premature vacuity, which was then the unhappiness of some persons, and which we have since seen to be the malady of a great number. The Regent said that he was born *ennuyée*; how many men have there been since, who, without being regents of the kingdom or sons of France, have likewise begun with *ennui* a life which the passions could only agitate and ravage without making it satisfactory. Massillon from this time shows that, with-

out having seen the Childe Harolds and the Renés, and
so many other illustrious persons successively disgusted,
he had known their malady as long as anybody, and that
he had learned its secret from Job and Solomon, if not
from himself. And what picture can be more striking
and more easily recognized than this illustration of a soul
finally devoted to capricious *ennui*, the offspring of pleasure:

"Your passions having tried everything and exhausted everything, nothing more remains to you than to devour yourselves; your whimsicalities (*bizarreries*) become the only resource of your *ennui* and of your satiety. Unable longer to vary the pleasures already quite exhausted, you can no longer find variety except in the eternal inequalities of your humor, and you incessantly blame yourselves for the void which everything that surrounds you leaves within you.

"This is not one of those idle illustrations which discourse employs, and in which one makes up with ornament for the lack of resemblance. Approach the great; look at one of those persons who have grown old by the indulgence of the passions, and whom long indulgence in pleasure has rendered equally incapable of vice and of virtue. What an eternal gloominess of temper! what a fund of ill-humor and caprice! Nothing pleases, because one can no longer please himself: we avenge upon everything about us the vexations which torment us; it seems as if we made it a crime in the rest of mankind that we are unable still to be as criminal as they; we secretly reproach them for all that which we can no longer permit in ourselves, and we substitute our ill-humor for our pleasures."

Certainly, it seems as if he who wrote that had suffered and known it all. Massillon had the gift which enabled him to describe all the states of the soul, as if he had experienced them himself.

And yet Massillon became so celebrated by his *Petit Carême* only because in that respect he chanced to be the organ of a social sentiment long repressed, which now found expression for the first time. A new reign, a new century, had just begun; along with the disorders which pervaded and scandalized the public morals, a great hope was cherished in all the souls that still remained virtuous. Lewis XIV having abused his mode of ruling, a new and gentler manner must be henceforth more effective and suited to the times: "Kings can be great only by rendering themselves useful to the peoples. . . . It is not the sovereign, it is the law, Sire, which must rule the peoples. . . . Men believe they are free only when they are governed by laws. . . . Yes, Sire, to be great in the opinion of men, one must be useful to men. . . . We must interest men in our glory, if we wish it to be immortal, and we can interest them in it only by our benefits." Such were the words with which Massillon, who in this repeated Fenelon, nourished his discourses, and which he uttered in the name of Christianity. It has been said that, in speaking thus, he alluded to, and indirectly satirized, Lewis XIV: I do not believe it. He would never have allowed himself to commit such an impropriety before the Villeroys, the Fleurys, the Du Maines, before those *old men*, those *wise men*, and those tried friends of the old reign, all those tutors of the royal child; but, in speaking for peace in opposition to conquests, he expressed the universal sentiment, that which those prudent men had been among the first to share with him. It was not at all against the honors paid to the august memory of Lewis XIV that Massillon protested in the portraits which he traced of a monarch who is the father of the people and their benefactor; he only proposed some kind of a reformation,—a peaceful and more humane transfiguration of Lewis XIV, —in that softened ideal of a great king.

Every precept, if one is not on his guard, runs great risk of being abused. By dint of continual repetition to the young king: "Be *tender*, humane, affable," Massillon, like Fenelon himself, trenched closely on the chimerical; he seemed to believe in that *love for the nourse* which the people do not have, and in which the great kings and those most reputed for their good nature, even Henry IV,* have never believed. Massillon, in this part of his *Petit Carême*, inaugurates that policy by which, doubtless, Lewis XV did not know how to profit in time, but which, as soon as one wished really to adopt it, succeeded so badly in the case of Lewis XVI, and in the case of Malesherbes,— those excellent men who confided too much, even touching this matter, in the general excellence of human nature. Massillon lays a little too much stress on this sentiment; he does not add any corrective; he does not add the proper qualification of firmness; and one must have dreamed of a pastoral monarchy after the style of the sixteenth century, in order to cry out with Lemontey: "The *Petit Carême* of Massillon, a masterpiece fallen from Heaven, like *Télémaque*, sweet and sublime lessons which kings should read, which the peoples should adore!" There is in this somewhat, indeed, of the fashion and dream of Salentum.

* In *L'Estoile* there is a saying of Henry IV, which is a bitter truth. It was a little after Châtel's attempt at assassination, in the early days of Henry's reign and of his entry into Paris. A procession was formed on the fifth of January, 1595, in which he took part. The people seemed to wish to recompense him and to avenge him for the late attack. Cries of "Long live the King!" resounded on all sides. "Never," says L'Estoile, "did one see a King so loudly applauded as was that good prince, that day, wherever he passed." One spoke of it to Henry IV, who replied by shaking his head: "*It is the mob;* if my greatest enemy were in my place, and they saw him passing by, they would do as much for him as for me, and would cry still louder than they do." A very similar answer is attributed to Cromwell, but from the lips of Henry IV the saying, it seems to me, has still more weight.

I will try to sum up the impressions which mingle with the admiration, so legitimate and so enduring, with which the *Petit Carême* inspires me. For the man of taste who reads it, there are wanting, I think, a little more strength in the pictures and a variety of style which would have given them more distinctness. For the christian, there is wanting, perhaps, toward the end, in the order of faith, I know not what flame and what sword's point, not opposed, however, to charity, but which one cannot mistake. Voltaire felt that sword's point in Pascal, and in Bossuet; he felt it less in Massillon. He had his work read to him at table, and it did not convert him: "The sermons of father Massillon," he wrote to Argental, who was a little astonished at it, "are one of the most *agreeable works* we have in our language. I love to have them read to me at table; the ancients did so, and I am very ancient. I am, besides, a very zealous worshipper of the Deity; I have always been opposed to atheism; I love the books which exhort to virtue, from Confucius to Massillon; and upon that subject I am not to be counselled but to be imitated."

It does not belong to me to play the rigorist, or to find fault with that magic of expression and language which prevented Voltaire, in this case, from taking offense at the ideas; still is not Massillon condemned somewhat by this very liking which Voltaire declares he had for him, and by the singular favor which he enjoyed of not displeasing the adversary? for, in spite of all, it is about this which Voltaire means to say: "In vain dost thou preach to me, thou art not one of my enemies!" He may be deceived, and he is deceived, but he seems at least to detect in him a more indulgent disposition than that of a Bossuet or a Bourdaloue.

It is not that the evil spirit was not rebuked from time to time incidentally: in that same *Petit Carême*, Massillon, as if he had had a presentiment of the author of *La Pucelle*, said: "These vaunted wits, who by their happy talents enabled their age almost to rival the ancients in taste and refinement, left to the world, as soon as their hearts were corrupted, only lascivious and pernicious works, whose poison, prepared by skillful hands, daily infects the public morals, and from which the ages following us will continue to imbibe the licentiousness and corruption of ours." How did Voltaire look when he heard this passage read to him at table?

In 1717 Massillon was appointed to the bishopric of Clermont, which was in the gift of the abbe de Louvois. As he was poor, one of his friends, a generous rich man, one of the Crozats, paid for his bulls. The consecration of Massillon took place on the twenty-first (and not on the sixteenth) of December, 1718, in the king's chapel, and the young prince wished to be present. There are hours when, after having for a long time waited for fortune, one has only to let it alone. Massillon was received into the French Academy on the twenty-third of February, 1719, in place of that same friend, the abbe de Louvois, who had already helped him to the bishopric of Clermont.* Honors are always paid for, in this world, by some compliance. A good deal has been said of that of Massillon, who consented to be one of the two bishops who took part in the consecration of cardinal Dubois, appointed archbishop of

* The tender connection and friendship of Massillon and the abbe de Louvois had existed for eighteen or twenty years. Two letters from Massillon to the abbe have been printed, which were written at Paris in 1701, during the young abbe's journey to Italy. (*Journal Général de l'Instruction Publique*, June 25, 1853.)

Cambray; the consecration took place, in a solemn manner, at Val-de-Grace (June, 1720). Duclos and Saint-Simon have given the only reasons, and the best ones, in excuse for his not having said *no*. Saint-Simon says:

"Dubois desired (for his second assistant) Massillon, the celebrated priest of the Oratory, whose virtue, knowledge, and great pulpit talents had made him bishop of Clermont. Massillon, driven into a corner, bewildered, without extraneous resources, felt the indignity of the proposal, stammered, and dared not refuse. What could a man so puny, in the estimation of the times, do when face to face with a Regent, his minister, and cardinal Rohan? He was, nevertheless, greatly blamed by the world, especially by good people of all parties; for on that point, the enormity of the scandal had united them. The most reasonable persons, who were numerous, contented themselves with pitying him, and it was at last very generally agreed that it was, in a certain sense, impossible for him to excuse himself and refuse to attend."

Note, in passing, this impartial testimony of the rarely indulgent Saint-Simon, to the merits and the proved virtue of Massillon. It was precisely on account of the virtue and respectability of Massillon that the abbe Dubois had chosen him.

Add to this that in the conduct of life this same virtue was never obstinate or intractable: there was something of Atticus in Massillon.

After these inevitable delays, Massillon, then fifty-eight years old, repaired to his diocese in 1721, and left it but once, when he went to Saint-Denis to deliver the funeral oration of the duchess of Orleans, mother of the Regent (1723). During the twenty-one years in which he resided in his diocese, he renounced preaching and eloquence, whether, as one has said, because his memory was wearied, or because he began to feel the natural indolence of old age: he limited himself to delivering, as occasion demanded, some charges and synodal discourses. Meanwhile he practiced the episcopal virtues, charity and toleration, then very rare on account of the lively disputes about the Bull. He mingled with that toleration a kind of amenity that belongs to the man of the world; he took pleasure in bringing together at his country-house Jesuits and Oratorians, the members of two societies that were little disposed to harmonize, and he made them play at checkers: it was the only war which he advised them to wage. He had the sacraments administered to the worthy niece of Pascal, Mademoiselle Marguerite Périer, who died at Clermont in 1733 at the age of eighty-seven, and whom a less wise curate wished to question touching certain articles, when she was on her death-bed. It was his principle to avoid scandal, above all things, when the church rule was not infringed. Persons not very friendly to Massillon found no other way of reproaching him than by calling him *that peaceful prelate*: it was this sort of taunt which the journal (Jansenist) of the *New Ecclesiastics* commonly addressed to him. Further details, which would exceed my plan, belong to that full and complete biography which I would provoke some one to write.

The last unfinished work of Massillon's old age was a series of *Moral Paraphrases of the Psalms*. Some beauties may be found in them, but they are more and more of the regular kind, and such as one anticipates even in their expansion; they are examples of Massillon's ordinary talent, without the movement and the energy which he infused into such developments in his discourses, as, for example, when he so powerfully paraphrased *De Profundis* in the sermon on *Lazarus*. I have sometimes thought, in the course of this study, upon the difference there is between Massillon and Bossuet when they make use of texts of Scripture. Massillon gives his moral paraphrase of a text which he unfolds verse by verse, and which he graduates; he puts his sheaf in order, and places it, in some manner, on the wheels of the sacred chariot; its march is regular, cadenced, harmonious; whilst the language of Bossuet is oftener confounded with the chariot itself, with the fiery wheel that bears the Prophet along.

Marmontel, who was destined at one period of his youth to the ecclesiastical calling, and who had studied for some time at Clermont, had occasion to visit the eloquent bishop, and in his Memoirs he has given a touching picture of his impressions, which must be generally faithful to the facts:

"In one of our walks at Beauregard, the bishop's country seat, we had the pleasure of seeing the venerable Massillon. The reception, so full of kindness, which that illustrious old man gave us, the lively and tender impression which his looks and the accents of his voice made upon me, is one of the sweetest recollections of my youth that remain to me. At that age when the mental and moral affections communicate with each other so suddenly, when thought and feeling act and react upon each other with such rapidity, there is no one who has not sometimes chanced, on seeing a great man, to stamp his forehead with the characteristic traits of his soul or genius. It was thus that in the wrinkles of that already withered face, and in those eyes which were going soon to close, I believed there was still visible the expression of that eloquence, so affecting, so tender, so lofty at times, so profoundly penetrating, with which I had just been enchanted in reading his Sermons. He permitted us to speak to him of it, and to pay him our homage for the religious tears which it had made us shed."

As Massillon's Sermons were not published in his lifetime, there seems to be an anachronism here: but it may be that there were some copies in circulation among the scholars at Clermont, or that an incomplete edition had fallen into their hands.

Massillon died on the eighteenth of September, 1742, in his eightieth year. He did not live long enough to see disclosed, along with the public scandals of Lewis XV, all the irony of the chaste promises and wishes with which the *Petit Carême* had saluted that royal infancy. With him expired the last, the most abundantly eloquent, and the most Ciceronian of the great voices which had filled and moved the age of Lewis the Fourteenth.

October 3, 1853.

PASCAL.

IN writing some pages upon *Pascal*, I labor under a disadvantage; it is that of having some time ago written a large volume of which he was almost entirely the subject. I shall try, in speaking now, before all the world, of a book which ranks among the classics, to forget what I have written of him that is of too special interest, and to limit myself to what will interest the generality of readers. The excellent work* which I have before me, and in which M. Havet has noted all the anterior labors, will aid me in this.

Pascal was great in heart as well as in mind, which great minds not always are; and all that he did in the sphere (*ordre*) of the mind and in the sphere of the heart bears a stamp of invention and of originality which attests force, depth, and an ardent, and, so to speak, ravenous pursuit of truth. Born in 1623 of a family full of intelligence and virtue, liberally educated by a father who was himself a superior man, he had received some admirable gifts, a special genius for arithmetical calculations and mathematical concepts, and an exquisite moral sensibility, which made him a passionate friend of goodness and foe of evil, — greedy of happiness, but of a noble and infinite happiness. His discoveries, even in childhood, are celebrated; wherever he cast his eye, he sought and found something

* Édition nouvelle avec Notes et Commentaires, par M. E. Havet. Desobry, 1852.

new; it was easier for him to make discoveries for himself than to study after the way of others. His youth escaped the levities and disorders which are the ordinary peril: his nature, he tells us, was very capable of tempests; but they spent themselves in the sphere of science, and especially in the order of the religious sentiments. His excessive mental labor had early rendered him subject to a singular nervous malady, which developed still more his keen natural sensibility. The acquaintance which he made with the gentlemen of Port-Royal supplied an aliment to his moral activity, and their doctrine, which was something new and bold, became for him a starting-point whence he set out in his own original way for a complete reconstruction of the moral and religious world. A sincere and passionate christian, he conceived an apology, a defense of religion by a method and by reasons which no one had yet discovered, and which was to carry defeat to the very heart of the sceptic. When thirty years old he applied himself to that work with the fire and precision which he put into everything: new and graver physical disorders which supervened, prevented him from executing it continuously, but he returned to it at every opportunity in the intervals of his pains; he threw upon paper his ideas, his views, his flashes. Dying at thirty-nine (1662), he was unable to arrange them in order, and his *Thoughts on Religion*, prepared by his family and friends, did not appear till seven or eight years afterward.

What was the character of that first edition of the *Thoughts?* One conceives it without difficulty, even though he may not have the proof from the originals. That first edition did not contain all that he had left; only the principal pieces were published in it, and in those that were published, scruples of various kinds, whether doctrinal or grammatical, caused certain passages to be corrected, softened, or explained, in which the vivacity and impatience of the author had been manifested in observations too blunt or too concise, and in a decisive style which, in such a matter, might be compromising.

In the eighteenth century, Voltaire and Condorcet seized upon some of the Thoughts of Pascal, as in war one tries to profit by the too advanced movements of a daring and rash hostile general. Pascal was only daring, not rash; but, since •I have compared him to a general, I will add that he was a general who was killed in the very moment of his operation; it remained unfinished, and, in part, exposed (*à découvert*).

In our day, in restoring the true text of Pascal, in giving his phrases in all their simplicity, with their firm and precise beauty, and also with their defiant boldness, and their everywhere singular familiarity, one has returned to a juster point of view, not at all hostile. M. Cousin was the first to urge that work of completely restoring Pascal, in 1843; M. Faugère has the merit of having executed it in 1844. Thanks to him, we have now the *Thoughts* of Pascal in conformity with the manuscripts themselves. This is the text which a very distinguished young professor, M. Havet, has just published in his turn, accompanying it with all the necessary helps, explanations, comparisons, commentaries; he has given a learned edition, and one that is truly classical in the best sense of the word.

Being unable to enter fully into the examination of Pascal's method, I would like to insist here, after the style of M. Havet, upon a single point, and show how, in spite of all the changes that have supervened in the world and in ideas, in spite of the repugnance which is more and more felt to certain views peculiar to the author of the *Thoughts*, we are to-day in a better position to sympathize with Pascal than one was in the time of Voltaire; how that which in Pascal scandalized Voltaire, scandalizes us less than the beautiful and heart-felt passages which are close to it, touch and ravish us. The reason is, that Pascal is not simply a reasoner, a man who presses his adversary in all directions, who defies him upon a thousand points which are commonly the pride and glory of the understanding; Pascal is at once a soul which suffers, which has felt, and which expresses its struggle and its agony.

There were unbelievers in the time of Pascal; the sixteenth century had engendered a sufficiently large number of them, especially among the lettered classes; they were pagans, more or less sceptical, of whom Montaigne is for us the most graceful type, and whose race we see continued in Charron, La Mothe-le-Vayer, Gabriel-Naudé. But these learned and sceptical men, as well as the freethinkers who were simply intellectual people and men of the world, like Theophile or Des Barreaux, took things little to heart; whether they persevered in their incredulity or were converted at the hour of death, we do not perceive in them that profound inquietude which attests a moral nature of a high order, and a mental nature stamped with the seal of the archangel; they are not, in a word, to speak like Plato, royal natures. Pascal is of this leading and glorious race; he has more than one sign of it in his heart and on his brow: he is one of the noblest of mortals, but he is sick, and he would be cured. He was the first man to introduce into the defense of religion the ardor, the anguish, and the lofty melancholy which others carried later into scepticism.

"I blame equally," he says, "those who take part in praising man, those who take part in blaming him, and those who make it a business to amuse themselves; and I can approve only those who *seek the truth with groans.*"

The method he employs in his *Thoughts* to combat unbelievers, and especially to rouse the indifferent man, and to excite desire in his heart, is full of originality and novelty. One knows how he begins. He takes man in the midst of nature, in the bosom of the infinite; considering him by turns in relation to the immensity of the heavens and in relation to the atom, he shows him alternately great and small, suspended between two infinities, between two abysses. The French language has no more beautiful pages than the simple and severe lines of that incomparable picture. Looking at man inwardly as he has looked at him outwardly, Pascal tries to show in the mind itself two other abysses, on one side an elevation toward God, toward the morally beautiful, a return movement toward an illustrious origin, and on the other side an abasement in the direction of evil, a kind of criminal attraction to vice. This, no doubt, is the christian idea of the original corruption and of the Fall; but Pascal, as he employs it, pushes it to such an extreme, and carries it so far, that he makes it in some sort his own: at the very beginning, he makes man a monster, a chimera, something incomprehensible. He makes the knot and ties it in an insoluble manner, in order that, later, only a God, descending like a sword, can cut it.

In order to vary the reading of Pascal, I have given myself the satisfaction of re-reading, along with his *Thoughts*, some pages of Bossuet and of Fenelon. I have taken Fenelon in the Treatise *On the Existence of God*, and Bossuet in the treatise *On the Knowledge of God and of One's Self;* and without seeking to investigate the difference (if there is any) of doctrine, I have noticed, before all, that of character and of genius.

Fenelon, as one knows, begins by seeking his proofs of the existence of God in the general aspect of the universe, in the spectacle of the marvels which manifest themselves in all the orders of creation; the stars, the different elements, the structure of the human body, all are to him a path by which to rise from contemplation of the work and from admiration of the art to a knowledge of the workman. There is a plan, and there are laws; then there is an architect and a legislator. There are visible ends, then there is a supreme design. After having confidently accepted this mode of interpretation by external things and the demonstration of God by nature, Fenelon, in the second part of his treatise, enters upon another order of proofs; he admits of philosophical doubt touching things without, and shuts himself up within himself to arrive at the same end by another road, and to demonstrate God's existence simply by the nature of our ideas. But in admitting the universal doubt of the philosophers, he is not frightened by this state of the case; he describes it slowly, almost complacently; he is neither hurried nor impatient, nor does he suffer like Pascal; he is not what Pascal in his search appears at the very first, that lost traveler who yearns for home, who, lost without a guide in a dark forest, takes many times the wrong road, goes, returns upon his steps, is discouraged, sits down at a crossing of the roads, utters cries to which no one responds, resumes his march with frenzy and pain, is lost again, throws himself upon the ground and wants to die, and reaches home at last only after all sorts of anxieties and after sweating blood.

Fenelon, in his easy, gradual, and measured march, has nothing like this. It is very true that at the very moment when he asks whether all nature is not a phantom, and when, to be logical, he puts himself in the position of absolute doubt, it is very true that he says to himself: "This state of suspense astonishes and frightens me; it throws me within myself, into a solitude that is profound and full of horror; it constrains me, *it keeps me as it were in the air;* it cannot endure, I admit; but it is the only reasonable state." At the moment when he says this, we see clearly, from the very manner in which he speaks and the lightness of the expression, that he is not seriously frightened. A little farther on, addressing himself to reason, and apostrophizing it, he demands of it: "How long shall I be in this state of doubt, which is *a kind of torment*, and which is, nevertheless, the only use I can make of reason?" This doubt, which is *a kind of torment* to Fenelon, is never admitted as a gratuitous supposition by Pascal, and in reality it appears to him the cruelest torture, that which is utterly abhorrent and revolting to nature itself. Fenelon, in placing himself in this state of doubt after the manner of Descartes, assures himself first of his own existence and of the certainty of certain primary ideas. He continues in this way of broad, agreeable, and easy deduction, mingled here and there with little bursts of affection, but without any storms of soul.

One thinks he perceives, in reading him, a light, angelic nature, which has but to let itself go, to remount of itself to its celestial principle. The whole is crowned with a prayer addressed to the infinite and good God, to whom he abandons himself with confidence, if sometimes his words have betrayed him: "Pardon these errors, O Goodness, who art not less infinite than all the other perfections of my God; pardon the stammerings of a tongue which cannot abstain from praising you, and the failings of a mind which you have made only to admire your perfection."

Nothing less resembles Pascal than this smooth and easy way. We hear nowhere the cry of distress, and Fenelon, in adoring the cross, does not cling to it, like Pascal, as to a mast in shipwreck.

Pascal, at the very outset, begins by rejecting the proofs of God's existence which are drawn from nature: "I admire," says he, ironically, "the *boldness* with which these persons undertake to speak of God, in addressing their discourses to the ungodly. Their first chapter is devoted to proving the existence of Deity by the works of nature." Continuing to develop his thought, he maintains that these discourses, which attempt to demonstrate God's existence by the works of nature, have really no effect except upon the faithful and those who already adore him. As for the other class, the indifferent, those who are destitute of living faith and graces, "to say to these persons that they have only to see the least of the things that surround them, and they will see God revealed, and to give them, as complete proof regarding that great and important subject, the course of the moon or the planets, and to pretend that one has finished his proof with such a discourse, is to give them occasion to believe that the proofs of our religion are very weak; and I see, by reason and by experience, that nothing is fitter to inspire them with contempt for it."

One may clearly judge by this passage how far Pascal neglected and even rejected with disdain half-proofs; and moreover he showed himself here more exacting than the Scripture itself, which says in a celebrated psalm: *Caeli enarrant gloriam Dei:*

"The heavens declare the glory of God, and the firmament sheweth his handy-work," etc.

It is curious to remark that the slightly contemptuous phrase of Pascal: "*I admire the boldness with which,*" etc., was originally printed in the first edition of his *Thoughts*, and the National Library has possessed for a short time a unique copy, dated 1669, in which one reads verbatim this phrase (page 150). But soon the friends, or the examiners and approvers of the book, were alarmed to see this exclusive way of proceeding, which was found here in contradiction to the Sacred Books; they took a proof before the work was published; they softened the phrase, and presented Pascal's idea with an air of precaution which the vigorous writer never assumes, even with regard to his friends and his auxiliaries. The single remark upon which I wish to insist here, is the open opposition of Pascal to that which will soon be the method of Fenelon. Fenelon, serene, confident, and tormented by no doubts, sees the admirable order of a starry night, and says with the Magi or the Prophet, with the Chaldean shepherd: "How powerful and wise must he be who makes worlds as innumerable as the grains of sand that cover the sea-shore, and who leads all these wandering worlds without difficulty, during so many ages, as a shepherd leads a flock!" Pascal considers the same sparkling night, and he perceives beyond it a void which his geometrical genius cannot fill; he cries: "The eternal silence of these infinite spaces frightens me." Like a sublime and wounded eagle, he flies beyond the visible sun, and, athwart its pale rays, he goes to seek, without attaining it, a new and eternal aurora. His plaint and his fright come from finding only silence and night.

With Bossuet, the contrast of method would not be less striking. Though in his Treatise on *The Knowledge of God*, the great prelate would not address himself to the young Dauphin, his pupil, and though he would speak to any reader whatever, he could not do otherwise. Bossuet takes his pen, and sets forth, with a lofty tranquillity, the points of doctrine, the double nature of man; the noble origin, the excellence and the immortality of the spiritual principle that is in him, and his direct connection with God. Bossuet teaches like the greatest of bishops; he is seated in his pulpit, he is reclining there. It is not a restless nor a sorrowful person who seeks, it is a master who indicates and establishes, the way. He demonstrates and develops the entire order of his discourse and of his conception without struggle and without effort: he experiences no pains in proving his point. He only in some way explores and promulgates the things of the mind like a sure man who has not fought for a long time the internal fights; it is the man of all authorities and of all stabilities who speaks, and who takes pleasure in viewing order everywhere or in immediately reëstablishing it by his word. Pascal insists upon the discord and upon the disorder inherent, according to him, in all nature. There, where the other extends and displays the august method (*auguste démarche*) of his teaching, he shows his wounds and his blood, and so far as he is more extravagant, he resembles us more nearly, he touches us more.

It is not that Pascal puts himself completely on a level with him whom he reclaims and directs. Without being a bishop or a priest, he is himself sure of what he says, he knows his end in advance, and lets his certainty, his disdains, his impatience, be plainly seen; he scolds, he rallies, he abuses the man who resists and who does not hear; but suddenly charity or frankness of nature gains the day; his despotic airs have ceased; he speaks in his own name and in the name of all; and he associates himself with the soul in pain, which is henceforth only the lively image of himself and of us also.

Bossuet does not spurn the glimmerings or the helps of the ancient philosophy, he does not insult it; according to him, all that which leads to the idea of the intellectual and spiritual life, all that aids in the exercise and development of the elevated part of ourselves, by which we are conformed to the First Being,— all this is good, and every time that an *illustrious truth* appears to us, we have a foretaste of that superior existence to which the rational creature is originally destined. In his magnificent language, Bossuet loves to associate, to unite the greatest names, and to weave in some sort the golden chain by which the human understanding reaches to the highest summit. This passage of sovereign beauty must be cited:

"He who sees Pythagoras, when ravished at having found the squares of the sides of an uncertain triangle, sacrifice a hecatomb in thanksgiving; he who sees Archimedes, intent on some new discovery, forgetting to eat and drink; he who sees Plato celebrate the felicity of those who contemplate the beautiful and the good, first in the arts, secondly in nature, and finally in their source and their beginning which is God; he who sees Aristotle praise those happy moments when the soul is possessed only of the knowledge of virtue, and judge such a life only to be worthy of being eternal, and of being the life of God; but (above all), he who sees the saints so ravished with that divine exercise of knowing, loving, and praising God, that they never abandon it, and that they extinguish all sensual desires in order to continue it during all the days of their lives; he who sees, I say, all these things, recognizes in intellectual operations the principle and practice of a life eternally happy."

That which leads Bossuet to God is rather the principle of human greatness than the sentiment of misery. He has a contemplation which rises gradually from truth to truth, and which has not to stoop incessantly from abyss to abyss. He has just painted to us that spiritual enjoyment of the highest kind, which begins with Pythagoras and Archimedes, passes on to Aristotle, and reaches and ascends even to the Saints; he seems himself, as seen in this last example, only to have ascended a degree nearer to the altar.

Pascal does not proceed thus; he strives to mark more clearly, and in an impassible manner, the difference of the spheres. He despises whatever there might have been in the ancient philosophy that was gradual and introductory to Christianity. The learned and moderate Daguesseau, in a plan of a work which he proposed to write after the style of the *Thoughts*, could say: " If one should undertake to work up the *Thoughts* of Pascal, it would be necessary to rectify in many places the imperfect ideas which he gives in it of the Pagan philosophy; the true religion has no need to suppose, in its adversaries or in its rivals, faults which are not theirs." Confronted with Bossuet, Pascal may exhibit, at the first glance, some austerities and a narrowness of doctrine which offend us. Not content to believe with Bossuet and Fenelon, and with all christians, in an unseen God, he loves to insist upon the mysterious character of that obscurity; he is pleased to declare expressly that God wishes to blind some and to enlighten others. He goes and dashes himself, at times, *s'aheurter* (that is his word), on rocks which it is wiser, as respects reason, and even as respects faith, to go round than to lay bare and openly announce; he will say, for example, of the prophecies cited in the Gospel: "You believe that they are reported to make you believe. No, it is to keep you from believing." He will say of miracles: "Miracles do not serve to convert, but to condemn." Like a too intrepid guide in a mountain journey, he purposely keeps close to the steeps and the precipices; one would think that he wished to defy giddiness. Pascal also, contrarily to Bossuet, is smitten with affection for little churches, for little reserved flocks of the elect, which leads to sectarianism: "I love," he says, "the worshippers unknown to the world and even to the Prophets." But along with and amid these roughnesses and these asperities of the way, what piercing words! what cries that touch us! what sensible truths for all those who have suffered, who have desired, lost, then refound the way, and who have never been willing to despair! "It is good," he cries, "to be wearied and fatigued by the useless search for the true good, that we may stretch out our arms to the Deliverer!" No one, better than he, has made men feel what faith is; perfect faith is "God perceptible to the heart, not to the reason. How far it is," says he, "from knowing God to loving him!"

This affectionate quality of Pascal, making its way through all that is bitter and severe in his doctrine and conduct, has so much the more charm and authority. The touching manner in which that great mind, suffering and praying, speaks to us of that which is most peculiar in religion, of Jesus-Christ in person, is fitted to win all hearts, to inspire them with I know not what that is profound, and to impress them forever with a tender respect. One may remain an unbeliever after having read Pascal, but he is no longer permitted to rail or to blaspheme; and, in that sense, it remains true that he has vanquished, on one side, the mind of the eighteenth century and Voltaire.

In a passage previously unpublished, and of which the publication is due to M. Faugère, Pascal meditates upon the agony of Jesus-Christ, upon the torments which that perfectly heroic soul, so firm when it wishes to be so, inflicted upon himself in the name and for the sake of all men: and here, in some verses of meditation and prayer by turns, Pascal penetrates into the mystery of that suffering with a passionateness, a tenderness, a piety, to which no human soul can remain insensible. He supposes all at once a dialogue in which the dying Deity begins to speak, and addresses his disciple, saying to him:

"Console thyself; thou wouldst not seek me, if thou hadst not found me. Thou wouldst not seek me, if thou didst not possess me; then do not disquiet thyself."

"I thought of thee in my agony; I shed such drops of blood for thee."

"Wouldst thou that it should always cost me the blood of my humanity, without thy shedding some tears? . . ."

This passage should be read in full and in its place.

J. J. Rousseau could not have heard it, I dare believe, without bursting into sobs, and perhaps falling upon his knees. It is by such burning, passionate passages, in which human charity breathes through the divine love, that Pascal has a stronger hold upon us to-day than any other apologist of his time. There is in that grief, in that passion, in that ardor, more than enough to atone for his harshnesses and extravagances of doctrine. Pascal is at once more violent than Bossuet and more sympathetic with us; he is more our contemporary in sentiment. The same day in which one has read *Childe Harold* or *Hamlet*, *René* or *Werther*, one will read Pascal, and he will enable us to cope with them, or rather he will make us perceive and comprehend a moral ideal and a beauty of heart which they all lack, and which, once caught sight of, is a despair also. It is already an honor for man to have such despairs regarding objects so high.

Some curious and some learned persons will continue to study all of Pascal thoroughly; but the resultant which appears to-day good and useful for minds simply serious and for honest hearts,— the advice which I come to give them after having read this last edition of the *Thoughts*, — is, not to pretend to penetrate too far into Pascal the individual and the Jansenist, to content one's self with divining him, and understanding him on that side, in some essential points, but to confine one's self with him to the spectacle of the moral struggle, of the tempest, and of the passion which he feels for goodness and for a worthy happiness. Dealing with him in this way, we shall sufficiently resist his somewhat narrow, opinionated and absolute logic; we shall lay ourselves open meanwhile to that flame, to that soaring disposition, to all that is tender and generous in him; we shall associate ourselves without difficulty with that ideal of moral perfection which he personifies so ardently in Jesus-Christ, and we shall feel that we have been elevated in the hours which we shall have passed face to face with that athlete, that martyr, and that hero of the invisible moral world: Pascal is for us all that.

The world moves on; it develops itself more and more in the ways which seem most opposed to those of Pascal, in the sense of positive interests, of physical nature investigated and subjected, and of human triumphs through industry. It is good that there should be somewhere a counterpoise; that, in some solitary closets, without pretending to protest against the movement of the age, some firm spirits, generous and not bitter, should say to themselves what is wanting to it, and in what direction it might complete and crown itself. Such reservoirs of lofty thoughts are necessary that the habit may not be absolutely lost, and that the practical may not use up the whole man. Human society, and, to take a plainer example, French society, appears to me sometimes like an indefatigable traveller who makes his journey and pursues his way in more than one costume, very often changing his name and dress. Since '89 we have been up and marching on: where are we going? who will tell us? but we are marching on incessantly. That Revolution, at the moment when one believed it arrested under one form, rose and pushed on under another: sometimes under the military uniform, sometimes under the black coat of the deputy; yesterday as a proletary, day before yesterday as a citizen. To-day it is, before all, industrial; and it is the engineer who leads and who triumphs. Let us not complain at all of this, but let us recollect the other side of ourselves, that which has so long formed the dearest honor of humanity. Let us go and see London, let us go visit and admire the Crystal Palace and its marvels, let us enrich it and make it proud with our products: yes, but on the way, on the return, let some persons repeat to themselves with Pascal these words which should be engraved on the frontispiece:

"All bodies, the firmament, the stars, the earth and its kingdoms, are not worth so much as the smallest of minds; for it knows all them and itself; and the bodies, nothing. All bodies together, and all minds together, and all their productions, are not worth the least movement of charity; that belongs to an order infinitely higher.

"From all bodies together one could not succeed in producing one little thought; that is impossible, and of another order. From all bodies and minds one could not obtain one movement of true charity; that is impossible, and of another, supernatural order."

It is thus that Pascal expresses himself in these brief and concise *Thoughts*, written for himself, a little abrupt, and which have sprung, as in a jet, from the very spring.

The present editor, M. Havet, has treated me with so much indulgence in a page of his Introduction, that, in concluding, I am somewhat embarrassed in coming to praise in my turn; he appears to me, however, to have proposed to himself and to have attained the principal end which I have indicated, and his learned edition is a service rendered to all. The philosophic and independent character which he has been anxious to give it cannot alter its value, and it rather adds to it in my eyes. Pascal's book, in the state in which it has come to us, and with the license or the looseness of the recent restitutions, cannot be for any one an exact and complete apologetic work: it can be only an ennobling kind of reading, which brings back the soul into the moral and religious sphere whence too many vulgar interests cause it to fall away. M. Havet has been constantly careful to maintain this lofty impression, and to disembarrass it from the sectarian questions in which Pascal's personal doctrines might involve it. His conclusion sums up well the very spirit of all his labor: "In general," says M. Havet, "we men of to-day, in our manner of understanding life, are wiser than Pascal; but if we would be able to boast of it, we should be, at the same time, like him, pure, disinterested, charitable."

March 29, 1852.

ROUSSEAU.

AFTER having spoken of the pure, airy, unemphatic, entirely fluid and free language which the closing seventeenth century had left to some extent as a legacy to the eighteenth, I would like to-day to speak of that language of the eighteenth century, as exemplified in the writer who did the most to improve it, who made it undergo, at least, the greatest revolution since Pascal, a revolution from which we of the nineteenth century begin to reckon. Before Rousseau and since Pascal there had been many trials of ways of writing, which were quite different from those of the eighteenth century; Fontenelle had his manner, if there had ever been a manner; Montesquieu had his, stronger, firmer, more striking, but a manner still. Voltaire alone had none, and his vivid, clear, rapid language ran, so to speak, almost from the spring. "You find," says he, somewhere, "that I express myself very clearly; I am like the little rivulets; they are transparent because they are not very deep." He said that laughing; one tells himself thus many half truths. The age, however, demanded more; it wished to be moved, warmed, rejuvenated by the expression of ideas and sentiments which it had not well defined, but which it was still seeking for. The prose of Buffon, in the first volumes of the *Natural History*, offered it a kind of image of what it desired, an image more majestic than lively, a little beyond its reach, and too much fettered to scientific themes. Rousseau appeared: the day when he became fully known to himself, he revealed at the same time to his age the writer who was best fitted to express with novelty, with vigor, with logic mingled with flame, the confused ideas which were fermenting and which desired expression. In laying hold of the language which it was necessary for him to conquer and command, he gave it a bent which it was henceforth to keep; but he gave back to it more than he took away, and, in many respects, he reinvigorated and regenerated it. Since Rousseau, it is in the mould of language established and created by him that our greatest writers have cast their own innovations, and tried to excel. The pure form of the seventeenth century, such as we love to recall it, has been little more than a graceful antiquity and a regret to people of taste.

Although the *Confessions* did not appear till after the death of Rousseau, and when his influence was fully dominant, it is in that work that it is most convenient for us to study him to-day with all the merits, the fascinations, and the faults of his talent. We shall try to do so, confining ourselves as far as possible to a consideration of the writer, but without interdicting ourselves from remarks upon the ideas and character of the man. The present moment is not very favorable to Rousseau, who is accused of having been the author and promoter of many of the ills from which we suffer. "There is no writer," it has been judiciously said, "better fitted to make the poor man proud." In spite of all, in considering him here, we shall try not to harbor too much of that almost personal feeling which leads some good spirits to have a grudge against him, in the painful trials we are passing through. Men who have such a range of influence and such a future must not be judged by the feelings and reactions of a day.

The idea of writing the *Confessions* seems so natural to Rousseau and so suitable to his disposition, as well as to his genius, that one would not believe that it had been necessary to suggest it to him. It came to him, however, in the first place, from his publisher, Rey, of Amsterdam, and also from Duclos. After the *Nouvelle Héloïse*, after the *Émile*, Rousseau, fifty-two years old, began to write his *Confessions* in 1764, after his departure from Montmorency, during his stay at Motiers in Switzerland. In the last number of the Swiss Review (October, 1850), there has just been published a beginning of the *Confessions*, taken from a manuscript deposited in the Library of Neuchâtel,—a beginning which is Rousseau's first rough draught, and which he afterward suppressed. In this first beginning, much less emphatic and less pompous than we read at the opening of the *Confessions*, we hear no peal of the *trumpet of the last Judgment*, nor does it finish with the famous apostrophe to the *Eternal Being*. Rousseau sets forth there more at length, but philosophically, his plan of portraying himself, of giving his confessions with rigorous truthfulness; he shows clearly wherein the originality and singularity of his design consist:

"No one can write a man's life but himself. The character of his inner being, his real life, is known only to himself; but in writing it, he disguises it; under the name of his life, he makes an apology; he shows himself as he wishes to be seen, but not at all as he is. The sincerest persons are truthful at most in what they say, but they lie by their *réticences*, and that of which they say nothing so changes that which they pretend to confess, that in uttering only a part of the truth they say nothing. I put Montaigne at the head of these *falsely-sincere* persons who wish to deceive in telling the truth. He shows himself with his faults, but he gives himself none but amiable ones; *there is no man who has not odious ones.* Montaigne paints his likeness, but it is a profile. Who knows whether some scar on the cheek, or an eye put out, on the side which he conceals from us, would not have totally changed the physiognomy?"

He wishes, then, to do what no one has planned or dared before him. As to style, it seems to him that he must invent one as novel as his plan, and commensurate with the diversity and disparity of the things which he he proposes to describe:

"If I wish to produce a work written with care, like the others, I shall not paint, I shall rouge myself. It is with my portrait that I am here concerned, and not with a book. I am going to work, so to speak, in the *dark room;* there is no other art necessary than to follow exactly the traits which I see marked. I form my resolution then about the style as about the things. I shall not try at all to render it uniform; I shall write always that which comes to me, I shall change it, without scruple, according to my humor; I shall speak of everything as I feel it, as I see it, without care, without constraint, without being embarrassed by the medley. In yielding myself at once to the memory of the impression received and to the present sentiment, I shall doubly paint the state of my soul, namely, at the moment when the event happened to me and at the moment when I describe it; my style, unequal and natural, sometimes rapid and sometimes diffuse, sometimes wise and sometimes foolish, sometimes grave and sometimes gay, will itself make a part of my history. Finally, whatever may be the way in which this book may be written, it will be always, by its object, a book precious for philosophers; it is, I repeat, an illustrative piece for the study of the human heart, *and it is the only one that exists.*"

Rousseau's error was not in believing that in thus confessing himself aloud before everybody, and with a sentiment so different from christian humility, he did a singular thing or even one of the most curious things as regards the study of the human heart; his error was in believing that he did a *useful* thing. He did not see that he did like the doctor who should set himself to describe, in an intelligible, seductive manner, for the use of worldly people and the ignorant, some infirmity, some well-characterized mental malady: that doctor would be partially guilty of, and responsible for, all the maniacs and fools whom, through imitation and contagion, his book should make.

The first pages of the *Confessions* are too strongly accented and very painful. I find in them, at the very beginning, "a void occasioned (*occasionné*) by a fault of memory"; Rousseau speaks there of the authors of his days (*auteurs de ses jours*); he brings at birth the germ of an inconvenience (*incommodité*) which the years have increased (*renforcée*), he says, and "which now sometimes gives him some *respites* only to," etc. etc. (*des relâches que pour*, etc. etc.) All this is disagreeable, and savors little of that flower of expression which we enjoyed the other day under the name of urbanity. And yet, close by these roughnesses of expression, and these crudities of the soil, we meet, strange to say, with a novel, familiar, and impressive simplicity!

"I felt before thinking; it is the common lot of humanity. I experienced it more than others. I know not what I did till I was five or six years old. I know not how I learned to read; I recollect only my first readings, and their effect upon me. My mother had left some romances; my father and I set to reading them after supper. The object, at first, was only to instruct me in reading, by means of amusing books, but soon the interest became so lively, that we read by turns without relaxation, and spent the night in that occupation. We could never leave off till at the end of the volume. Sometimes my father, hearing the swallows in the morning, said, quite ashamed: '*Let us go to bed; I am more of a child than you.*'"

Note well that swallow; it is the first, and it announces the new spring-time of the language; one does not see it begin to appear till in Rousseau. It is from him that the sentiment of nature is reckoned among us, in the eighteenth century. It is from him also that is dated, in our literature, the sentiment of domestic life; of that homely, poor, quiet, hidden life, in which are accumulated so many treasures of virtue and affection. Amid certain details, in bad taste, in which he speaks of robbery and of eatables (*mangeaille*), how one pardons him on account of that old song of childhood, of which he knows only the air and some words stitched together, but which he always wished to recover, and which he never recalls, old as he is, without a soothing charm!

"It is a caprice which I wholly fail to comprehend, but it is utterly impossible for me to sing it to the end, without being checked by my tears. I have a hundred times planned to write to Paris, to have the rest of the words sought for, if any one there knows them still: but I am almost sure that the pleasure which I take in recalling that air would vanish in part, if I had proof that other persons than my poor aunt Susy have sung it."

This is the novelty in the author of the *Confessions*, this is what ravishes us by opening to us an unexpected source of deep and domestic sensibility. We read together the other day Madame de Caylus and her *Recollections*; but of what memories of childhood does she speak to us? whom did she love? for what did she weep in quitting the home in which she was born, in which she was reared? Has she the least thought in the world of telling us of it? These aristocratic and refined races, gifted with so exquisite a tact and so lively a sensibility to raillery, either do not

love these simple things, or dare not let it be seen that
they do. Their wit we know well enough, and we enjoy
it; but where is their heart? One must be plebeian, and
provincial, and a new man like Rousseau, to show himself
so subject to affections of the heart and so sensitive to
natural influences.

Again, when we remark with some regret that Rousseau forced, racked, and, so to speak, ploughed the language, we add immediately that he at the same time sowed and fertilized it.

A man of a proud, aristocratic family, but a pupil of
Rousseau, and who had hardly more than he the sentiment and fear of the ridiculous, M. de Chateaubriand, has
repeated in *René* and in his *Memoirs* that more or less
direct manner of avowals and confessions, and he has
drawn from it some magical and surprising effects. Let
us note, however, the differences. Rousseau has not the
original elevation; he is not entirely,— far from it!—
what one calls a *well-born* child; he has an inclination to
vice, and to low vices; he has secret and shameful lusts
which do not indicate the gentleman; he has that extreme
shyness which so suddenly turns into the effrontery of the
rogue and the *vagabond*, as he calls himself; in a word, he
has not that safeguard of honor, which M. de Chateaubriand had from childhood, standing like a watchful sentinel by the side of his faults. But Rousseau, with all
these disadvantages which we do not fear, after him, to
mention by their name, is a better man than Chateaubriand, inasmuch as he is more human, more a man, more
tender. He has not, for example, that incredible hardness
of heart (a hardness really quite feudal), and that thoughtlessness in speaking of his father and his mother. When

he speaks of the wrongs done him by his father, who, an honest man, but a man of pleasure, thoughtless, and remarried, abandoned him and left him to his fate, with what delicacy does he mention that painful matter! With what deep feeling is all that depicted! It is not of chivalric delicacy that I speak; it is of the real, the heart-felt, that which is moral and human.

It is incredible that this inner moral sentiment with which he was endowed, and which kept him so much in sympathy with other men, should not have apprised Rousseau how far he derogated from it in many a passage of his life and in many a phrase which he affects. His style, like his life, contracted some of the vices of his early education and of the bad company which he kept at first. After a childhood virtuously passed in the circle of the domestic hearth, he became an apprentice, and as such underwent hardships which spoiled his tone and deprived him of delicacy. The words *rogue, vagabond, ragamuffin, knave*, have nothing that gives him any embarrassment, and it even seems as if they returned with a certain complacency to his pen. His language preserves always something of the bad tone of his early years. I distinguish in his language two kinds of debasement: the objection to one of them is merely that it is provincial, and bespeaks a Frenchman born out of France. Rousseau will write without scowling: "*Comme que je fasse, comme que ce fût,*" etc., instead of saying "*De quelque manière que je fasse, de quelque manière que ce fût,*" etc.; he articulates strongly and roughly: he has, at times, a little *goître* in his voice. But that is a fault which one pardons him, so far has he succeeded in triumphing over it in some happy pages; so far, by force of labor and emotion, has he softened his organ of speech, and learned how to give to that cultivated and laborious style mellowness and the appearance of a first gush. The other kind of debasement and corruption which one may note in him is graver, inasmuch as it touches the moral sense: he does not seem to suspect that there are certain things the mention of which is forbidden, that there are certain ignoble, disgusting, cynical expressions, which a virtuous man never uses, and which he ignores. Rousseau, at some time, was a lackey; we perceive it, in more than one place, in his style. He hates neither the word nor the thing. "If Fenelon were living, you would be a Catholic," said Bernardin de Saint-Pierre to him one day, on seeing him affected by some ceremony of the Catholic worship. "Oh! if Fenelon were living," cried Rousseau, all in tears, "I should seek to be his lackey, that I might deserve to be his *valet de chambre*." We see the lack of taste even in the emotion. Rousseau is not only a workman in respect to language, an apprentice before becoming a master, who lets us see in passages marks of the solderings: he is morally a man who, when young, had the most motley experiences, and whom ugly and villainous things do not make heart-sick when he names them. I shall say no more of this essential vice, this stain which it is so painful to have to notice and to censure, in so great a writer and so great a painter, in such a man.

Slow to think, prompt to feel, with ardent and suppressed desires, with suffering and constraint each day, Rousseau reaches the age of sixteen, and he paints himself to us in these terms:

"I reached thus my sixteenth year, restless, dissatisfied with everything and with myself, without a liking for my condition, without the pleasures of my age, devoured by desires of whose object I was ignorant, shedding tears without occasion, sighing without knowing why; finally, cherishing tenderly my chimeras from inability to see anything about me which was of equal value. On Sundays, my playmates came for me, after the church service, to go and play with them. I would willingly have escaped them, if I could; but, once engaged in their sports, I was more ardent, and I went farther than the rest,—*being difficult to stir and to restrain.*"

Always in extremes! We here recognize the first form of the thoughts, and almost the phrases of René, those words which are already a music and which sing still in our ears:

"My disposition was impetuous, my character unequal. By turns noisy and joyous, silent and sad, I gathered my young companions about me; then, suddenly abandoning them, I went and seated myself apart, to contemplate the fugitive cloud, or to hear the rain fall on the foliage."

Again:

"When young, I cultivated the Muses; there is nothing more poetic than a heart of sixteen years, in the freshness of its passions. The morning of life is like the morning of the day, full of purity, of hopes, and of harmonies."

René, indeed, is no other than this young man of sixteen transposed, exiled amid different natural scenery, and in the midst of a different social condition; no longer an engraver's apprentice, son of a citizen of Geneva, of a citizen of the *lower class*, but a cavalier, a noble traveller at large, smitten with the Muses; all, at the first view, wears a more seductive, a more poetic color; the unexpected character of the landscape and of the frame-work heightens the character, and denotes a new manner; but the first evident type is where we have indicated it, and it is Rousseau who, in looking into himself, has found it.

René is a more pleasing model for us, because in it all

the vile aspects of humanity are concealed from us; it has a tint of Greece, of chivalry, of Christianity, the reflections of which cross each other on its surface. Words, in that masterpiece of art, have acquired a new magic; they are words full of light and harmony. The horizon is enlarged in all directions, and the rays of Olympus play upon it. Rousseau has nothing comparable with this at the first view, but he is truer at heart, more real, more living. That workman's son, who goes to play with his comrades after the *preaching*, or to muse alone if he can, that little youth with the well-shaped form, with the keen eye, with the fine physiognomy, and who arraigns all things more than one would like,— he has more reality than the other, and more life; he is benevolent, tender, and compassionate. In the two natures, that of René and that of Rousseau, there is a spot that is diseased; they have too much ardor mingled with a tendency to inaction and idleness,— a predominance of imagination and of sensibility, which turn back and prey upon themselves; but, of the two, Rousseau is the more truly sensitive, as he is the most original and the most sincere in his chimerical flights, in his regrets, and in his pictures of a possible but lost ideal felicity. When, at the end of the first book of the *Confessions*, quitting his country, he pictures to himself in a simple and touching manner the happiness which he could have enjoyed there in obscurity; when he tells us: "I should have passed in the bosom of my religion, of my country, of my family, and of my friends, a sweet and peaceful life, such as my disposition required, in regular labor suited to my taste and in a society after my heart; I should have been a good christian, a good citizen, a good father of a family, a good friend, a good workman, a good man in every respect; I should have loved my situation, *I should have honored it, perhaps*, and, after having passed an obscure and simple, but even and pleasant life, I should have died peacefully in the bosom of my family; soon forgotten no doubt, I should have been regretted, at least, as long as I should have been remembered;" when he speaks to us thus, he does indeed convince us of the sincerity of his wish and of his regret, so profound and lively is the sentiment that breathes through all his words, of the quiet, unvarying, and modest charm of a private life!

Let none of us who, in this age, have been more or less afflicted with the malady of reverie, do like those ennobled persons who disown their ancestry, and let us learn that before being the very unworthy children of the noble *René*, we are more certainly the grandchildren of citizen Rousseau.

The first book of the *Confessions* is not the most remarkable, but we find Rousseau in it already, quite complete, with his pride, his vices in their germ, his odd and grotesque humors, his meannesses and his obscenities (you see that I note everything); with his pride also, and that firm and independent spirit which exalts it; with his happy and healthy childhood, his suffering and martyred youth, and the apostrophes to society and avenging reprisals (one foresees them), with which it will inspire him at a later day; with his tender sentiment of domestic happiness and family life, which he had so little opportunity of enjoying, and also with the first breaths of spring-time, a signal of the natural revival which will appear in the literature of the nineteenth century. We run a risk to-day of being too little impressed by these first picturesque pages of Rousseau; we are so spoiled by colors, that we forget how fresh and new those first landscapes then were, and what an event it was in the midst of that very witty, very refined, but arid society, which was as devoid of imagination as of true sensibility, and had in its own veins none of the sap which circulates, and, at each season, comes back again. French readers, accustomed to the factitious life of a *salon* atmosphere,— the *urbane* readers, as he calls them,— were astonished and quite enraptured to feel blowing from the region of the Alps these fresh and healthy mountain breezes which came to revive a literature that was alike elegant and dried up.

It was time for this revival, and hence it is that Rousseau was not a corrupter of language, but, on the whole, a regenerator.

Before him La Fontaine alone, among us, had had as keen a relish for nature, and had known that charm of reverie in the fields; but the example had little effect; the people let the good man come and go with his fables, and kept in their *salons*. Rousseau was the first person who compelled all these fashionable people to go out of them, and to quit the great alley of the park for the true walk in the fields.

The beginning of the second book of the *Confessions* is delightful and full of freshness: Madame de Warens appears to us for the first time. In painting her, Rousseau's style becomes gentle and gracefully mellow, and at the same time we discover a quality, an essential vein which is innate and pervades his whole manner,— I mean sensuality. "Rousseau had a voluptuous mind," says a good critic; women play in his writings a great part;

absent or present, they and their charms occupy his mind, inspire him and affect him, and something relating to them is mingled with all that he has written. "How," says he of Madame de Warens, "in approaching for the first time a lovely, polished, *dazzling* woman, a woman of a superior condition to mine, whose like I had never met, . . . how did I find myself at once as free, as much at my ease, as if I had been perfectly sure of pleasing her?" This facility, this ease, which he will not usually feel when he finds himself in the presence of women, will always be found in his style when he paints them. The most adorable pages of the *Confessions* are those concerning that first meeting with Madame de Warens, those, also, where he describes the welcome of Madame Basile, the pretty shopkeeper of Turin: "She was brilliant and elegantly attired, and, in spite of her gracious air, that splendor had overpowered me. But her welcome, which was full of kindness, her compassionate tone, her soft and endearing manners, soon put me at my ease; I saw that I had succeeded, and that made me more successful." Have you never observed that brilliancy and splendor of complexion, like a ray of the Italian sun? He then relates that vivid and mute scene, which nobody has forgotten, that scene of gestures, seasonably checked, all full of blushes and young desires. Join to this the walk in the environs of Annecy with Mademoiselles Galley and de Graffenried, every detail of which is enchanting. Such pages were, in French literature, the discovery of a new world, a world of sunshine and of freshness, which men had near them without having perceived it; they presented a mixture of sensibility and of nature, one in which no sensuality appeared, except so far as it was permissible and necessary to deliver us at last from the false metaphysics of the heart and from conventional spiritualism. The sensuality of the brush, in that degree, cannot displease; it is temperate also, and is not masked, which renders it more innocent than that of which many painters have since made use.

As a painter, Rousseau everywhere manifests the sentiment of *reality*. He shows it every time that he speaks to us of beauty, which, even when it is imaginary, like his Julia, assumes a body and perfectly visible forms, and is by no means an airy and intangible Iris. That he has this sense of reality appears from his wishing that every scene which he recollects or invents, that every character he introduces, should be enclosed and move in a well determined place, of which the smallest details may be traced and retained. One of the things which he found fault with in the great novelist Richardson, was, that he did not connect the recollection of his characters with a locality the pictures of which one would have loved to identify. See also how he has contrived to naturalize his Julia and his Saint-Preux in the Pays-de-Vaud, on the border of that lake about which his heart never ceased to wander. His sound, firm mind continually lends its graver to the imagination, that nothing essential to the sketch may be omitted. Finally this sense of *reality* is noticeable, again, in the care with which, amid all his circumstances and his adventures, happy or unhappy, and even the most romantic, he never forgets to speak of repasts and the details of a good, frugal cheer, fitted to give joy alike to heart and mind.

This trait is also a material one; it is related to that citizen-like and popular character which I have noted in

Rousseau. He had been hungry in his lifetime; he notes in his *Confessions*, with a feeling of thankfulness to Providence, the last time that it was his lot to experience literal want and hunger. Nor will he ever forget to introduce these incidents of real life and of the common humanity, these *heart-matters*, even into the ideal picture of his happiness, which he will give at a later day. It is by all these true qualities combined in his eloquence, that he seizes and holds us.

Nature, sincerely enjoyed and loved for herself, is the source of Rousseau's inspiration, whenever that inspiration is healthy, and not of a sickly kind. When he sees Madame de Warens again, on his return from Turin, he stays some time at her house, and from the room that is given him he sees gardens and discovers the country: "It was the first time," he says, "since I was at Bossey (a place where he was sent to be boarded in his childhood), that I had *something green before my windows*." Till then, to have or not to have *something green* under one's eyes, had been a matter of great indifference to French literature; it belonged to Rousseau to make it perceive it. It is from this point of view that one might characterize him by a word: he was the first who put *something green* into our literature. Living thus, at the age of nineteen, near a woman whom he loved, but to whom he dared not declare his passion, Rousseau abandoned himself to a sadness which yet had nothing gloomy in it, and which was tempered by a flattering hope. Having gone to walk out of town, on a great *fête* day, whilst the people were at vespers,—

"The sound of the bells, which has always strangely affected me, the song of the birds, the beauty of the day, the softness of the landscape, the *scattered and rural* houses, in which I fixed in imagination our common abode, all this affected me with such a vivid, tender, sad, and touching impression, that I saw myself, as it were, in ecstasy transported to that happy time and to that happy sojourn, in which my heart, possessing all the felicity that could please it, enjoyed it with inexpressible rapture, without even dreaming of the pleasure of the senses."

This is what the child of Geneva felt at Annecy in the year 1731, whilst at Paris people were reading the *Temple of Gnidus*. On that day he discovered the reverie, that new charm which had been left as a singularity to La Fontaine, and which he was going, himself, finally to introduce into a literature that was till then polite or positive. *Reverie*,—such is his novelty, his discovery, his own America. The dream of that day was realized by him some years afterward, in his sojourn at the Charmettes, in that walk by day from Saint-Louis, which he has described as nothing like it had ever before been depicted:

"Everything seemed to conspire to promote the happiness of that day. It had rained just before; there was no dust, and *the streams were running well;* a gentle fresh breeze stirred the leaves, the air was pure, the horizon cloudless, serenity reigned in the sky as in our hearts. We took our dinner at a peasant's house, and shared it with his family, who blessed us heartily. These poor Savoyards are such good people!"

With this kindly feeling, and in this observant and simply truthful way, he continues to unfold a picture in which all is perfect, all is enchanting, and in which only the name of *Mamma* applied to Madame de Warens morally wounds and pains us.

That period at the Charmettes, in which this still young heart was permitted to open for the first time, is the divinest of the *Confessions*, and it will never return, even when Rousseau shall have retired to the Hermitage. The description of those years at the Hermitage, and of the passion which came to seek him there, is very fascinating also, and is more remarkable perhaps than all that precedes it; he will justly exclaim, however: *It is no longer the Charmettes there!* The misanthropy and the suspicion of which he is already the victim, will pursue him in that period of solitude. He will be thinking continually there of the Parisian world, of the society at D'Holbach's; he will enjoy his retreat in spite of them, but that thought will poison his purest enjoyments. His disposition will sour, and will contract during these years a henceforth incurable disorder. He will have, no doubt, some delicious moments then, and afterward, even to the end; he will find again, in Saint-Peter's island, in the middle of lake Bienne, an interval of calmness and of forgetfulness which will furnish him with inspiration for some of his finest pages,— that fifth Walk of the *Reveries*, which, with the third Letter to M. de Malesherbes, cannot be separated from the divinest passages of the *Confessions*. Nevertheless, nothing will equal in lightness, freshness, and joyousness the description of life at the Charmettes. Rousseau's true happiness, of which no one, not even himself, could rob him, was the ability thus to evoke and to retrace, with the precision and vividness which characterized his recollection, such pictures of youth, even in the years that were fullest of troubles and distractions.

The pedestrian journey, with its impressions at each moment, was also one of the inventions of Rousseau, one of the novelties which he imported into literature: it has since been greatly abused. It was not just after he had enjoyed his trip, but much later, that he thought of relating his experiences. It was only then, he assures us, when he traveled on foot, at a beautiful season, in a beautiful country, without being hurried, having for the goal of his journey an agreeable object which he was not in too great haste to attain,— it was then that he was entirely himself, and that ideas of his which were cold and dead in the study, came to life and took flight:

"Walking has something in it that animates and brightens my ideas; I am scarcely able to think when I keep one position; my body must be in full swing before my mind can be so. The sight of the country, the succession of agreeable objects, the open air, the good health I gain by walking, the freedom of the inn, the removal from everything that makes me feel my dependence, from everything that reminds me of my situation, all this sets my soul free, gives me a greater audacity of thought, casts me, in some way, into the immensity of beings where I may combine, choose, and appropriate them at will, without hindrance and without fear. I dispose, as a master, of all nature. . . ."

Do not ask him to write, at these moments, the sublime, foolish, pleasant thoughts which pass through his mind: he likes much better to taste and to relish than to speak of them: "Besides, did I carry with me paper and pens? If I had thought of all that, nothing would have come to me. I did not foresee that I should have ideas; they come when it pleases them, not when it pleases me." Thus, in all that he has since related, we should have, if we may believe him, only distant recollections and feeble remains of himself, as he was at those moments. And yet what could be at once more true, more precise, and more delicious? Let us recall that night which he passes in the starlight, on the bank of the Rhone or the Saone, in a hollow way near Lyons:

"I slept voluptuously on the sill of a kind of niche or false door opened in a terrace wall. The canopy of my bed was formed of the tops of the trees; a nightingale was just above me, I fell asleep under his song, my sleep was sweet, my waking was more so. It was broad day; my eyes, as they opened, saw the water, the verdure, a wonderful landscape. I rose and roused myself; I felt hungry; I proceeded gaily toward the city, resolved to lay out for a good breakfast two six-blank pieces* which were yet left to me."

All the native Rousseau is there, with his reverie, his ideality, his reality; and that *six-blank piece* itself, which comes after the nightingale, is not too much to bring us back to the earth, and make us feel all the humble enjoyment which poverty conceals within itself when it is joined with poetry and with youth. I desired to extend the quotation as far as this six-blank piece, to show that when we are with Rousseau we are not merely keeping company with *René* and with *Jocelyn*.

The picturesque in Rousseau is temperate, firm, and clear, even in the softest passages; the coloring is always laid upon a well-drawn outline; that Genevese citizen shows in this that he is of pure French extraction. If he lacks at times a warmer light and the splendors of Italy and Greece; if, as about that beautiful Geneva lake, the north wind comes sometimes to chill the atmosphere, and if at times a cloud suddenly casts a grayish tint upon the sides of the mountains, there are days and hours of clear and perfect serenity. Improvements have since been made upon this style, and persons have believed that they have paled and surpassed it; they have certainly succeeded in respect to certain effects of colors and sounds. Nevertheless, the style remains still the surest and the firmest which one can offer as an example in the field of modern innovation. With him the centre of the language has

* A *blanc* is an old French copper coin. Six *blancs* made one and a half pence in English money. [TR.

not been too much displaced. His successors have gone farther; they have not merely transferred the seat of the Empire to Byzantium, they have often carried it to Antioch, and even to mid-Asia. With them the imagination in its pomp absorbs and dominates all.

The portraits in the *Confessions* are lively, piquant, and *spirituels*. Bach, the friend, Venture, the musician, Simon, the *jugemage*, are finely seized and observed; they are not so easily dashed off as in *Gil Blas*, they are rather engraved; Rousseau has here recalled his first trade.

I have been unable to do more than hurriedly to indicate the leading particulars in which the author of the *Confessions* remains a master, to salute this time the creator of the reverie,— him who has inoculated us with the sentiment of nature and with the sense of reality, the father of the literature of the heart, and of internal painting (*la peinture d'intérieur*). What a pity that misanthropic pride should be mingled with these excellences, and that cynical remarks should cast a stain upon so many charming and genuine beauties! But these follies and vices of the man cannot overcome his original merits, nor hide from us the great qualities in which he shows himself still superior to his descendants.

MADAME GEOFFRIN.

AFTER all that I have said of the women of the eighteenth century, there would be too great a *lacuna* if I did not speak of Madame Geoffrin, who was one of the most celebrated, and whose influence was greater than that of any other. Madame Geoffrin wrote only four or five letters that have been published; many true and piquant sayings of hers are quoted; but this would not be enough to keep her memory alive; that which properly characterizes her and entitles her to the recollection of posterity, is the fact that she had the completest, the best organized, and, if I may say it, the best managed, the best appointed *salon* there has been in France since *salons* came in vogue, that is to say, since the *hôtel Rambouillet*. The *salon* of Madame Geoffrin was one of the institutions of the eighteenth century.

There are persons, perhaps, who imagine that, to form a *salon*, it is sufficient to be rich, to have a good cook, a comfortable house situated in a good neighborhood, a great desire to see people, and affability in receiving them. Such a lady, however, only succeeds in crowding people together pell-mell, in filling her *salon*, not in creating it; and if she is very rich, very active, and strongly inspired with the kind of ambition that seeks to shine, and if she is at the same time well informed regarding the list of invitations that should be made, and determined at whatever cost to draw to her house the kings or queens of the season, she may attain to the glory which some Americans win in Paris every winter: they have brilliant *routs*, people attend them, hurry through them, and the next winter forget them. How far from this way of crowding people together, is the art of a legitimate establishment! This art was never better understood or practiced than in the eighteenth century, amidst the regular and quiet society of that time, and no one pushed it farther, had a greater conception of it, or employed it with more perfection and finish in all its details, than Madame Geoffrin. A Roman cardinal could not have lavished upon it more shrewdness, a greater degree of fine and quiet skill, than she expended upon it for thirty years. It is especially while studying this art, that one becomes convinced that a great social influence always has an adequate cause, and that, underlying these celebrated successes, which, after a long lapse of time, are summed up in a simple name which one repeats, there have been much labor, study and talent; in the case of Madame Geoffrin, it must be added, much good sense.

Madame Geoffrin appears only as an old person at the start, and her youth steals away from us into a distance which we shall not attempt to penetrate. Plebeian and very plebeian by birth, born in Paris in the last year of the seventeenth century, Marie-Thérèse Rodet was married on the nineteenth of July, 1713, to Pierre-François Geoffrin, an influential citizen, who was one of the lieutenant-colonels of the national guard at that time, and one of the founders of the glass manufacture. A letter of Montesquieu's, written in March, 1748, shows us Madame Geoffrin gathering at that date very good company at her house, and already the centre of that circle which was to continue and increase for twenty-five years. Whence sprang this person who was so distinguished and so clever, and who seems by no means to have been destined to such a *rôle*, either by her birth or by her worldly position? What had been her early education? The empress of Russia, Catherine, put that question one day to Madame Geoffrin, and was answered by a letter which must be joined to all that Montaigne has said upon education:

"I lost my father and my mother while I was yet in the cradle. I was brought up by an old grandmother, who had much talent and a well-formed head. She had received very little education; but her mind was so enlightened, so adroit, so active, that it never failed her; it always supplied the place of knowledge. She spoke so agreeably of things which she was unacquainted with that nobody wished that she understood them better; and when her ignorance was too evident, she extricated herself by pleasantries which disconcerted the pedants who would have humiliated her. She was so content with her lot, that she regarded knowledge as something very useless to a woman. She would say: 'I have done so well without it, that I have never felt the want of it. If my granddaughter is a fool, knowledge would make her presuming and insupportable; if she has mind and sensibility, she will do as I have done, she will supply her lack of knowledge by address and tact; and when she becomes wiser she will learn for what she is best fitted, and she will learn it very quickly.' She therefore, in my childhood, made me learn only to read; but she made me read a good deal; she taught me how to think by making me reason; she taught me how to acquire a knowledge of men, by asking me to tell what I thought of them, and by telling me also her opinion of them. She obliged me to give her an account of all my impulses and all my sentiments, and she corrected them with so much sweetness and indulgence, that I never concealed from her any of my thoughts or feelings: my inner self was as visible to her as my outer. My education was unremitting. . . ."

I have said that Madame Geoffrin was born at Paris: she never left it, except to make in 1766, at the age of sixty-seven, her famous journey to Warsaw. Beyond this, she had never quitted the suburbs; and even when she went into the country to visit a friend, she habitually returned at evening, and did not sleep away from home. She believed that there is no better atmosphere than that of Paris, and wherever she might have been, she would have preferred her Saint-Honoré street gutter, as Madame de Staël regretted that of Bac street. Madame Geoffrin adds one name more to the list of Parisian geniuses who have been gifted with affable and social qualities in so high a degree, and who are easily civilizers.

Her husband appears to have been of little account in her life, beyond securing to her the fortune which was the starting-point and the prime instrument of the consideration which she knew how to acquire. M. Geoffrin is represented to us as old, and sitting in silence at the dinners which were given at his house to literary people and savants. It is related that attempts were made to get him to read some work of history or travels, and as a first volume was always given to him without his noticing it, he was pleased to find that "the work was very interesting, but that the author repeated himself a little." It is added that when reading a volume of the *Encyclopædia*, or of Bayle, which had been printed in double columns, he would read a line of the first column and then the corresponding line of the second, which made him say that "the work appeared to him well enough, but a little abstract." These are such stories as we should expect to be told of a husband who was eclipsed by a famous wife. One day a stranger asked Madame Geoffrin what had become of that old gentleman who formerly was always present at her dinners, but was no longer seen there. ".It was my husband; he is dead."

Madame Geoffrin had a daughter, who became the marchioness of La Ferte-Imbault, an excellent woman, it is said, but who lacked the calm good sense and the perfect propriety of her mother, and of whom the latter said when showing her: "When I look at her, I seem like a hen who has hatched a duck's egg."

Madame Geoffrin, then, resembled her grandmother, and, with this exception, she appears to have been unlike any of her family. Her talent, like all talents, was entirely personal. Madame Suard represents her as easily commanding respect "by her lofty stature, by her silvery hair covered with a cap tied under the chin, by her dress, so dignified and so becoming, and her looks in which judgment was mingled with goodness." Diderot, who had just played a game of piquet with her at the house of Baron Holbach, in Grandval, where she had gone to dine (October, 1760), wrote to a friend: "Madame Geoffrin was very well. I notice always the noble and simple taste with which that woman is dressed: it was, that day, in a simple stuff, of a sober color, with large sleeves,— with the smoothest and the finest linen, and the most fastidious neatness in every respect." Madame Geoffrin was then sixty-one years old. This old lady's dress, so exquisitely modest and simple, was peculiar to her, and recalls a similar art of Madame Maintenon. But Madame Geoffrin did not have to husband and to preserve the remains of a beauty which still shone forth by gleams in the twilight; at an early day she frankly acknowledged herself to be old, and suppressed the after-season. Whilst the majority of women are busy in beating a retreat in good order, and in prolonging their yesterday's age, she voluntarily got the start of time, and installed herself without grudging in her to-morrow's age. "All other women," said a person, in speaking of her, "dress, as it were, the day before; it is only Madame Geoffrin who is always dressed, as it were, to-morrow."

Madame Geoffrin is supposed to have taken her lessons in high life at Madame Tencin's, and to have been formed in that school. People quote that saying of Madame de Tencin, who, seeing Mme. G., not long before Madame T.'s death, assiduously visiting her, said to her visitors: "Do you know what Madame Geoffrin comes here for? She comes to see what she can gather from my inventory." That inventory was worth the trouble, since it was composed at the very beginning of Fontenelle, Montesquieu, and Mairan. Madame de Tencin is much less remarkable as the author of sentimental and romantic stories, in writing which she had, perhaps, the assistance of her nephews, than for her intriguing spirit, her adroit management, and the boldness and comprehensiveness of her judgments. Though she was not a very estimable person, and some of her actions border on criminality, one found himself captivated with her look of sweetness and almost of goodness, if he approached her. Even when her own interests were by no means concerned, she would give you unerring practical advice, by which you might profit in life. She knew the end of the game in everything. More than one great politician would have done well, even in our days, to have kept in mind this maxim, which she was accustomed to repeat: "Intellectual people make a great many mistakes in conduct, because they never believe the world to be as stupid as it is." The nine letters of hers which have been published, and which were addressed to the duke of Richelieu during the campaign of 1743, show her to have been full of ambitious intrigues, striving to win power for herself and her brother the cardinal, at that brief period when the king, liberated by the death of cardinal Fleury, had no chief mistress. Never was Lewis XV judged more profoundly, and with more enlightened and justifiable sentiments of contempt than in those nine letters of Madame de Tencin. In the year 1743 this intriguing woman has some flashes of penetration which pierce the horizon. "Unless God visibly interferes," she writes, "it is physically impossible that the state should not fall to pieces." It is this clever mistress whom Madame Geoffrin consulted, and from whom she received some good counsels, particularly the one never to decline anybody's acquaintance, to reject any friendly advances; for if nine acquaintances out of ten prove to be of no value, a single one may compensate for all the rest; and then, as that woman so fertile in expedients says again: "Everything is serviceable in housekeeping, when one knows how to use the tools."

Madame Geoffrin, then, inherited, to some extent, the *salon* and method of Madame de Tencin; but, in confining her abilities to a private sphere, she enlarged them to a remarkable degree and in a way entirely honorable. Madame de Tencin moved heaven and earth to make her brother a prime minister; Madame Geoffrin laid politics aside, never intermeddled with religious matters, and, by her infinite art, by her skill in following and leading, became herself a kind of clever administrator and almost a great *minister of society*, one of those ministers who are the more influential because they are not such titularly, and are more permanent.

She had at the beginning a complete conception of that machine which is called a *salon*, and knew how to organize it completely with its smooth, imperceptible wheel-work, skillfully put together and kept agoing by continual care. She not only comprehended in her solicitude literary people, properly so called, but she looked after artists, sculptors, and painters, to bring them all into communication with each other and with the people of the world; in a word, she conceived the idea of the Encyclopædia of the age acting and conversing around her. She had every week two regular dinners, that of Monday being for artists: there one saw the Vanloos, the Vernets, the Bouchers, the La Tours, the Viens, the Lagrenés, the Soufflots, the Lemoines, distinguished amateurs and patrons of the arts, and *littérateurs* like Marmontel to keep up the conversation, and promote mutual intercourse. On Wednesday was the dinner of the men of letters: one saw there D'Alembert, Mairan, Marivaux, Marmontel, the chevalier Chastelleux, Morellet, Saint-Lambert, Helvetius, Raynal, Grimm, Thomas, D'Holbach, and Burigny, of the Academy of Inscriptions. One woman only was admitted with the mistress of the house: it was Mademoiselle de Lespinasse. Madame Geoffrin had observed that several women at a dinner distract the guests, disperse and scatter the conversation: she loved unity and to be herself the centre. At evening, Madame Geoffrin's house was still kept open, and the entertainment ended with a little supper, very simple and very elegant, given to five or six intimate friends at most, including this time some women who were the flower of the great world. Not a stranger of distinction lived in or passed through Paris without aspiring to be admitted at Madame Geoffrin's. Princes came there simply as private persons; ambassadors did not budge from the place when once they had set foot there. Europe was represented there in the persons of the Caraccioli, the Creutzes, the Galianis, the Gattis, the Humes, and the Gibbons.

It is seen already that of all the *salons* of the eighteenth century, it is Madame Geoffrin's which is the completest. It is more so than that of Madame Du Deffand, who, since the defection of D'Alembert and others in the train of Mademoiselle de Lespinasse, has lost nearly all the men-of-letters. The *salon* of Mademoiselle Lespinasse, with the exception of five or six friends who formed its base, was itself made up of people who had little mutual intimacy, who had been taken here and there, and whom that witty and intelligent woman assorted with infinite art. The *salon* of Madame Geoffrin, on the contrary, represents to us the great centre and resort of the eighteenth century. In its pure influence and in its lively regularity, it forms a counterpoise to the little dinners and licentious suppers of Mademoiselle Quinault, Mademoiselle Guimard, and the financiers, the Pelletiers, the la Popelinières. Toward the end of its existence, this *salon* sees formed, in emulation and a little in rivalry of it, the *salons* of Baron D'Holbach and of Madame Helvetius, partly composed of the flower of Madame Geoffrin's guests, and partly of some heads which Madame Geoffrin had found too lively for admission to her dinners. The age became weary, at last, of being restrained and led in leading-strings by her; it wanted to speak of everything in loud tones and to its heart's content.

The spirit which Madame Geoffrin carried into the management and the economy of that little empire which she had so liberally planned, was a natural, precise, and shrewd spirit, which descended to the smallest details, a spirit that was at once ingenious, active, and gentle. She had the carvings in her rooms planed off: it was the same with her morally, and *Nothing in relief* seemed to be her motto. "My mind," said she, "is like my legs; I love to walk on level ground, and I do not wish to climb a mountain, to have the pleasure of saying when I have reached the top: *I have climbed that mountain.*" She loved simplicity, and, when it was necessary, she could affect it. Her activity was of that kind which displays itself chiefly in good order, that kind of discreet activity which acts upon all points almost silently and insensibly. Mistress of her house, she has an eye upon everything; she presides, she scolds too, but it is a scolding which is peculiar to her; she wishes people to be silent at times; she keeps order in her *salon*. With a single word: *There, that will do*, she arrests in time the conversations which are straying upon dangerous themes and the wits that are getting heated; they fear her, and go and have their uproar elsewhere. It is a principle of hers never to talk herself except when it is necessary, and to intervene only at certain moments, without engrossing the conversation too long. She then introduces certain wise maxims, some piquant stories, some anecdotal and acted morality, commonly pointed by some striking expression or very familiar illustration. All this, she knows, comes fitly only from her own lips: she says also that "she would have nobody else preach her sermons, tell her tales, or touch her tongs."

Having early taken her position as an old woman and as the *mamma* of the people whom she receives, she has a means of government, a little artifice, which becomes at last a bad habit and a madness: it is to scold; but she knows how to do it. Not everyone is scolded by her, who wishes to be; it is the highest proof of her favor and of her superintendence. The guest she likes the best is the best scolded. Horace Walpole, before having passed, with banners flying, into the camp of Madame Du Deffand, wrote from Paris to her friend Gray:

"(January, 1766). Madame Geoffrin, of whom you have heard much, is an extraordinary woman, with more common sense than I almost ever met with. Great quickness in discovering characters, penetration in going to the bottom of them, and a pencil that never fails in a likeness,—seldom a favorable one. She exacts and preserves, spite of her birth, and their nonsensical prejudices here about nobility, great court and attention. This she acquires by a thousand little arts and offices of friendship, and by a freedom and severity which seem to be her sole end of drawing a concourse to her, for she insists on scolding those she inveigles to her. She has little taste and less knowledge, but protects artisans and authors, and courts a few people to have the credit of serving her dependents. She was bred under the famous Madame Tencin, who advised her never to refuse any man; for, said her mistress, though nine in ten should not care a farthing for you, the tenth may live to be an useful friend. She did not adopt or reject the whole plan, but fully retained the purport of the maxim. In short, she is an epitome of empire subsisting by rewards and punishments."

The office of majordomo of her *salon* was usually confided to Burigny, one of her oldest friends, and one of the best scolded of all. When there was any infraction of the rules, and an imprudent speech escaped, it was upon him that she freely laid the blame, for not maintaining good order.

People laughed at this, they joked her about it, but they submitted to this government, which was always strict and exacting, but tempered with much goodness and beneficence. This right of correction she ensured by settling from time to time upon you some good little life-annuity, without forgetting the annual present of the velvet breeches.

Fontenelle did not appoint Madame Geoffrin his testamentary executrix without good reasons. Madame Geoffrin appears to me, after a careful study of her character, to have been, in the constitution of her mind, in her habitual behavior, and in the kind of influence she exerted, a female Fontenelle, a Fontenelle more actively benevolent (we shall return to this trait presently), but a real Fontenelle in prudence, in her views and provisions concerning her own happiness, and in her way of speaking at pleasure familiarly, epigrammatically, and ironically without bitterness. She is a Fontenelle who, for the very reason that she is a woman, has more vivacity, and livelier and more affectionate impulses. But, like him, she loves, above everything else, repose, and walking upon level ground. Everything about her that is of a fiery nature disquiets her, and she believes that reason itself is wrong when it is passionate. She one day compared her mind to "a *folded scroll*, which opens and unrolls gradually." She was in no hurry to unroll the whole at once: "Perhaps at my death," she said, "the scroll will not be entirely laid open." This wise slowness is a distinctive trait of her mind and of her influence. She feared movements that are too abrupt and changes that are too sudden: "there is no need," said she, "of pulling down the old house, before we have built us a new one." She tempered, as well as she could, the already fiery age, and tried to discipline it. It was a bad sign with her, if a person who had belonged to her dinner-parties, did anything to send him to the Bastille; Marmontel saw that he had greatly lowered himself in her esteem, after his *Belisarius* affair. In a word, she continued to represent the already philosophic, but still moderate spirit of the first part of the century, so long as it did not cease to recognize certain bounds. I can easily picture to myself that constant study of Madame Geoffrin by an illustration: she had had a wig added (a marble wig, if you please,) to Falconet's bust of Diderot.

Her beneficence was great as well as ingenious, and, in her case, it was a true gift of nature: she had the *giving humor*, as she said. *To give and to forgive* was her motto. Her kindness was unfailing. She could not help making presents to everybody, to the poorest man of letters as well as to the empress of Germany, and she made them with that art and exquisite delicacy which do not permit one to refuse without a kind of rudeness. Her sensibility was perfected by the practice of kindness and by an exquisite social tact. Her benevolence, like all her other qualities, had something singular and original in it, which was seen only in her. A thousand charming, unexpected sayings of hers have been quoted, by which Sterne might have profited; I will recall but one. Some one observed to her one day, that everything at her house was perfect, except the *cream*, which was not good. "What can I do?" said she, "I cannot change my milk-woman." "Why, what has that milk-woman done, that she cannot be changed?" "I have given her two cows." "A fine reason!" all cried out. And, in truth, one day when that milk-woman was weeping in despair at having lost her cow, Madame Geoffrin had given her two cows, the additional one being to console her for having wept so much, and from that day, also, she could not comprehend that she could ever change that milk-woman. Many persons would have been just as capable of giving her a cow, or even two cows; but to keep the ungrateful or negligent milk-woman, in spite of her bad cream, is what they would not have done. Madame Geoffrin did it for herself, that she might not spoil the memory of a charming deed. She wanted to do good in her own way; it was her distinctive quality. Just as she scolded, not to correct people, but to please herself, so she gave, not to make people happy or grateful, but, mainly, for her self-satisfaction.

Her good offices were marked, in a manner, by a degree of bluntness and oddity; she had an aversion to thanks: "Thanks," one has said, "provoked in her an amiable and almost serious anger." She had upon this point a complete theory pushed to paradox, and she went so far as to extol ingratitude in all possible ways. One thing that is clear is, that, even in giving, she wished *not to let her left hand know what her right hand did*, and that she knew how to enjoy *all alone* the satisfaction of obliging people. Shall I say it? I think I recognize here, even in the midst of an excellent nature, that streak of egoism and of dryness which was inherent in the eighteenth century. The pupil of Madame de Tencin, the friend of Fontenelle, reappears even at the moment when she yields to her heart's propensity; she yields to it, but still without abandonment, and while coolly planning everything. We know also of a beautiful act of benevolence done by Montesquieu, after which he abruptly and almost rudely stole away from the thanks and the tears of the person obliged. Contempt of men peeps out too much here, even in the benefactor. Is it, then, well in taking one's time to despise them, to choose precisely the moment when one is uplifting them, when one pities them, and when one is making them better?

In Saint-Paul's admirable chapter on Charity, we read, among the other characteristics of that divine virtue: "*Caritas non quæret quæ sua sunt. . . . Non cogitat malum.* Charity seeks not her own. . . . She thinks no evil." Here, on the contrary, this mundane and social beneficence seeks its own pleasure, its private enjoyment, and its own satisfaction, and a little malice and irony, also, mingle with it. I am aware of all that may be said in behalf of this charming and respectable virtue, even when it thinks only of itself. Madame Geoffrin, when one took her to task about this, had a thousand happy answers, shrewd like herself: "Those," said she, "who oblige others rarely, have no need of customary maxims; but those who oblige often must oblige in the way most agreeable to themselves, *because it is necessary to do conveniently what one wishes to do every day.*" There is a touch of Franklin in this maxim, of Franklin correcting and thickening a little the too spiritual meaning of Charity as defined by Saint-Paul. Let us respect, let us honor, then, the native and deliberate liberality of Madame Geoffrin; but let us remember, however, that in all that goodness and beneficence there is wanting a certain celestial flame, as in all that talent and in all that social art of the eighteenth century there was wanting a flower of imagination and poetry, a *fond* of light equally celestial. Never does one see in the distance the blue of the sky or the brightness of the stars.

We have been able already to form an idea of the mould and quality of Madame Geoffrin's mind. Her dominant quality was justness and good sense. Horace Walpole, whom I love to quote, a good judge and one who will be regarded with little suspicion, had seen Madame Geoffrin a good deal, before visiting at Madame Du Deffand's; he liked her exceedingly, and never speaks of hers but as one of the best heads, one of the best *understandings* he has met with, and the person who has the best knowledge of the world. Writing to Lady Hervey after an attack of the gout which he had just had, he said:

"Madame Geoffrin came and sat two hours last night by my bedside: I could have sworn it had been my Lady Hervey, she was so good to me. It was with so much sense, instruction, and correction! The manner of the latter charms me. I never saw anybody in my days that catches one's faults and vanities and impositions so quick, and explains them to one so clearly, and convinces one so easily. I never liked to be set right before! You cannot imagine how I taste it! I make her both my confessor and director, and begin to think I shall be a reasonable creature at last, which I had never intended to be. The next time I see her, I believe I shall say, 'Oh, Common Sense, sit down: I have been thinking so and so; is it not absurd?'—for t'other sense and wisdom, I never liked them; I shall now hate them for her sake. If it was worth her while, I assure your ladyship she-might govern me like a child."

Every time he meets her he speaks of her as being reason itself.

We begin to form an idea of the kind of singular and scolding charm which the good sense of Madame Geoffrin cast about her. She loved to reprimand her visitors, and she made them, for the most part, enjoy the lecture. It is true that if one did not submit to it, if one stole away when she desired to give advice and reproof, she was not pleased, and a little drier accent informed you that she was wounded in her weak place, in her pretension to be your mentor and director.

The following note of hers to David Hume has lately been published, as a sample of her way of abusing (*bourrer*) people when she was pleased with them; I suppress only the orthographical errors, for Madame Geoffrin had no knowledge of orthography, and did not conceal the fact:

> "All you need, my fat rogue, to become a perfect fop, is to play the *beau rigoureux*, by making no reply to a *billet doux* which I sent to you by Gatti. And, to assume all possible airs, you wish to give yourself that of being modest."

Madame de Tencin called the talented people of her world her *cattle* (*bêtes*); Madame Geoffrin continued to treat them somewhat on the same footing and as a pedagogue treats his pupils. She was a scold by profession, by her right as an old woman, and *par contenance*.

She judged her friends, her visitors with perfect honesty, and some terrible sayings of hers have been preserved, which escaped her when she was no longer jesting. It is she who said of the abbe Trublet, who was called in her presence a man of talent (*un homme d'esprit*): "He a man of talent! he is *a fool rubbed over with talent*" (*frotté d'esprit*). She said of the duke of Nivernais: "He has failed in everything, *failed* as a warrior, *failed* as an ambassador, *failed* as an author," etc. Rulhière read in her *salons* his manuscript anecdotes of Russia; she would have been glad if he had thrown them into the fire, and she offered to indemnify him for so doing by a sum of money. Rulhière was indignant, and talked largely of all the great sentiments of honor, of disinterestedness, and love of truth; she replied only in these words: "Do you wish for more?" We see that Madame Geoffrin was gentle only when she was pleased to be so, and that her benignity of disposition and her beneficence concealed a bitter experience.

I have already quoted Franklin in speaking of her. She had certain maxims which seem to have sprung from the same calculating, ingenious, and thoroughly practical good sense, as his. She had had this maxim engraved upon her counters: "Economy is the source of independence and liberty"; and also this: "We must not let the grass grow in the pathway of friendship."

Her mind was one of those acute ones which are wont to judge at the first view, and completely at a glance, and which rarely return to that which they have once missed. There are some minds which have a slight dread of fatigue and *ennui*, and whose sound and sometimes penetrating judgment is not continuous. Madame Geoffrin, endowed in the highest degree with this kind of mind, differed entirely in this from Madame du Châtelet, for example, who loved to follow out and to exhaust an argument. These delicate and rapid minds are especially fitted to know the world and men; they love to look about, rather than at one object. Madame Geoffrin needed, in order to avoid weariness, a great variety of persons and things. Haste in all its forms paralyzed her; too great prolongation even of a pleasure rendered it unendurable to her; even "when society was most agreeable, she only wished that she could enjoy it at her own time and as she pleased." A visit which threatened to be prolonged and to last for ever, made her turn deadly pale. One day when she saw the good abbe *de Saint-Pierre* installing himself at her house for a whole winter's evening, she was frightened for a moment, but drawing inspiration from the desperate situation, she did so well that she utilized the worthy abbe, and made him amusing. He was completely astonished at it himself, and when, as he withdrew, she complimented him upon his good conversation, he replied: "Madame, I am but an instrument upon which you have well played." Madame Geoffrin was a skillful artist.

In all this I am only quoting and condensing the Memoirs of the times. It is a greater pleasure than is supposed, to re-read these authors of the eighteenth century that are regarded as secondary, and who are simply excellent in plain prose. There is nothing else so agreeable, so dainty, and so elegant, as the pages which Marmontel has consecrated in his Memoirs to Madame Geoffrin and to pictures of that society. Morellet himself, when he speaks of her, is not an excellent painter, but a perfect analyst; the hand that writes is indeed a little clumsy, but the pen is neat and delicate. Even Thomas, who is regarded as bombastic, is very agreeable and very happy in expression, when speaking of Madame Geoffrin. People are always declaring that Thomas is inflated; but we ourselves have become, in our ways of writing, so inflated, so metaphorical, that Thomas, when re-read, appears to me simple.

The great event of Madame Geoffrin's life was the journey she made to Poland (1766) to see the king Stanislaus Poniatowski. She had known him when a young man at Paris, and had remembered him as well as so many others in her acts of kindness. He had hardly ascended the throne of Poland, when he wrote to her: *Mamma, your son is king;* and he earnestly begged her to come and visit him. Notwithstanding her already advanced age, she did not refuse; she went by way of

Vienna, and was there the object of marked attentions by the sovereigns. It has been thought that a little diplomatic commission slipped in among the main objects of this journey. We have some charming letters of Madame Geoffrin written from Warsaw; they ran the rounds of Paris, and it was ungenteel at the time to be ignorant of them. Voltaire chose that time to write to her as to a power; he entreated her to interest the king of Poland in the Sirven family. Madame Geoffrin had a good head, and this journey did not turn it. Marmontel, in his letters to her, had appeared to believe that these attentions paid by monarchs to a merely private person, were going to produce a revolution in ideas; Madame Geoffrin set him right in the matter:

"No, my neighbor," she replied (*neighbor*, because Marmontel was living in her house), "no, not a word of all that: nothing of that which you are thinking of will ever take place. Everything will remain in the condition in which I found it, and you will also find my heart to be still, as you have known it, very susceptible of friendship."

Writing also to D'Alembert from Warsaw, she said, felicitating herself upon her lot, and without enthusiasm:

"This journey made, I feel that I shall have seen enough of men and of things to be convinced that they are everywhere nearly the same. I have my storehouse of reflections and comparisons well furnished for the rest of my life."

She adds, with a sensibility alike touching and elevated, concerning her royal pupil:

"It is a terrible position, to be king of Poland. I dare not say how unfortunate I find him: alas! he feels it only too often. All that I have seen since I quitted my Penates, will make me thank God for having been born *a Frenchwoman and a private citizen.*"

On returning from this journey, during which she had

been loaded with honors and consideration, she redoubled her clever modesty. We may believe that that modesty of hers was but a gentler manner, and full of taste, of manifesting her self-love and her glory. But she excelled in that discreet and adjusted manner. Like Madame de Maintenon, she belonged to the race of *glorious modest* persons. When she was complimented and questioned about her journey, whether she replied or did not reply, there was no affectation either in her words or her silence. Nobody knew better than she, better than that plain Parisian woman, the art of dealing with the great, of obtaining from them what is wanted, without either keeping in the background or making a parade, and of keeping, in everything and with everybody, an air of ease within the limit of propriety.

Like all powers, she had the honor of being attacked. Palissot tried twice to traduce her upon the stage, under the title of the patron of the Encyclopædists. But of all attacks, the sharpest must have been the publication of Montesquieu's familiar Letters, which the abbe Guasco had printed in 1767, to annoy her. Some words of Montesquieu against Madame Geoffrin indicate plainly enough what one might otherwise suspect, that a little intrigue and manœuvring always creep in where there are men to be governed, even when women themselves are charged with the task. Madame Geoffrin had also the credit of having the publication arrested, and the passages in which she was noticed were cancelled.

There were some singular circumstances connected with Madame Geoffrin's last sickness. While sustaining the *Encyclopædia* with her gifts, she was always more or less religious. La Harpe relates that she had at her service a Capuchin confessor, an easy-going (à *très-large manche*), confessor, for the convenience of her friends who might have need of him, for, as she was not pleased if one of her friends did anything to send him to the Bastille, she was equally displeased when one died without confession. As for herself, while she lived with the philosophers, she went to the mass, as one goes in prosperity, and she had her seat at the church of the Capuchins, as other persons would have had their *petite maison*. Age strengthened this serious or becoming disposition. At the end of a Jubilee which she followed up too strictly in the summer of 1776, she fell into a paralytic state, and her daughter, taking advantage of this circumstance, shut the door on the philosophers, whose influence upon her mother she dreaded. D'Alembert, Marmontel, Morellet, were rudely excluded; so rumor said. Purgot wrote to Condorcet: "I pity that poor Madame Geoffrin for being obliged to suffer this slavery, and to have her last moments poisoned by her vile daughter." Madame Geoffrin was no longer her own mistress; even when she came to her senses, she felt that she must choose between her daughter and her friends, and blood won the day: "My daughter," said she, smiling, "is like Godfrey de Bouillon, she wants to defend my tomb against the Infidels." She secretly sent to these same Infidels her regards and regrets; she sent them presents. Her reason was enfeebled; but the mould of her mind never changed, and she revived enough to utter some of those sayings which showed that she was still like herself. Her friends talked by her bedside upon the means which governments might employ to render the people happy, and each person began to invent great things: "Add to it," she said, "the care of procuring pleasures, a thing with which one does not sufficiently occupy himself."

She died in the parish of Saint-Roch, October 6, 1777. The name of Madame Geoffrin, and the peculiar influence she exerted, have naturally called to mind another amiable name, which it is too late to compare here with hers. The Madame Geoffrin of our days, Madame Recamier, had, in a greater degree than the other, youth, beauty, poetry, grace, the star on the forehead, and, let us add, a goodness not more ingenious, but more angelic. The quality which Madame Geoffrin showed, in addition, in the administration of a larger and more important *salon*, was a judgment which was firmer and, in some sense, more at home,— which was at less pains and expense, and sacrificed less, to please others; it was that singular good sense, of which Walpole has given so good an idea, a mind not only refined and acute, but just and *penetrating*.

July 22, 1850.

JOUBERT.

A PERSON was astonished one day that Geoffroy could return again and again to the same theatrical piece, and make so many articles upon it. One of his witty brethren, M. de Feletz, replied: "Geoffroy has three ways of making an article: *to assert, to re-assert, and to contradict himself* (*dire, redire, et se contradire*)." I have already spoken more than once of M. Joubert, and to-day I would like to speak of him again, without repeating and without contradicting myself. The new edition* which is now publishing will furnish me with the occasion and perhaps with the means of doing so.

The first time that I spoke of M. Joubert, I had to answer this question, which one had a right to ask me: "Who is M. Joubert?" To-day the question will no longer be asked. Although he may not be destined ever to become popular as a writer, the first publication of his two volumes of "Thoughts and Letters," in 1842, sufficed to give him a place, at the very outset, in the esteem of connoisseurs and judges, and to-day it is only necessary to extend a little the circle of his readers.

His life was simple, and I recall it here only for those who love to know what kind of a man one speaks of when he treats of an author. M. Joubert, who was born in 1754 and died in 1824, was, in his life-time, as little of

* Of his "Pensées, Essais, Maximes et Correspondance."

an author as possible. He was one of those happy spirits who pass their lives in thinking, in talking with their friends, in dreaming in solitude, in meditating upon some work which they will never accomplish, and which will come to us only in fragments. These fragments, by their quality, and in spite of some faults of a too subtle thought, are in this instance sufficiently meritorious to entitle the author to live in the memory of the future. M. Joubert was, in his day, the most delicate and the most original type of that class of honest people which the old society alone produced,—spectators, listeners who had neither ambition nor envy, who were curious, at leisure, attentive, and disinterested, who took an interest in everything, the true *amateurs* of beautiful things. "To converse and to know, —it was in this, above all things, that consisted, according to Plato, the happiness of private life." This class of connoisseurs and of amateurs, so fitted to enlighten and to restrain talent, has almost disappeared in France since every one there has followed a profession. "We should always," said M. Joubert, "have a corner of the head open and free, that we may have a place for the opinions of our friends, where we may lodge them provisionally. It is really insupportable to converse with men who have, in their brains, only compartments which are wholly occupied, and into which nothing external can enter. Let us have hospitable hearts and minds." Go, then, to-day, and demand intellectual hospitality, welcome for your ideas, your growing views, of hurried, busy minds, filled wholly with themselves, true torrents roaring with their own thoughts! M. Joubert, in his youth, coming in 1778 at the age of twenty-four from his province of Périgord to Paris, found there what one finds no longer to-day; he lived there as one lived then: he *chatted.* What he did in those days of youth may be summed up in that single word. He chatted then with famous people of letters; he knew Marmontel, La Harpe, D'Alembert; he knew especially Diderot, by nature the most gracious and the most hospitable of spirits. The influence of the latter upon him was great, greater than one would suppose, seeing the difference in their conclusions. Diderot had certainly in M. Joubert a singular pupil, one who was pure-minded, finally a Platonist and a christian, smitten with the *beau idéal* and saintliness; studying and adoring piety, chastity, modesty, and never finding, to express himself upon these noble subjects, any style sufficiently ethereal, nor any expression sufficiently luminous. However, it is only by that contact with Diderot that one can fully explain the inoculation of M. Joubert with certain ideas, then so new, so bold, and which he rendered truer by elevating and rectifying them. M. Joubert had his Diderot period when he tried everything; later, he made a choice. Always, even at an early day, he had tact; taste did not come to him till afterward. "Good judgment in literature," said he, "is a very slow faculty, which does not reach the last point of its growth till very late." Reaching that point of maturity, M. Joubert was sufficiently just to Diderot to say that there are many more *follies of style* than *follies of thought* in his works. It was especially for his interest and initiation in art and literature that he was indebted to Diderot. But, in falling into a soul so delicate and so light, those ideas of literary reform and of the regeneration of art, which in Diderot had preserved a kind of homely and prosaic, a smoky and declamatory character, were brightened and purified, and assumed an ideal character which approximated them insensibly to the Greek beauty; for M. Joubert was a Greek, he was an Athenian touched with the Socratic grace. "It seems to me," said he, "much more difficult to be a modern than to be an ancient." He was especially an ancient in the calmness and moderation of his sentiments; he disliked everything that was sensational, all undue emphasis. He demanded a lively and gentle agreeableness, a certain internal, perpetual joy, giving to the movement and to the form ease and suppleness, to the expression clearness, light and transparency. It is principally in these that he made beauty consist:

"The Athenians were delicate in mind and ear. They never would have endured a word fitted to displease, even though one had only quoted it. One would say that they were always in good humor when writing. They disapproved in style of the austerity which reveals hard, harsh, sad, or severe manners."

He said again:

"Those proud Romans had a hard ear, which it was necessary to caress a long time to dispose them to listen to beautiful things. Hence that oratorical style which one finds even in their wisest historians. The Greeks, on the contrary, were endowed with perfect organs, easy to put in play, and which it was only necessary to touch in order to move them. Again, the simplest dress of an elegant thought sufficed to please them, and in descriptions they were satisfied with pure truth. They observed especially the maxim, *Nothing in excess.* Much choice and purity in the thoughts; words assorted and beautiful by their own harmony; finally, the sobriety required to prevent anything from weakening an impression,— these formed the character of their literature."

Upon Pigalle and modern statuary as opposed to the ancient, one might cite from him thoughts of the same kind, whole pages which mark at once and very clearly in what respect he agrees with Diderot, and wherein

he separates from him. Thus, then, about the epoch of
'89, there was in France a man already at maturity,
thirty years old, eight years older than André Chénier,
and fourteen years older than Chateaubriand, who was
fully prepared to comprehend them, to unite them, to
furnish them with incitements and new views, to enable
them to extend and complete their horizon. This was
the part, indeed, of M. Joubert touching M. de Chateaubriand, whom he knew in 1800, on the return of the
latter from London. M. de Chateaubriand, at that fine
period of his life (that fine period, for me, is the literary period, and extends from *Atala*, by *René*, by *The
Martyrs*, even to the *Last of the Abencerrages*), M. de
Chateaubriand had then, as a poet, a happiness which
very few persons enjoy: he found two friends, two distinct critics, Fontanes and Joubert, made expressly for
him, to inform him or to guide him. One has commonly
but one guardian angel, he then had two: one entirely
guardian, Fontanes, restraining him in private, defending
him when necessary before everybody, covering him with
a buckler in the *melée;* the other, rather fitted to incite
and to inspire,— M. Joubert, who encouraged him in an
undertone, or murmured to him sweet counsel in a contradiction full of grace. The best, the finest criticism to
be made upon the first and great literary works of M.
de Chateaubriand, might still be found in the Letters
and Thoughts of M. Joubert. This is not the place
to examine and to disentangle that criticism; I shall,
nevertheless, touch somewhat upon it presently.

The life of Joubert is all in his thoughts; but one
would not say of that life the little that is to be said of
it, if he did not speak of Madame de Beaumont. That

daughter of the old minister, M. de Montmorin, who escaped during the Reign of Terror from the fate of the rest of her family, and who found favor on account of her weakness and paleness, was one of those touching beings who only glide through life, and who leave there a trace of light. M. Joubert, who was already married, and who spent a part of the year at Villeneuve-sur-Yonne, had met her in Burgundy at the door of a cottage, where she had taken refuge. He was immediately attached to her; he loved her. He would have loved her with a sentiment livelier than friendship, if there had been for this exquisite soul a livelier sentiment. Madame Beaumont, still young, had infinite grace. Her mind was quick, solid, exalted; her form delicate and aërial. She had formerly known and appreciated André Chénier. Rulhière had had a seal engraved for her which represented an oak with this device: "A breath agitates me; nothing shakes me." The device was just; but the image of the oak may seem somewhat proud. Be this as it may, that frail and graceful shell, that *sensitive reed*, which seemed to abandon itself to the least breath, enclosed a strong, ardent soul, capable of a passionate devotion. Struck in her tenderest place, victim of an ill-assorted union, she had little love for life; mortally attacked, she felt that it was fleeing from her, and she hastened to give it up. While waiting for death, her noble mind was prodigal of itself, happy in scattering sweet approvals about her. One has said of Madame de Beaumont that she loved merit as others love beauty. When M. de Chateaubriand, coming to Paris, was presented to her, she immediately recognized that merit under its most seductive form of poetry, and she adored it. Hers was, after his sister Lucille's, the first great devotion which that figure of René inspired,—that figure which was to inspire more than one other afterward, though none of greater value. With what feeling she inspired M. Joubert, it would be difficult to define: it was an active, tender, perpetual solicitude, without excitement, without uneasiness, full of warmth, full of radiance. That too lofty spirit, which knew not how to move slowly, loved to fly and perch itself near her. He had, as he said, a chilly mind; he loved to have it pleasant and warm about him; he found in her society the serenity and the warmth of affection, which he desired, and he drew strength from the indulgence. As she despised life, he preached to her constantly upon the care and love of it; he would have had her learn again to hope. He wrote to her:

"I am paid for desiring your health, since I have seen you; I know its importance, since I have it not. That, you say, will be the sooner done with. Yes, sooner, but not soon. One is a long time dying, and if, roughly speaking, it is sometimes agreeable to be dead, it is frightful to be dying for ages. Finally, we must love life while we have it: it is a duty."

He repeats to her this truth of morality and of friendship in all its forms; he wished, if possible, to lessen and to moderate the activity which was consuming her and wasting her frail organs. He wished to insinuate Madame de La Fayette's sentiment of resignation: *It is enough to be.*

"Be quiet in love, in esteem, in veneration, I pray you with joined hands. It is, I assure you, at this moment the only way to commit but few mistakes, to adopt but few errors, to suffer but few ills." "To live," he said to her again, "is to think and to be conscious of one's soul; all the rest, eating, drinking, etc., although I value them, are but preparations for living, the means of preserving life. If one could do without them, I could easily resign myself thereto, and I could very well dispense with my body, if one would leave me all my soul."

He had reasons for speaking thus, he of whom one has said that he had the appearance of a soul which has encountered a body by chance, and which gets along with it as it can. He commended to that lovely friend repose, immobility, that she should follow the only regimen which he found good for himself,— to remain a long time in bed and to *count the joists*. He added:

"Your activity disdains such a happiness; but see if your reason does not approve of it. Life is a duty; we must make a pleasure of it, so far as we can, as of all other duties. If the care of cherishing it is the only one with which it pleases Heaven to charge us, we must acquit ourselves gaily and with the best possible grace, and poke that sacred fire, while warming ourselves by it all we can, till the word comes to us: *That will do.*"

These tender recommendations were useless. Madame de Beaumont had so little attachment to life, that it seemed as if it depended only upon herself whether she should live. Pure illusion! she was but too really attacked, and she herself had but little to do to hasten her end. She decided to go to the waters of Mont-Doré in the summer of 1803, and thence to set out for Rome, where she rejoined M. de Chateaubriand; shortly after her arrival there she died. One should read the letter of M. Joubert, written during that trip to Rome. He had not believed in that departure; he had secretly hoped that she would shrink from so much fatigue and such occasions of exhaustion. The last letter which he addressed to her (October 12, 1803,) is filled with an anxious tenderness; one perceives in it a kind of revelation, long withheld, which he finally made to himself; he had never before confessed to himself, so plainly, how much he loved her, how necessary she was to him. He wrote:

"All my mind has returned to me; it gives me many pleasures; but a despairing reflection corrupts them; I have you no longer, and surely I shall not have you for a long time within reach, to hear what I think. The pleasure I formerly had in speaking is entirely lost to me. I have made a vow of silence; I remain here for the winter. My inner life is going to be spent wholly with (*entre*) Heaven and myself. My soul will preserve its wonted habits, but I have lost its delights."

In conclusion, he cries:

"Adieu, adieu, cause of so many pains, who hast been for me so often the source of so many blessings. Adieu! preserve yourself, take care of yourself, and return some day among us, if only to give me for a single moment the inexpressible pleasure of seeing you again."

In the two preceding years (1800–1803) there had been formed about Madame de Beaumont a little *réunion*, often spoken of, which was very short in duration, but which had life and activity, and which deserves to hold a place by itself in literary history. It was the hour when society was everywhere regenerated, and many *salons* then offered to those who had recently been exiled and shipwrecked the enjoyments, so desired, of conversation and intellectual intercourse. There were the philosophic and literary circles of Madame Suard and Madame d'Houdetot, and that of the abbe Morellet (held by his niece, Madame Chéron); there, properly speaking, literary people and philosophers held sway, who directly prolonged the last century. There were the fashionable *salons*, of a more varied and diverse composition; the *salon* of Madame de la Briche; that of Madame de Vergennes, where her daughter, Madame de Remusat, distinguished herself; that of Madame de Pastoret, that of Madame de Staël when she was at Paris; and yet others, of which each had its hue and its dominant tone.

But, in a corner of Neuve-du-Luxembourg street, a *salon* much less visible, much less exposed, gathered together some friends in intimate union about a lady of superior quality. In that place were to be found youth, the new sentiment, and the future. The *habitués* of the place were M. de Chateaubriand, even his sister Lucille for a whole winter, M. Joubert, Fontanes, M. Molé, M. Pasquier, Chênedollé, M. Greneau de Mussy, one M. Jullien, well instructed in English literature, Madame de Ventimille. These were the body of the assemblage: the others whom one might name came only as it happened. The sunstroke which followed the eighteenth brumaire had made itself felt more in this corner of the world than elsewhere; one loved, one adopted with pleasure every kind of genius, every new talent; one enjoyed them as enchanters; imagination had flowered again, and one might have inscribed on the door of the place the saying of M. Joubert: "Admiration has reappeared, and rejoiced a saddened earth."

These happy meetings, these complete reunions here below, last but a day. After the loss of Madame de Beaumont, M. Joubert continued to live and to think, but with less delight; he conversed often of her with Madame de Vintimille, the best female friend whom she had left; but such a reunion as that of 1802 was never formed again, and, at the end of the Empire, politics and business had loosened, if not dissolved, the ties of the principal friends. M. Joubert, isolated, living with his books, with his dreams, noting his thoughts on unconnected bits of paper, would have died without leaving anything finished or enduring, if one of the relatives of the family, M. Paul Raynal, had not had the pious care to collect these fragments, to set them in a certain order, and to make of them a kind of series of precious stones. These are the volumes of which a second edition is published to-day.

Since I have spoken of precious stones, I will say, right at the beginning, that there are too many of them. An English poet (Cowley) has said: "One concludes by doubting whether the milky-way is composed of stars, there are so many of them!" There are too many stars in the heaven of M. Joubert. One would like more intervening spaces and more repose. "I am like Montaigne," said he, "unfit for continuous discourse. Upon all subjects, it seems to me, I either lack intermediate ideas, or they weary me too much." These intermediate ideas, if he had given himself the trouble to express them, would not have wearied us, it seems, but would rather have given us repose in reading him. One is conscious in his writings of an effort,—often happy, yet an effort. "If there is a man," he says, "tormented with the accursed ambition of putting a whole book into a page, a whole page into a phrase, and that phrase into a word, it is I." His method is always to express a thought in an image; the thought and the image make, for him, but one thing, and he believes that he has grasped the one only when he has found the other. "It is not my phrase that I polish, but my idea. I stop till the drop of light which I need is formed and falls from my pen." This series of thoughts, then, are only drops of light; the mind's eye is at last dazzled by them. "I would like," says he, defining himself with marvellous correctness, "I would like to infuse exquisite sense into common sense, or to render exquisite sense common." Good sense alone wearies him; the ingenious without good sense rightly appears to him contemptible; he wishes to unite the two, and it is no small undertaking. "Oh! how difficult it is," he cries, "to be at once ingenious and sensible!" La Bruyère, before him, had felt the same difficulty, and had avowed it to himself at the beginning: "All is said, and one comes too late, now that there have been men for seven thousand years, and men, too, that have thought." M. Joubert recognizes this likewise: "All the things which are easy to say well have been perfectly said; the rest is our business or our task: painful task!" I indicate at the outset the disadvantage and the fault; these books of maxims and of condensed moral observations, such as that of La Bruyère, and especially such as M. Joubert's, cannot be read consecutively without fatigue. It is the mind distilled and fixed in all its sugar; one cannot take much of it at once.

The first chapters of the first volume are not those which please me most; they treat of God, of creation, of eternity, and of many other things. To the peculiar difficulty of the subjects is added that which springs from the subtlety of the author. Here it is no longer with Plato that we have to do, but with Augustin in large doses, and without any connection in the ideas. Unquestionably it will be well, one day, to make of all these metaphysical chapters a single one, much abridged, into which shall be admitted only the beautiful, simple, acceptable thoughts, rejecting all those which are equivocal or enigmatical. On these terms one may make of M. Joubert's volumes, not a library book as to day, but (that which would be so easy to make by selection) one of those beautiful little books which he loved, and which would justify in every respect his device: *Excel, and thou shalt live!*

It is when he returns to speak of manners and of arts, of antiquity and of the century, of poetry and of criticism, of style and of taste,— it is in treating all these subjects that he pleases and charms us, that he appears to us to have made a notable and novel addition to the treasure of his most excellent predecessors. Taste, for him, is *the literary conscience of the soul.* Not more than Montaigne does he love the book-like or bookish style (*style librier ou libresque*), that which savors of ink, and which one never employs except when writing: "There should be, in our written language, voice, soul, space, a majestic air, words that subsist all alone, and which carry their place with them." This life which he demands of the author, and without which style exists only on paper, he wishes also in the reader: "The writers who have influence are only men who express perfectly what others think, and who reveal in minds ideas or sentiments that were striving to come forth. It is in the depths of minds that literatures exist." Again, he who relished the ancients so well, the antiquity of Rome, of Greece, and of Lewis XIV, does not demand impossibilities of us; he will tell us to appreciate that antiquity, but not to return to it. In respect to expression, he prefers again the sincere to the beautiful, and truth to appearance:

"*Truth* in style is an indispensable quality, and one which suffices to recommend a writer. If, upon all sorts of subjects, we should write to-day as men wrote in the time of Lewis XIV, we should have no truth in style, for we have no longer the same dispositions, the same opinions, the same manners. A woman who would write like Madame de Sevigné would be ridiculous, because she is not Madame de Sevigné. The more the way in which one writes partakes of the character of the man, of the manners of the time, the more must the style differ from that of the writers who have been models only by having manifested preëminently, in their works, either the manners of their epoch or their own character. Good taste itself, in that case, permits one to discard the best taste, for taste, even good taste, changes with manners."

If this is already the case, so far as we are concerned, with the style of the age of Lewis XIV, how will it be with that of remote antiquity, and can one hope to return to it? M. Joubert contents himself with desiring that we should prize and tenderly regret that which will never return:

"In the luxury of our writings and of our life, let us at least love and regret that simplicity which we have no longer, and which, perhaps, we can no longer have. While drinking from our gold, let us regret the ancient cups. Finally, that we may not be corrupted in everything, let us cherish that which is better than ourselves, and let us, in perishing, save from the shipwreck our tastes and our judgments."

What M. Joubert demands, above all, of the moderns, is, not to insist upon their faults, not to follow their inclinations, not to throw themselves in that direction with all their strength. The visionary and fickle nature, the sensual, the bombastic, the colossal, especially displease him. We have had a high opinion for some years of what we call force, power. Often when I have chanced to hazard some critical remark upon a talent of the day, one has replied to me: "What matters it! that talent has power." But what kind of power? Joubert is going to reply for me: "Force is not energy; some authors have more muscles than talent. Force! I do not hate it nor do I fear it; but, thanks to Heaven, I am entirely disabused in regard to it. It is a quality which is praiseworthy only when it is concealed or clothed. In the vulgar sense Lucan had more of it than Plato, Brebeuf more than Racine." He will tell us again: "Where there is no delicacy, there is no literature. A writing in which are found only force and a certain fire without splendor, announces only character. One may produce many such, if he has nerves, bile, blood, and boldness." M. Joubert adores enthusiasm, but he distinguishes it from explosiveness, and even from fervor (*verve*), which is but a secondary quality in inspiration, and which *excites* (*remue*) whilst the other *moves* (*émeut*): "Boileau, Horace, Aristophanes, had fervor; La Fontaine, Menander, and Virgil, the gentlest and the most exquisite enthusiasm that ever was." Enthusiasm, in that sense, might be defined a kind of *exalted peace*. Fine works, according to him, do not intoxicate, but they enchant. He exacts agreeableness and a certain amenity even in the treatment of austere subjects; he requires a certain charm everywhere, even in profundity: "It is necessary to carry a certain charm even into the deepest investigations, and to introduce into those gloomy caverns, into which one has penetrated but for a short time, the pure and antique light of the ages that were less instructed but more luminous than ours." Those words *luminous* and *light* reappear frequently in his writings, and betray that winged nature that loved the heavens and high places. The brilliant, which he distinguishes from the luminous, does not seduce him: "It is very well that thoughts should shine, but it is not necessary that they should sparkle." What he most of all desires in them is splendor, which he defines a quiet, inner brilliancy, uniformly diffused, and which penetrates the whole body of a work.

There is much to be drawn from the chapters of M. Joubert upon criticism and upon style,— from his judgments upon different writers; in these he appears original, bold, and almost always correct. He astonishes at the first impression; he generally satisfies when one reflects upon his sayings. He has the art of freshening stale precepts, of renewing them for the use of an epoch which holds to tradition only by halves. On this side he is essentially a modern critic. In spite of all his old creeds and his regrets for the past, we distinguish immediately in him the stamp of the time in which he lives. He does not hate a certain appearance of elaborate finish, and sees in it rather a misfortune than a fault. He goes so far as to believe that "it is permissible to avoid simplicity, when to do so is absolutely necessary for agreeableness, and when simplicity alone would not be beautiful." If he desires naturalness, it is not the vulgar naturalness, but an exquisite naturalness. Does he always attain it? He feels that he is not exempt from some subtlety, and he excuses himself for it: "Often one cannot avoid passing through the subtle to rise and reach the sublime, as to mount to the heavens one must pass through the clouds." He rises often to the highest ideas, but it is never by following the high-roads; he has paths that are unseen. Finally, to sum all up, there is singularity and an individual *humor* in his judgments. He is an indulgent *humorist*, who sometimes recalls Sterne, or rather Charles Lamb. He has a manner that leads him to say nothing, absolutely nothing, like another man. This is noticeable in the letters he writes, and does not fail to be wearisome at last. It appears by all marks that Joubert is not a classic but a modern, and it is by this title that he appears to me fitted, better perhaps than any other person, to give emphasis to good counsel, and to pierce us with his shafts.

I have sometimes asked myself what would be a sensible, just, natural French rhetoric, and it happened to me, once in my life, to have to treat the subject in a course of lectures to some young people. What did I have to do to avoid falling into routine, and also risking too much by novelty? I began quite simply with Pascal, with the "thoughts" on literature, in which the great writer has set down some of the observations which he made upon his own art; I read them aloud, at the same time commenting on them. Then I took La Bruyère, at the chapter on the *Works of the Mind*. I next went to Fenelon, for his *Dialogues on Eloquence*, and for his *Letter to the French Academy*. I read cursorily, choosing the points, and commenting on them always by means of examples, and without confining myself to the living. Vauvenargues, on account of his *Thoughts* and his *Literary Characters*, came next. I then borrowed of Voltaire his articles on *Taste* and *Style* in the *Philosophical Dictionary*, his *Temple of Taste*, and some passages of his letters in which he judges Boileau, Racine, and Corneille. In order to extend the horizon a little at this moment, I joined some considerations upon the genius of Goethe and upon the English taste of Coleridge. Marmontel, in his *Elements of Literature*, furnished me next with the article on *Style*, an excellent piece. I was careful not to forget Buffon upon the same subject, who crowned the whole. Then, the classic circle completed, I gave M. Joubert to my young people for a kind of dessert, for recreation, and for a little final debauch, a debauch worthy of Pythagoras! And so my French rhetoric found itself complete.

On the whole, if we must characterize M. Joubert, he had all the delicacy which one can desire in a mind, but he had not all the power. He was one of those meditative and fastidious minds that "are incessantly distracted from their work by immense perspectives and distant prospects of celestial beauty of which they would like to show everywhere some image or some ray." He had in too high a degree the sentiment of the perfect and of the complete: "To perfect one's thought," cried he, "that takes time, that is rare, that imparts an extreme pleasure; for perfected thoughts enter minds easily; they need not even be beautiful to please, it suffices that they be finished. The condition of the soul which has had them communicates itself to other souls, and conveys to them its own repose." He had sometimes that sweet enjoyment of finishing his thoughts, but never that of joining them together and forming a monument.

A philosopher of that time, himself an exceedingly intellectual man, was accustomed to distinguish three kinds of minds thus:

"The first, at once powerful and delicate, which excel as they understand it, execute what they conceive, and attain both the great and the true beautiful; a rare elect among mortals!

"The second, whose chief quality is delicacy, and who feel their idea to be superior to their execution, their intelligence greater still than their talent, even when this last is very real. They are easily disgusted, disdain the easily obtained suffrages, love better to judge, to taste, and to abstain, than to remain below their idea and themselves. When they write, it is in fragments, it is for themselves alone, it is at long intervals, and in rare moments; they have for their apportionment only an internal fecundity, which has few confidants.

"Finally, the last kind of minds comprises those who, more powerful and less delicate or less exacting, go on producing and diffusing themselves, without being too much disgusted with themselves and with their works; and it is very happy that it is so with them, for, otherwise, the world would run the risk of being deprived of many thoughts which amuse and which charm it, which console it for the want of those greater ones that will not come."

Is it necessary to say that M. Joubert, like M. Royer-Collard, belongs to the second class of these minds, to those who look upward and produce chiefly within?

Naturally the conversation of these men is superior to what they leave in writing, and which exhibits but the smallest part of themselves. I have been permitted to gather some flashes of the conversation of M. Joubert from the papers of Chênedollé, who took notes of them on leaving him. Would one know how Joubert talked about M. de Chateaubriand and about Bernardin de Saint-Pierre, while comparing the excellences of the two? The last week has been entirely consecrated to M. de Chateaubriand, and there has been a great festival of eloquence on his account.* Nevertheless, if I do not deceive myself, and if I see clearly in respect to certain symptoms, the moment is approaching when his high renown will have to undergo one of those general insurrections which long-continued monarchies, universal monarchies, at the final reckoning, never escape. What it will be necessary to do then, to maintain the just rights of his renown, will be, in wise criticism as in wise war, to abandon without difficulty all the parts of that vast domain which are not truly beautiful, nor susceptible of being seriously defended, and to entrench one's self in the portions which are entirely superior and durable. These portions which I call truly beautiful and inexpugnable, will be *René*, some scenes of *Atala*, the story of Eudore, the picture of the Roman Campagna, some fine pictures in the *Itinéraire*; to these will be joined some political and especially some polemical pages. Well, here

---

*On the sixth of December (1849) there was a great session at the French Academy for the reception of M. Noailles, who came to replace and to celebrate M. de Chateaubriand; M. Patin had replied to him.

is what M. Joubert said, one day in February, 1807, while walking with Chênedollé before the column of the Louvre, as *René, Paul et Virginie* and *Atala* came to his recollection:

"The work of M. de Saint-Pierre resembles a statue of white marble, that of M. de Chateaubriand a bronze statue cast by Lysippus. The style of the former is more polished, that of the latter more colored. Chateaubriand takes for his theme heaven, earth, and hell: Saint-Pierre chooses a well-lighted earth. The style of the one has the fresher and younger look; that of the other has the more ancient look: it has the appearance of belonging to all times. Saint-Pierre seems to choose the purest and richest terms in the language: Chateaubriand borrows from all sources, even vicious literatures, but he works a real transmutation, and his style resembles that famous metal which, at the burning of Corinth, was formed by the mingling of all the other metals. The one has a varied unity, the other a rich variety.

"There is a reproach to be made against both. M. de Saint-Pierre has given to matter a beauty which does not belong to it; Chateaubriand has given to the passions an innocence which they do not have, or which they have but once. In *Atala* the passions are covered with long white veils.

"Saint-Pierre has but one line of beauty which turns and returns indefinitely upon itself, and is lost in the most graceful windings: Chateaubriand employs all the lines, even the defective ones, the breaks of which he makes contribute to the truth of the details and to the pomp of the whole.

"Chateaubriand produces with fire; he melts all his thoughts in the fire of heaven.

"Bernardin writes by moonlight, Chateaubriand by the light of the sun."

I will add nothing after such thoughts so worthy of memory, except that, when a new edition of M. Joubert is prepared, they should be added to it.

December 10, 1849.

GUIZOT.

M. GUIZOT has twice addressed the public, as a writer, since February, 1848: the first time in January, 1849, by his pamphlet, *On Democracy in France;* the second time, in these latter days, by the *Discourse* * which we have now to notice, and which has a double end in view. This *Discourse*, indeed, is designed to serve as an introduction to a new edition of the *History of the English Revolution*, which appears at this time; but it has also an evident reference to the present political situation, and almost a direct discussion of it. In discussing strictly this question: "Why did the *English Revolution succeed?*" the eminent historian evidently provokes every thinking reader to ask himself this other question: "Why has the French Revolution miscarried thus far? Why, at least, did it not succeed in the same sense as the English, and why is its final adjustment yet to be made?"

If M. Guizot's discourse were purely political, I might let it pass without believing it to belong to my province, thus remaining faithful to my office and to my taste, which are agreed to adhere to literature; but this *Discourse* is political only in its meaning and object; it is purely historical in form and appearance, and as such I cannot neglect it without seeming to be unequal to an important occasion, and almost to an opportunity. It is

* Discours sur l'Histoire de la Révolution d'Angleterre.

impossible for the newspaper critic, who commonly has to hunt for or to create subjects of interest, to evade so important ones when they directly confront him. If I should pass by this *Discourse* in silence, to speak of a book of poetry, or of an old or new novel, the public would have a right to think that literary criticism acknowledges its incompetency, that it knows its business only to a certain trifling extent; that there are subjects from which it is interdicted as too difficult or too thorny; and I have never thus regarded that criticism, which is light, no doubt, and, so far as possible, agreeable, but firm and serious when it should be, and as far as it should be.

However (and I will frankly confess it at the outset, in order that I may be so much the more at my ease afterward), I have felt a momentary embarrassment on finding myself prepared to express a direct opinion upon a work whose import is so real, and consequently upon an eminent man of whom there is so much to be said, and whom one cannot consider by halves. The writings of M. Guizot form a complete chain; you cannot touch a link, without moving, without shaking all the rest. And then we have to do, in this case, with a living writer! M. Guizot is not one of those men who are divided, and of whom one can say: I will speak of the historian, of the man of letters, without touching the politician. No, to his honor we must admit, and it is one of the very causes of his personal importance, he is one; literature and history itself have been with him only a means of action, of teaching, of influence. He adopted early certain ideas and systems, and in all ways, by the pen, by speech, in the professor's chair, on the platform, in power and out of power, he has left nothing undone to naturalize those ideas and to make them prevail in our country. And at this moment what is he doing still? Fallen yesterday, he lifts up his banner again to-day; only he raises it now in the historic form. Once more he ranges his ideas and his reasons in order of battle, as if he had never been attacked. To make an end of these precautions, which were yet indispensable, I shall not pretend to forget that Guizot has counted for much in our destinies, that, in determining them, he has been a heavy weight. The accident of February, that immense catastrophe in which we all shared and by which we were shipwrecked, will be present to my memory. I should tell a falsehood if I should say that this last lesson of history is not joined, in my opinion, to all the others which we owe to M. Guizot, to complete them, to correct them, and to confirm me in certain judgments, which I shall try to express here as fitly as possible.

M. Guizot is one of the men of our day who, early and on every occasion, have labored the most and written the most, and upon all sorts of subjects; one of those whose information is the most various and vast, who are best acquainted with the ancient and the modern languages and with belles-lettres; and yet he is not a *littérateur* properly so called, in the exact sense which that word conveys to me. Napoleon wrote to his brother Joseph, then king of Naples, who was very fond of literary people and of savants: "You live too much with men of letters and savants. They are coquets with whom one must have a commerce of gallantry, but he must never dream of making a wife or a minister of any of them." This is true of many literary persons, of some even of those whom, in our day, we have seen made ministers. But it is not true either of M. Guizot or M. Thiers. Both are politicians who began by being writers; they made their start in literature, they return to it when necessary, they honor it by their works; but they do not belong, strictly speaking, to the family of *littérateurs*, that race which has its special qualities and faults. M. Guizot, perhaps, is farther from belonging to it than anybody else. There is no mind to which one can less properly apply that word *coquet*, which Napoleon used; it is a mind which, in everything, cares the least for form, for fashion. Literature has never been his end, but his means. He has no literary ambition, so far as it makes one inquisitive, easy to distract, excitable, easy to irritate, easy to amuse and console. He does nothing trivial, nothing useless. He goes in all matters to the fact, to the end, to the main point. If he writes, he does not trouble himself about a chimerical perfection; he seeks to say well what he means, and as he means it; he does not hunt for a better form of expression, thus losing time and wasting his energies. He is not smitten with an ideal which he would realize. An executive mind, he gathers his forces and his ideas with vigor and with ardor, and sets himself resolutely to work, caring little for the form, and attaining it often by the nerve and decisiveness of his thought. When a work is done, he rarely returns to it; he does not resume it in order to revise it at leisure, to retouch it and polish it up, to improve the inexact or weak parts, and to amend the imperfections of the first draught; he passes on to another. He thinks of the present and of the morrow.

Such he was at the beginning, before he was in office, such in the intervals of his political life. When the Restoration took place, he felt that, under a peaceful government, which admitted the right of discussion and of speech, he was one of those whom their natural vocation and their merit call to take part in the affairs and in the deliberations of the country. All the while that he wrote a great deal, as much from taste as from an honorable necessity, he felt that he belonged to the class who become ministers and who govern. From the very first day he set his eye upon a lofty position, and he prepared himself for it with energy.

While waiting, however, for the hour to come when he should be an orator and a minister, he taught at the Sorbonne; he was the greatest professor of history that we have had. He founded a school; that school reigns; it reigns in part over the very persons who think they are combating it. In his *Essays on the History of France*, in his *History of Civilization in Europe and in France*, Guizot has developed his principles and his points of view. More precise than the Germans, generalizing more than the English, he became European by his writings before becoming such by the part he played as a public man. From the first day that he set foot in history, M. Guizot brought to it his instinct and his habits of mind; he professed to regulate it, to organize it. His first design, in crossing that vast ocean of past things, was to discover and trace a determinate direction, without being too straitened, and without diminishing the diversity of the whole. To act impartially, to admit all the constituent elements of history, royal, aristocratic, communal, or ecclesiastic, to exclude no one of them henceforth, on condition of classifying them all and making them march under one law,— that was his ambition. It was vast, and if we may judge by the effect produced, M. Guizot has succeeded. He has been praised as he deserved. He has not been controverted as he ought. Daunou alone made some timid but judicious observations. No firm spirit, in the name of the school of Hume and Voltaire, in the name of that of experience and good sense, in the name of human humility, has come forth to declare the objections which would not have detracted from his solid merits as a thinker and classifier, which would have left untouched many of the positive portions of his work, but which would have given birth to some doubts concerning the foundation of his exorbitant pretensions.

I am one of those who doubt, indeed, whether it is granted to man to comprehend with this amplitude, with this certainty, the causes and the sources of his own history in the past; he has so much to do to comprehend it even imperfectly at the present time, and to avoid being deceived about it at every hour! Saint Augustine has made this very ingenious comparison: Suppose that a syllable in the poem of the *Iliad* were endowed, for a moment, with a soul and with life: could that syllable, placed as it is, comprehend the meaning and general plan of the poem? At most, it could only comprehend the meaning of the verse in which it was placed, and the meaning of the three or four preceding verses. That syllable, animated for a moment, is man; and you have just told him that he has only to will it, in order to grasp the totality of the things which have occurred on this earth, the majority of which have vanished without leaving monuments or traces of themselves, and the rest of which have left only monuments that are so incomplete and so truncated!

This objection does not address itself to M. Guizot only,

but to the whole doctrinaire school of which he has been the organ and the most active and influential worker. It addresses itself to many other schools, also, which believe themselves distinct from that, and which have split upon the same rock. The danger is very real to any person, especially, who would pass from history to politics. History thus seen from a distance,— mark the fact!— undergoes a singular metamorphosis, and produces an illusion, the worst of all because one believes it a reality. Under this more or less philosophical arrangement which one gives to history, the deviations, the follies, the personal ambitions, the thousand strange accidents which compose it, and of which those who have observed their own times know that it is composed,— all this disappears, is neglected, and is judged but little worthy of being taken into the account. The whole acquires, after the fact, a rational appearance which is deceptive. The fact becomes a view of the mind. One judges henceforth only from above; he puts himself, insensibly, in place of Providence. He finds in all the individual accidents inevitable chains, *necessities*, as they are called. But if he afterward proceeds from study to practice, he is tempted to forget, in dealing with present things, that one has incessantly to deal with human passions and follies, with human inconsistency. He desires at the present time, and even at the very hour, certain net results, as he fancies that they existed in the past. He deals authoritatively with experience. In this age of sophists in which we live, it is in the name of the philosophy of history that each school (for each school has its own) comes imperiously to demand the innovation, which, in its eyes, is no more than a rigorous and legitimate conclusion. It is well to see how, in the name of that pretended historic experience which is nothing more than logic, each one presumptuously arrogates the present and claims the future as his own.

M. Guizot knows better than we these inconveniences, and he would combat them, if there were occasion, in his own masterly way. But he has not been exempt from these errors himself, and, by his ascendency, he has authorized these general ways of viewing events. His philosophy of history is by far too logical to be true, and none the less so for being more specious than others, and for resting upon facts. I see in it only an artificial method, convenient for keeping an account of the past. All the forces which have not produced their effect, and which, nevertheless, might have produced it, are suppressed. All those which can be recovered and gathered together, are arranged in the best order, and under complex names. All the lost causes, which have not had their representative, or which have been finally vanquished, are declared to have been born feeble, and from the outset doomed to defeat. And often what a trifle has prevented them from being triumphant! The very old facts are the ones which lend themselves most readily to this kind of systematic history. They are no longer living, they reach us scattered, piecemeal; they permit themselves to be commanded and trained at will, when a capable hand attempts to arrange and reconstruct them. But modern history offers more resistance. M. Guizot knows it well. In his *History of Civilization in Europe*, it is only when he comes to the sixteenth century, that he entertains any doubts about the advantages of hasty generalizations; it is only then, also, that these objections start up of themselves on all sides, and we reënter the stormy and variable atmosphere of modern and present times. The generalization which seems profound in respect to far distant ages, would seem shallow and rash in respect to nearer ones. Let us well understand each other: I admire that far-reaching and ingenious force of mind which recreates, which restores all of the past that can be restored, which gives it a meaning, if not the true, at least a plausible and probable meaning, which controls the disorder in history, and which furnishes useful bases and directions for its study. But what I would point out as a danger, is the habit of wishing to draw conclusions from a past thus recreated and reconstructed,— from a past artificially simplified,— concerning the moving, various, and changing present. For myself, when I have read some of these lofty lessons, so clear and so trenchant, upon the *History of Civilization*, I speedily reopen a volume of the *Memoirs* of Retz, that I may come back to the real world of intrigue and of human masquerades.

We touch here upon one of the essential reasons why the historian, even the great historian, is not necessarily a great politician or a statesman. These are talents which approximate, which resemble each other, and which one is tempted to confound, but which in some important respects differ. The historian is employed to describe the malady when the sick man is dead. The statesman is employed to treat the sick man while he is still living. The historian deals with "facts accomplished" and simple results (at least, relatively simple): the politician confronts a certain number of results, of which more than one may chance at any moment to vanish.

Some recent facts have demonstrated this last truth. I appeal here to everybody's good sense, and say: In politics, there are several different ways in which a thing that is begun may turn out. When the thing is done, we see only the event. That which passed under our eyes in February is a notable example. The thing might have turned out in many different ways. Fifty years hence one will maintain perhaps (according to the method of the *doctrinaires*) that it was a necessity. In a word, there are many possible defiles in the march of human affairs. In vain does the absolute philosopher tell you: "In history I love the main roads; I believe only in the main roads." Good sense replies: "These main roads are most frequently made by the historian. The main road is made by enlarging the defile which one has passed, and at the expense of the other defiles which one might have passed."

A positive mind, that knows how to combine the practical result and the abstract view, M. Guizot did not care to embarrass himself very long with these historic formulas in which a German professor would have dwelt forever. He stated them, but he did not shut himself up in them. In 1826, he knew how to choose, as material for history, a subject which was most happy in its analogies to our own political situation, and which, besides, was in all respects most fitting to his abilities: he undertook the *History of the English Revolution*. Two volumes only of that History have appeared thus far, and the recital goes only to the death of Charles I. M. Guizot, after a long interruption, resumes his task to-day, and he signalizes his return to it by the remarkable *Discourse* which one may read. Amid the interruptions and the chasms, there is this in common between the beginning in 1826 and the resumption in 1850, that he published the History then as a lesson given to that time, and it is also by the title of a lesson given to our own time, that he returns to his task to-day. In 1826 the lesson was addressed to royalty which wanted to be absolute, and to the *ultras*. In 1850 it is addressed to the democracy. But why, then, a lesson always? Does not history, thus presented, run a risk of going out of the way and of being made a little to order?

Be this as it may, the two published volumes of this *History of the English Revolution* have a real interest, and offer a grave and manly recital, a series of facts that form a firm and dense tissue, with great and lofty parts. The scenes of the death of Strafford and the trial of Charles I are treated simply, and with great dramatic effect. That which was more difficult, and which M. Guizot excels in setting forth, is the debates, the discussions, the disagreements of parties, the parliamentary side of the history, the state of the ideas in the different groups at a given moment; he understands in a masterly way this marshalling of ideas. Sprung from a Calvinist family, he has kept up a certain austere tone of theirs, a talent for comprehending and reproducing those tenacious natures, those energetic and gloomy inspirations. The habits of race and early education stamp themselves on the talents and reappear in the speech, even when they have disappeared from the habits of our life; we keep their fibre and their tone. The men, the characters, are expressed, as we meet them, by vigorous strokes; but the whole lacks a certain splendor, or rather a certain continuous animation. The personages do not live with a life of their own; the historian takes them, seizes them, and gives their profile in brass. His plan implies a very bold and confident execution. He knows what he wants to say, and where he wants to go. The ridiculous and ironical side of things, the sceptical side, of which other historians make too much, has with him no place. He shows plainly a kind of moral gravity in men amid their manœuvrings and intrigues; but he does not set the contradiction in a sufficiently strong light. He gives us, on the way, many stale maxims, but none of those moral reflections which instruct and delight, which recreate humanity and restore it to itself, like those which escape incessantly from Voltaire. His style, which is emphatically his own, is sad and never laughs. I have given myself the pleasure of reading at the same time the corresponding pages of Hume: one would not believe that the same history was treated, so different is the tone! What I remark especially is, that it is possible for me, in reading Hume, to check him, to contradict him sometimes: he furnishes me with the means of doing so by the very details he gives, by the balance he strikes. In reading Guizot this is almost impossible, so closely woven is the tissue, so interlinked is the whole narrative. He holds you fast and leads you to the end, firmly combining the fact, the reflection, and the end in view.

How far, even after these two volumes, and regarding his writings as a whole, is M. Guizot a historical painter? How far and to what extent is he properly a narrator? These would be very interesting questions to discuss as literary ones, without favor and without prejudice; and, whatever fault one might find with M. Guizot, it would necessarily be accompanied with an acknowledgment of a peculiar originality, which belongs only to him. Even when he narrates, as in his *Life of Washington*, it is of a certain abstract beauty that he gives us an impression, not of an external beauty that is designed to please the eyes. His language is strong and ingenious; it is not naturally picturesque. He uses always the graver, never the brush. His style, in the fine passages, is like reflections from brass and, as it were, of steel, but reflections under a gray sky, and never in the sunlight. It has been said of the worthy Joinville, the ingenuous chronicler, that his style *savors still of his childhood*, and that "worldly things are created for him only on the day when he sees them." At the other extremity of the historic chain, with Guizot, it is quite the contrary. His thought, his very recital, assumes spontaneously a kind of abstract, half-philosophical appearance. He communicates to everything that he touches, a tint, so to speak, of an anterior reflection. He is astonished at nothing; he explains whatever he presents to you, he gives the reason for it. A person who knew him well said of him: "That which he has known only since morning, he appears to have known from all eternity." In fact, an idea in entering that lofty mind loses its freshness; it instantly fades, and becomes in a manner antique. It acquires premeditation, firmness, weight, temper, and sometimes a gloomy splendor.

All this being said, it is just to admit that in the second volume of the *History of the English Revolution*, there are passages of a continuous narrative which are irreproachable. It is when M. Guizot abandons himself to his favorite manner, as in the late *Discourse*, that everything in his writing naturally turns into reflections. The very description of a fact is already a result.

But we cannot properly estimate M. Guizot as a writer, unless we also speak of the orator. The one is closely connected with, and has reacted on, the other. Generally, it is the writer (as Cicero has observed) that contributes to form the orator. In Guizot, it is rather the orator that has contributed to perfect the writer, and some one has gone so far as to say that it is upon the marble of the tribune that he has finished polishing his style. M. Guizot, in his first attempts, did not always write well; at least, he wrote very unequally. As soon, however, as his feelings were roused, in his polemical articles, in his pamphlets, he had much point and sharpness. For a long time I have heard it said that M. Guizot did not write well. It is necessary to think twice before denying that he has a certain quality; for, with that tenacious and ardent will of his, he may not be long in winning the very quality which one denies to him, and in saying, "Here it is!" As a professor, M. Guizot spoke well, but with nothing extraordinary in his manner; there was clearness, a perfect lucidity of expression, but along with repetitions of abstract terms; very little elegance, little warmth. One has always the warmth of his ambition. The ambition of M. Guizot was not to feel at ease, and at home, as it were, till it entered upon the parliamentary stage, into the heart of political struggles; it was then that he became wholly himself and began to grow. He needed some apprenticeship still; but from 1837 he displayed all his talent. He had not merely what I call the warmth of his ambition; he had at moments its flame in his speech. That flame, however, burst forth chiefly in his look, gesture, and action. His speech, taken separately, has force and nerve rather than fire. I check myself in these praises. One cannot, if he is patriotic, confine himself here to the literary point of view; for — is it possible to forget it? — that speech has translated itself into acts, it has had too real consequences. That marvellous faculty of authority and serenity (to take a word which he affects), that sovereign art of imparting to things an apparent simplicity, a deceitful clearness, which is purely fanciful, was one of the principal causes of the illusion which destroyed the last administration. Eloquence, to that extent, is a great power; but is it not also one of those *deceitful powers* of which Pascal has spoken? In the last years of the preceding administration, there were two very distinct atmospheres, that within the Chamber and that without. When the eloquence of M. Guizot had reigned within, when it had refilled and renovated that artificial atmosphere, it was believed that the storms had been conjured away. But the atmosphere without was so much the more charged, and out of equilibrium with the air within. Hence the final explosion.

The style of M. Guizot has come forth from these trials of the tribune firmer and better tempered than before; his thought has come forth unmodified. The present *Discourse*, which he has just published, attests this statement. This *Discourse* is written with a master's hand, but it has also a master's tone. He views the English Revolution in its whole course, from the beginning of the troubles under Charles I till after the reign of William III, and even till the complete consolidation of the Settlement of 1688. Looking at the direct intention which is visible in the picture, and which appears formally in the conclusions, it is clear that in the eyes of the eminent historian, all the lessons which that English Revolution, already so fertile in real or false analogies, may furnish us, are not exhausted. This prepossession with the English government and with the English remedy applied to our malady, does not seem to me less grave an error, and one that has been already sufficiently fatal, because it is a more specious one and touches us more nearly. For example, much has been said, under the preceding constitutional government, of the *land of law:* "The *land of law* is the one for us; ours is the *land of law.*" To what has this led? In England, such a saying is significant; for there, before everything else, one has respect for law. In France, it is to other instincts that one must appeal, it is other feelings that one must lay hold of, to maintain even the land of law. The Gallic people are rapid, tumultuous, inflammable. Is it necessary to recall to the historian who has known and described the two countries, these essential differences of genius and of character? Yet it is through the character rather than through the ideas that men are governed. A foreigner, a man of genius, was accustomed to divide human nature into two parts, *human nature in general* and *the French nature,* meaning that the latter so sums up and combines in it the inconstancies, the contradictions, and the caprices of the other, that it forms a variety, and a kind of distinct species. M. de la Rochefoucauld, who had seen the Fronde and all its changes, said one day to cardinal Mazarin: "Everything happens in France!" It was the same moralist, a contemporary of Cromwell, who was the author of that other saying, which is so true, and which too many systematic historians forget: "Fortune and humor govern the world." Understand by *humor* the temperament and character of men, the stubbornness of princes, the complaisance and presumption of ministers, the irritation and the spite of party chiefs, the turbulent disposition of the peoples, and say, you who have had experience of public affairs, and who speak no longer in front of the stage, if that is not to a great extent true. It is then only with the utmost discreetness, it seems to me, that one should propose general remedies made up only of speculations. M. Guizot, after having considered in his masterly way the English and the American Revolutions, recognizes in them three great men, Cromwell, William III, and Washington, who remain in history as the chiefs and representatives of those sovereign crises that determined the fate of two powerful nations. He characterizes them, one after the other, by broad outlines. All three succeeded, the last two the most completely, Cromwell less so: he succeeded only in maintaining his own position, and founded nothing. M. Guizot attributes this difference to the fact that William III and Washington, "even amidst a revolution, never accepted nor acted upon the revolutionary policy." He believes that Cromwell's misfortune was in having at first, by the necessity of his position, to adopt and practice a policy whose alloy rendered his power always precarious. M. Guizot concludes from this that, under all forms of government, whether a monarchy or a republic is concerned, an aristocratic society or a democratic, the same light shines forth from the facts; ultimate success is obtained, he says, only in the name of the same principles and by the same means. The revolutionary spirit is as fatal to the great persons whom it raises up as to those whom it casts down.

M. Guizot will permit me here to say that this conclusion, while it is generally true, is perfectly vague and sterile. To say generally to those who govern a state, that they must not be in any degree revolutionary, is not to give any indication whatever of the ways and means, the contrivances necessary to preserve it; for it is in the detail of each situation that the difficulty lies, and that there is a field for skill. If you go and say to a commander of an army: "Adopt only the defensive method, never the offensive," will he be much better prepared to gain a battle? As if there were no moments, also, when, to defend Rome, it is necessary to go and attack Carthage!

In what relates to men in particular, the conclusion of M. Guizot appears to me much too absolute. Cromwell, you say, only half succeeded, because he was revolutionary. I will add that Robespierre afterward fell through the same cause, and for other reasons besides. But Augustus succeeded in both characters. He was by turns Octavius and Augustus; he proscribed and he founded an empire. And as that same Augustus tells us so eloquently by the mouth of the great Corneille:

> Mais l'exemple souvent n'est qu'un miroir trompeur;
> Et l'ordre du Destin, qui gène nos pensées,
> N'est pas toujours écrit dans les choses passées.
> Quelquefois l'un brise où l'autre est sauvé,
> Et par où l'un périt un autre est conservé.

This is the only practical philosophy of history: nothing absolute, an experience always called in question again, and the unexpected concealing itself in resemblances.

Bossuet has the habit, in his views, of introducing Providence, or rather he does not introduce it: it reigns,

with him, in a continual and sovereign way. I admire
that religious inspiration in the great bishop; but, prac-
tically, it has led him to divine right and sacred politics.
In the modern historians, who have risen to general and
purely rational views, Providence intervenes only at intervals, and, so to speak, at the great moments. The more
discreet and rare that intervention is, as described by
them, the more real reverence it attests; for, in many
cases, when one is prodigal of it, it may seem much rather
an implement of discourse, an oratorical and social effect,
than a heart-felt and truly sincere exaltation. This is
not the case with M. Guizot. He has from the beginning
cherished the religious sentiment, a turn of mind and, as
it were, habitual gesture directed toward Providence.
For a man, however, who reverences and worships it to
such a degree, he makes, I think, too frequent and too
familiar use of that mysterious intervention. He says:

"The fall of Clarendon has been ascribed to the faults of
his character, and to certain faults or checks of his policy, at
home or abroad. *This is to ignore the greatness of the causes
which decide the fates of eminent men. Providence, which imposes
upon them a task so hard, does not treat them so rigorously as
to refuse to pardon their weaknesses, and inconsiderately to over-
throw them*, on account of certain wrongs they have done, or
certain defeats of their policy. Richelieu, Mazarin, Walpole, had
their defeats, committed faults, and experienced checks as grave
as those of Clarendon. But they understood their time; the aims
and efforts of their policy were in harmony with its needs, with
the general condition and movement of minds. Clarendon was
deceived about his epoch; he did not recognize the meaning of
the great events in which he took part. . . ."

So, you appear to believe that Providence proceeds
with more ceremony when it deals with those *eminent
men* whom one calls Mazarin or Walpole, than when it

deals with simply honest private people! You leave to these last the petty causes and the paltry accidents which decide their destiny. As for the others, the real statesmen, the ambitious men of high rank, you believe that they never succumb except from motives worthy of them, — worthy of the painful sacrifice to which they subject themselves in governing us. In a word, you believe that Providence thinks twice before it causes them to fall. For myself, I believe that at the moment that it looks at the matter, a single glance and a single rule answers with it for all. But of that rule we are profoundly ignorant.

I might select again some other assertions equally absolute, equally gratuitous, and which make me doubt the intrinsic reasonableness of this imposing philosophy. But if one examines the *Discourse* with respect to the subject itself of which it treats, that is to say, the English Revolution, there is much to praise. When I question the possibility of man's attaining to the thousand distant and various causes, I am far from objecting to that order of considerations and conjectures by which, within determinate limits, one tries to connect effects with their causes. It is the noble science of Machiavelli and Montesquieu, when they both treat of the Romans. The English Revolution, considered in its proper elements and in its limits, that Revolution which presents itself to us, as it were, shut up in an enclosed field, lends itself better than any other, perhaps, to such a study, and M. Guizot is better fitted than any other person to treat it properly, without mingling with it those disputed conclusions which each one draws for himself. We might point out in his *Discourse* some portraits vigorously and saliently drawn, notably those of Monk and Cromwell. Finally,— need it be said?—the talent which shows us all this is masterly. But even when we consider only the conclusions concerning the English Revolution, the chain of causes and effects, as there set forth, will appear too extended. The author, at each decisive crisis, is not content with explaining it; he declares that it could not have taken place otherwise. It is habitual for him to say: "It was too soon . . . it was too late . . . God was beginning simply to execute his laws and to give his lessons" (page 31). What do you know about it?

Let us remain men in history. Montaigne, who loved it better than any other reading, has given us the reasons for his predilection, and they are ours. He loved, he tells us, only the simple and ingenuous historians who recounted facts without choice or selection, *in good faith;* or, among the other more learned and nobler historians, he loved only the best, those who know how to choose and to say that which is worthy of being said. But the *intermediate* ones (as he calls them) "spoil all for us; they wish to chew the mouthfuls for us; they lay down rules for judging, and consequently for bending history to their fancy; for since the judgment leans to one side, they cannot help turning and twisting the narration according to that bias." That is the rock, and a talent, even of the first order, does not save one from it. At least, an experience absolutely perfect is necessary to guard one against it, as it seems to me. The superior men, who have been acquainted with public affairs, and who have relinquished them, have a great *rôle* still to fill, but on condition that that *rôle* be quite different from the first, and that it even be no longer a *rôle*. Initiated as they have been into the secret of things, into the vanity of good counsels, into the illusion of the best minds, into human corruption, let them sometimes tell us something of these things; let them not disdain to make us touch with our finger the little springs which have often played at the greatest moments. Let them not always force (*guindent*) humanity. The lesson which springs out of history must not be direct and stiff; it must not be fired off at us point-blank, so to speak, but should sweetly exhale and insinuate itself. It should be savory, as we said lately regarding Commynes; it is a lesson entirely moral. Do not fear to show these mean things in your great pictures; the dignity will find its way into them afterward. The nothingness of man, the littleness of his most exalted reason, the inanity of that which once appeared wise, all the labor, study, talent, accomplishment, and meditation that are needed to frame even an error,—all this leads back also to a severer thought, to the thought of a supreme force; but then, instead of speaking in the name of that force which baffles us, we bow down, and history yields all its fruit.

February 4, 1850.

THE ABBE GALIANI.

IN speaking some time ago of Madame d'Épinay, I had occasion to notice the abbe Galiani, with whom that lady carried on a correspondence during the last twelve years of her life. The abbe Galiani is one of the liveliest, the most original, and the gayest figures of the eighteenth century; he wrote a good number of his works in French; he belongs to our literature as truly as any stranger naturalized among us, almost as truly as Hamilton himself. But, at the same time that he entered so well into the ideas and tastes of French society, he knew how to preserve his own manner, physiognomy, and gesture, and also an independence of thought which prevented him from abounding in any of the commonplaces of the time. He prided himself on having a way of looking at things which was peculiar to him, and such was the fact, for he did not see like anybody else. The eighteenth century, judged in the person of the abbe Galiani, reappears to us in entirely new aspects.

The abbe Ferdinand Galiani, born in the kingdom of Naples on the tenth day of December, 1728, and brought up in the city of Naples by an uncle who was an archbishop, manifested the most precocious talents for letters and for every kind of science; but, physically, he was never able to rise above four feet and a half in stature. In that little body, so well formed and so handsome, dwelt nothing but talent, grace, lively fancy, and pure wit; the gaiety of the mask covered much good sense and many profound ideas. In 1748, Galiani, at the age of twenty, became celebrated in his country by a poetic pleasantry, a funeral Oration on the public executioner who had just died; it was a burlesque parody on the Academical Eulogiums, which were far more bombastic in Italy than elsewhere. The academicians of Naples, turned into ridicule, made an uproar which increased the success of the ingenious satire. Galiani, about that time, gave himself up to the gravest studies; he published at the age of twenty-one a book upon *money;* he rendered to an illustrious savant, then very old and almost blind, — the abbe Intieri,— the service of describing in his name, in a small, substantial, and very practical treatise, a new way of *preserving grain.* He gave his attention also to antiquities and to natural history. Having made a collection of volcanic stones and other things thrown up by Vesuvius, he added to it a learned dissertation, and presented it to pope Benedict XIV, who was not ungrateful. Upon one of the boxes sent to the address of the *Most Holy Saint Peter,* Galiani took care to write these words from the Gospel: "Make these stones to become bread" (*Fac ut lapides isti panes fiant*). The amiable Benedict XIV took the hint, and, in exchange for the stones, gave Galiani a benefice. That little four-foot-and-a-half man, so gay, so foolish, so sensible, and so learned, was now a mitred abbe, and had the title of *My Lord* (*monseigneur*).

He came to Paris in 1759 as secretary of the Italian embassy, and, with the exception of certain brief absences, he resided there till 1769, that is to say, for ten years:

he considered that he had lived a true life only during that time. Distinguished from the very first day by the singularity of his stature, he at once disconcerted jeering curiosity and changed it to friendliness by the vivacity and piquancy of his repartees. He was the delight of the social circles, which appropriated him to themselves; his private friends, especially Grimm and Diderot, deeply appreciated the novelty and reach of his views and his lights: "That little being, born at the foot of Mount Vesuvius," cried Grimm, "is a true phenomenon. He joins to a luminous and profound *coup d'œil* a vast and solid erudition,— to the views of a man of genius the playfulness and charm of a man who seeks only to be amused and pleased. It is Plato with the animation and gestures of harlequin." Marmontel likewise said of him: "The abbe Galiani was personally the prettiest little harlequin that Italy had produced; but upon the shoulders of that harlequin was the head of Machiavelli." That name, harlequin, which is repeated here, is characteristic of Galiani. French-like as he was, and as he wished to be, he did not cease to be an Italian, a Neapolitan, a fact which must never be forgotten in judging of him; he had the peculiar genius of the soil, facetiousness, pleasantry, a taste for parody. In an article of his upon *Punchinello*, he represents him as born in the country, not far from the place where the *atellan* farces of antiquity had their origin. He seems to think that the spirit of those ancient farces may have been perpetuated in the modern original, and the little abbe himself had inherited something of their buffoonery and license. He had great, lofty, sublime thoughts, worthy of Vico if not of Plato, worthy of *Magna Græcia*, and suddenly these thoughts were put to flight by buffooneries, jests, fooleries, or something worse: "You see," said he pleasantly, "that I am two different men kneaded together, who, nevertheless, do not entirely occupy the room of one."

To-day the abbe Galiani loses much; we should have heard him. He did not tell his stories; he played them, he had some of the qualities of the *mime*. *Apropos* to every serious theme, in politics, in morality, and in religion, he had some apologue, some good story to tell, a lively, foolish, unexpected story, which made you *laugh yourself to tears*, as he said, and which often concealed a profound moral reflection. He made a little play of it, an acting show, bustling about, throwing himself to and fro, carrying on a dialogue in each scene with the most artless gracefulness, making the spectators, even Madame Necker and Madame Geoffrin, put up with liberties and even indecencies. He painted himself to admiration in a letter to the latter person, written at Naples. In writing it he mentally sees himself again at Madame Geoffrin's, and he depicts himself to us as he was when there in times past: "See me then as ever, the abbe, the little abbe, your *little thing*. I am seated in the comfortable arm-chair, moving my feet and arms like a demoniac, my wig awry, talking much, and saying things which one deems sublime and attributes to me. Ah, madame, what a mistake! It was not I who said so many beautiful things; your arm-chairs are so many tripods of Apollo, and I was the Sibyl. Be assured that upon chairs of Neapolitan straw I utter only stupid things." No, he did not utter stupid things; but, at Naples, the kind of talent which he had in the highest degree, was more common than at Paris; one took less notice in

Naples of the play, the action, because it was a more customary thing, and one did not know how to separate from it all the excellent and unique ideas which Galiani veiled under this guise. This gesticulating petulance which appeared so curious at first at Paris, was vulgar in Toledo street and its neighborhood; Galiani lacked *listeners* and the circle for himself alone: "Paris," he often cried in accents of despair after having quitted that city, "Paris is the only place where I am listened to." Having once retired to his own country, that country which he nevertheless loves, and of which he is one of the living curiosities, he dies of *words returned* to him unheard. Galiani is a true Neapolitan virtuoso, but one who cannot do without a Parisian auditory.

And how he was relished there! Let one be in La Chevrette at Madame d'Épinay's, at Grand Val with baron D'Holbach; if one feels a little sad, and the day lowers, if the conversation languishes, if the rain falls, the abbe Galiani enters, "and with the pleasant abbe, gaiety, imagination, wit, sportiveness, everything that causes the pains of life to be forgotten. The abbe has an exhaustless fund of sayings and pleasant sallies," adds Diderot; "he is a treasure on a rainy day. I said to Madame d'Épinay, that if they made such persons at the toy-shops, everybody living in the country would want to have one." Of these happy sayings and sallies of the abbe, he has preserved a large number. Some one was speaking of the trees in the park at Versailles, and it was remarked that they were tall, straight and slender: "*Like the courtesans*," added the abbe Galiani. Fond of music, and of exquisite music, as the Neapolitans are, as the friend of Paisiello should be, he disliked the French opera of the time, which made too much noise; and when, after the burning of the hall of the Palace-Royal, the opera had been transferred to the Tuileries, and some one complained that the hall was bad for hearing: "How happy it must be!" cried Galiani. But many people, or at least more persons than one, have these sallies which spring out of the occasion, which last but for a moment and are followed by a long silence; but with the abbe Galiani there was no silence; he sustained the conversation almost alone; he enlivened it with the maddest, merriest fancies, which were yet replete with fine good sense. In this he had no parallel in his class. Diderot, in his letters to Mademoiselle Voland, has preserved some of the abbe's good stories, that of the *porco sacro*, the apologue of the tall and fat monk in the mail-coach, the story of the archbishop counterfeiting a duchess in bed before a cardinal who visits her, and the colics of the false duchess and what follows,— in fine, a thousand untranslatable fooleries, which, narrated by Diderot himself, have remained in the state of mere rough sketches. All this is spoken, is played and improvised, but it cannot be written. The ancients had the *mimes* (little dramatic pieces) of Sophron, which have been lost; we have lost the *mimes* of Galiani. Diderot, however, has very well reported the apologue of *The Cuckoo, the Nightingale*, and *the Ass*, and one may read it in his works; but of the apologues of Galiani I prefer to repeat the one I find reported in the Memoirs of the abbe Morellet, and which is quite famous:

One day at baron D'Holbach's, after dinner, the assembled philosophers had talked of God at the top of their voices, and had said things fitted "to bring down thunderbolts upon the house a hundred times, if they ever fell for such a reason." Galiani had listened patiently to all this intrepid dissertation; finally, tired of seeing the whole company taking but one side of the question, he said:

"Gentlemen philosophers, you travel very fast; I begin by telling you that, if I were the pope, I would hand you over to the Inquisition, and, if I were king of France, to the Bastille; but as I have the happiness to be neither the one nor the other, I will come back to dinner next Thursday, and you shall hear me as I have had the patience to hear you, and I will refute you."

"*On Thursday!*" they all cried with one voice, and the challenge was accepted. Morellet continues:

"Thursday arrives. After dinner, the coffee having been taken, the abbe seats himself in an arm chair, with his legs crossed like a tailor's, as usual; and, as it is warm, he takes his wig with one hand, and gesticulating with the other, he begins nearly thus:

"'I will suppose, gentlemen, the person among you who is most thoroughly convinced that the world is the work of chance, to be playing with three dice, I do not say in a gambling-house, but in the best house in Paris, and his antagonist throwing double-sixes once, twice, three times, four times, in fine continually.

"'However short the game, my friend Diderot, if he should thus lose his money, would say without hesitation, without a moment's doubt: '*The dice are loaded;* I am in a den of thieves.'

"'Ah, philosopher! how is this? Because in ten or twelve throws the dice have fallen from the box in such a way as to make you lose six francs, you firmly believe that it is in consequence of an adroit contrivance, of an artificial combination, of a well-planned trick; and yet, when you see in this universe so prodigious a number of combinations, a thousand and thousand times more difficult, and more complicated, and more constant, and more useful, etc., you never suspect that nature's dice are also *loaded,* and that there is, up above there, a great knave (*fripon*) who makes a sport of overreaching you.'"

Morellet gives only the outline of this exposition, which from the lips of Galiani was assuredly (and one will believe it without difficulty) the most piquant thing in the world, and as good as the most amusing play.

Here are our philosophers painted from life; here we have them, like all the epicureans in the world, making a *play* of the gravest questions of destiny and human morality, a pure joust or game of their leisure hours, in which the *for* and the *against* are treated with equal levity, and yet utterly astonished afterward (I speak of those who survived, like the abbe Morellet), if one day all these doctrines burst forth, and falling upon the street, are recapitulated in Revolution Place at the festivals of Reason and the other goddesses. The people, however, only translated there the reasoning of the subtlest thinkers; they translated it coarsely, after the usual way of translators, but without much misconstruction.

Galiani, in this dispute, has the appearance of playing a noble part; he seems to plead in favor of order and the supreme Ordainer, against the dogmatic and excessively brutal atheism of his friends: let us not, however, after this facetious sermon, form too edifying an idea of his performances. He had too much acuteness and good sense not to be shocked by the absolute theories of D'Holbach: "In reality," he thought, "we do not know enough of nature to form a system of it." He accused those pretended systems of nature of destroying all the illusions that are natural and dear to man; and as D'Holbach's book appeared about the time when the abbe Terray issued a decree of bankruptcy, he said: "That M. Mirabaud (D'Holbach's pseudonym) is a true abbe Terray of metaphysics. He makes reductions and suspensions, and causes the bankruptcy of knowledge, of pleasure, and of the human mind."

In philosophy the true system of the abbe Galiani is this: he believes that man, when his mind is not too much subtleized by metaphysics and excessive reflection, lives in *illusion*, and was made to live in it: "Man," he tells us, "was made to enjoy effects without the ability to divine causes; man has five organs framed expressly to indicate to him pleasure and pain; he has not a single organ to apprise him of the truth or falsehood of anything." Galiani does not believe then in absolute truth for man, in truth worthy of the name: relative truth, which is only an *optical illusion*, is the only kind, according to him, for which man should seek. According to him, also, there is an illusion in morality as in physics; it produces results which, relatively to society and man, may be beautiful and good. It is because the human eye was fashioned so as to see the heavens round and vaulted, that man afterward invented the cupola, the dome of the temple, sustained by columns, which is a beautiful thing to see. So in morality, our internal illusions regarding liberty and the first cause have given birth to religion, morality, and law, all of which are useful things, natural to man, and even true if you please, but their truth is purely relative and wholly dependent on the configuration, on the first illusion.

We see to what such a way of looking at things leads him, in religion and morality. But if he prides himself upon being himself unaffected by illusory views and relative impressions, he is not furious to destroy those of other persons, a characteristic in which he differs essentially from his friends, the French philosophers of the eighteenth century. He would quite agree with any one who should say: "I seem to be, in life, in an apartment between the cellar and the attic. There is a flooring which conceals the girders, and, if one has means, he also puts a carpet under his feet. One tries also to adorn his ceiling, to hide the laths. If one could have upon that ceiling a beautiful fresco, a sky painted by Raphael, it would be so much the better. So with the illusions of life and its deceitful perspectives; it is necessary to respect them, and at times to be pleased with them, even when we know too well what there is beyond them."

This, in all its reality, is the theology of the abbe Galiani, and I do not give it, even when viewed from the illusory standpoint, of which he made so much, as very beautiful or consoling; the sum total, he admits, is equal to *zero*. But in his scepticism there is none of the arrogance and intrepidity of doctrine which offends us in his friends. When Madame Geoffrin fell sick, in 1776, after some devotional excesses which she had committed during the Jubilee exercises, Galiani wrote to Madame d'Épinay:

"I have mused over that strange metamorphosis (of Madame Geoffrin), and I have found that it was the most natural thing in the world. Incredulity is the greatest effort which the mind of man can make against its own instinct and its taste. He strives to deprive himself forever of all the pleasures of the imagination, of all taste for the wonderful; he tries to empty the whole sack of knowledge (and man would know all), to deny or to doubt always and to doubt everything, and to remain in an utter impoverishment of all sublime ideas, knowledge, and information. What a frightful void! what nothingness! what an effort! It is, then, demonstrated that the great majority of men, and especially of women (whose imagination is double that of man), could not be incredulous, and those who could be so, would be able to sustain the effort only while enjoying the greatest strength and youthfulness of soul. If the soul should grow old, a certain degree of credulity would reappear."

He adds also that the sceptic, he who persists in being so at all seasons, "performs a real feat; that he resembles a rope-dancer, who performs the most incredible feats in the air, vaulting about his cord; he astonishes and frightens all the spectators, and nobody is tempted to follow or imitate him." He concludes that we should never persecute true unbelievers, quiet and sincere unbelievers; wait, and do not regard them, and there is every chance that a moment will come when the effort against nature will begin to be relaxed, and the unbeliever will be such no longer.

When one heard him talk politics, one said that he was equally luminous and charming. When we read to-day the observations upon political themes that drop from his pen in his *Correspondence*, allowance must be made for the bold ideas, the paradoxes, the necessity of amusing himself, which always tormented him, his mania for predicting and prophesying, and finally for the perpetual buffooneries which are mingled with all that he writes. With him a piece of grave and profound reasoning turns suddenly into a joke. Nevertheless, amid all these faults, which to-day are very perceptible, there is much good sense, many ideas, horizons of wide extent, and vistas at every instant.

The two contemporaries with whom he was the most intimate, and with whom he had the most affinity in heart and mind, Grimm and Diderot, were his enthusiastic admirers, and spoke of him as a true genius. Galiani himself seems to have no aversion to that way of looking at him, and he does not fear to say off-hand, without guarding his language: *Montesquieu and I.* Other contemporaries seem to have been more struck with his faults. The wise and shrewd David Hume writes to the able Morellet:

"The abbe Galiani returns to Naples; he does well to quit Paris before I go there, for I should certainly have put him to death for all the ill things he has said of England. But it has turned out as his friend Caraccioli had predicted, who said that the abbe would remain two months in that country, that nobody would have a chance to speak but he, that he would not suffer an Englishman to edge in a syllable, and that on his return he would pronounce upon the character of the nation, and would continue to do so for the rest of his days, as if he had known and studied that character exclusively."

Galiani had at a certain moment a great success and a real triumph. "About the year 1750," says Voltaire, "the nation, satiated with verses, tragedies, comedies, operas, romances, romantic histories, moral reflections more romantic still, and theological disputes about Grace and convulsions, set itself at last to reasoning about *grain*. People forgot even the vines, to talk only of wheat and rye. . . ." Grain, and all that is connected with that trade, was, then, very fashionable during the sojourn of the abbe Galiani in France. Was it necessary to grant it a free exportation? Should the exportation be regulated or forbidden? The economic sect was then established, and enlightened men gave great attention and respect to these systematic views. Galiani, who was very much at home in such discussions, and who had studied these questions before coming to France, was horrified by absolute ideas upon such subjects, and, above all, by the dogmatic, trenchant, mysterious, and wearisome way in which the economists presented theirs. He set himself to reasoning and jesting on the matter. It appears that it was to some pleasantry in which he allowed himself to indulge upon this subject,— pleasantries of which M. Choiseul was the victim, and which related to the concessions which that minister had made to the new ideas,— that the abbe owed his recall from France, which had been requested of the Neapolitan Court by Choiseul himself. Be that as it may, Galiani, on leaving, shot his arrow; he left in manuscript his *Dialogues upon the Grain Trade*, which appeared in 1770, and of which Diderot revised the proofs. That was the fireworks and the bouquet with which the witty abbe brilliantly crowned the period of his Parisian life. We can form no idea to-day of the success of those Dialogues; the women doted upon them, they thought they understood them; they were then economists, as they were afterward electricians, as they had previously been believers in Grace, as they are to-day to some extent Socialists: they are always following the fashion of the day or of the morrow. These Dialogues of Galiani have been compared to the *Brief Letters* of Pascal; that is saying a good deal. They are less easy to read to-day than the *Provincial Letters*, which are themselves a little wearisome in some passages. Galiani chose the dialogue form of composition, as being the most French-like style: "That is the natural style," said he. "The language of the most social people in the world, the language of a nation which speaks more than it thinks, of a nation which needs to speak in order to think, and which thinks only in order to speak, should be the language best fitted for dialogue." With regard to the subject-matter,— in combating the absolute ideas and reasonings of the economists, Galiani aimed to give a glimpse of the political ideas which should rule and even dominate in these matters. When he said of a man: "He is an economist, and nothing more," he believed that he had pronounced sentence upon him, and excluded him from the sphere of statesmen. "He is a good man to compose memoirs, journals, or dictionaries," added he,—"to give occupation to printers and booksellers, to amuse the idle; but as to governing the state, he is good for nothing." A statesman, according to him, should not only have a thorough knowledge of special subjects, but he should also know the matter *par excellence* upon which he has to operate, that is to say, the human heart. "You are a delicate anatomist of man," says the Marquis of the Dialogues to the Chevalier. The latter replies: "That is what one should be, when one would speak of men. They must be well understood by him who presumes to govern them." He denied that Turgot himself had that knowledge and that art, and with far more reason he affirmed the same of the men of the economic school. Galiani did not have to wait for the alarm and trumpet-peal of the French Revolution, in order to distrust the optimist and rationalistic statesmen, the honest people so well known in the time of Lewis XIV and afterward, who too often forget the true, real, and always perilous circumstances of every political society. "Believe me," said he, "do not fear the rogues, nor the wicked men, for sooner or later they are unmasked; fear the honest man who is deceived; he acts in good faith, he means well, and everybody trusts him; but unhappily he is deceived concerning the means of doing good to his fellow men." Galiani's friends, and the abbe himself, were accustomed to say of his work on grain: "It is not so much a work on the Grain-Trade as a work on the Science of Government: one should know how to read the *white* in it, and *between the lines.*" The French Government charged the abbe Morellet with the task of replying to Galiani, and the former abbe, who was as tall as the other was short, as didactic and heavy with the pen as the other was light and sparkling, replied in such a way as to win no readers. He has none of the waggeries which the malicious Neapolitan, during that dispute, addressed from afar to his patient and slow adversary. Turgot, whose economic principles were very much concerned in the discussion, has given his opinion of Galiani's book, and without despising its agreeable qualities, has written some words which clearly mark the opposite nature of their views, inspirations, and doctrines. "I do not like any better," says he, after some criticisms upon Galiani's hop-and-skip method, designed to puzzle the reader, "I do not like to see him always so prudent, so hostile to enthusiasm, so very much in sympathy with all the *Ne quid nimis,* and with all those people who enjoy the present, who are very much at ease, who let the world wag, because it goes very well with them,— people who, having their bed well made, are unwilling that any one should disturb it." Turgot touches here on one of the weaknesses of the little mitred and beneficed abbe.

Galiani believed in a *secret* doctrine in everything, in a secret intention which few people are called upon to penetrate, and which even men of great talent do not suspect. He pretended, in his half-serious, half-jesting way, in which the thought is duplicated with the joke, that there are three kinds of reasonings or *resoundings* (*résonnements*): 1. The reasoning of *dunces* (*cruches*); they are, as he believed, the most ordinary kind, those of the mass of men; 2. The reasonings or *resoundings* of bells (*cloches*); these are the kind employed by many poets and orators, by people of high talents, but who, according to the abbe, are influenced too much by appearances, by the majestic and resounding forms of the human illusion. He dared to range in this class of reasonings those of Bossuet and Jean-Jacques Rousseau. 3. Finally, there are, according to him again, the reasonings of *men*, of the true sages, of those who have cracked the nut (like the abbe Galiani), and who have found that it contains nothing. I think that in his most serious moments he would have defined the sage as "he who, in the hours of reflection, disengages and divests himself completely of all relative impressions, and who accounts for his own proper accident, his own *nothing*, amidst the universality of things."

The abbe Galiani quitted Paris, no more to return, in the summer of 1769, and it is at this date that his correspondence with Madame d'Épinay begins; it is by means of her that he is reattached to his Parisian friends, and he will very often have occasion to repeat to her: "I am lost if you fail me."

This little Machiavelli, who affected a lack of feeling, who boasted that he never wept in his life, and that he had seen with dry eyes his father, mother, sister, all his friends, pass away (he calumniated himself), wept and sobbed on quitting Paris, on quitting, as he said, "that amiable nation which has loved me so much." It was necessary to tear him away from it, since of himself he never would have had strength to leave it. His entire Correspondence is but one long regret. The city of Naples, which has so many attractions for one who has seen it but once, and in which one would like to die, appeared to him but a place of exile. "Life there has a killing uniformity. What can one do with himself in a country where they dispute about nothing, *not even about religion?*" He finds occupation there, nevertheless, and of a more serious kind than he pretends. A servant of the king, Counsellor-Secretary of Commerce, he judges, or professes to judge, difficult cases; he applies himself in the intervals of duty to letters and study; he revises, corrects, and prepares new editions of his early writings: "they are all in Italian; there are dissertations, versés, prose, antiquarian researches, detached thoughts: all this writing is, indeed, very youthful, *still it is mine.*" He artlessly reveals to us, in these things of the mind, his parental tenderness. He also applies himself to new tasks; he pushes still farther his studies on Horace, upon whom he had already commented with a rare taste, sharpened with paradox; he thinks of drawing from his favorite poet a complete moral philosophy. He gives himself up, with a passion which one loves to recognize, to his Neapolitan dialect, maintaining its superiority and priority to the other Italian dialects; he compares it to the *Doric* of the Greeks. Among the celebrated poets and prose-writers in that *patois*, one would find, I imagine, more than one type of Galiani remaining in the pure state, and not cut out after the French fashion. Having become a Neapolitan again, the abbe, that he may not lose the habit, begins again to make fun of fools, the literary pedants of the town, and, under the title of *The Imaginary Socrates*, he constructs a theatrical piece, an opera bouffe, the verses of which are composed by another person, and the music by the illustrious Paisiello. The piece causes a *furore*, and it is thought that its representation must be forbidden. Amidst these mental diversions, and sports with his cat which furnishes him with a thousand occasions for philosophic and playful observations, Galiani punctiliously performs his duties as a public man and as head of a family. He has three nieces whom he does not spare in his Correspondence (*My nieces are stupid, and a cat is all the company I have*), three nieces who are demanding with a hue-and-cry to be married, and of whom he is, as he says, the *jockey*. While he seems thus to be laughing at them, he marries them in a very fatherly way. Meanwhile the poor abbe grows old, and sooner than other persons, as if in his case, owing to his extreme vivacity of spirit, everything was more rapid, — as if the scantier stuff must be more quickly consumed. He loses his teeth; he, the epicure, can no longer eat; and,— O wo above all others! — he can no longer *talk*, he stammers. "But imagine what that means, the abbe *dumb!*"

By a contradiction which is not rare, this epicurean, who will allow to men no generous springs of action, and who dissects and decomposes all that appear such, shows in his own affairs a noble, elevated soul, and all the pride of an honorable man. The ministers are successively changed; his fortune, which is good certainly, but not on a level with his talents, is impaired at the same moment. What matters it to him that his friend Sambucca becomes minister in place of Tanucci? "A minister is attached only to people who are devoted to him, and I cannot devote myself to any one; I cannot even give myself to the Devil,—*I am my own!*"

In the same way this man who affects insensibility experiences all the inquietudes of friendship; he feels its cruel pains in the losses which are his lot. It is true that the number of his genuine friends, of those to whom he is really attached and bound by secret fibres, lessens with the years. Learning through Madame d'Épinay the death of one of his Parisian friends, the Marquis of Croismare, he is astonished that he is affected less than he would have believed: "This phenomenon has astonished me,— has almost made me horrified at myself,— and I have desired to investigate its cause. It is not absence; it is not that my heart has changed or hardened; it is because one is attached to the life of another person only in the degree that he is attached to his own, and one is attached to life only in proportion to the pleasures it yields him. I understand now why peasants die tranquilly, and so stupidly see others die. A man sent to Bicêtre, to remain there forever, would hear of all the deaths in the universe without regret." This theory, which is perhaps very true, is found to be at fault in respect to him, as soon as he is confronted with a great loss, which really takes hold of the heart: he has not yet reached the state of insensibility which he imagines: "Time," he remarks, "effaces the little furrows, but the deep impressions remain. I know now who are the persons that interested me most at Paris; during my first years there I did not distinguish them." The day when he loses Madame d'Épinay, on that day only does his heart break, and his Parisian life close; Galiani the Parisian dies with her, Galiani the Neapolitan continues to vegetate. A Parisian woman, Madame du Bocage, proposed to replace Madame d'Épinay as his correspondent, in order to keep him apprised of things and persons; he refuses this diversion and alleviation, and with an accent which one cannot disregard, cries:

"There is no more happiness for me; I have lived, I have given wise counsels, I have served the state and my master, I have held the place of father to a numerous family, I have written to make my fellow-men happy; and now, at that age when friendship becomes most necessary, I have lost all my friends! I have lost all! One does not survive his friends."

Bravo! amiable abbe, it is thus that you nobly disagree with your avowed principles, with your pretense of dryness, and it is for this that one loves you!

The abbe Galiani died according to the forms and the proprieties of his cloth and his country, not without having perpetrated, even at the last hour, some pleasantry in the style of Rabelais. We might add his name to the list of celebrated men who have died jesting. He was less than fifty-nine years old when he expired, October 30, 1787.

His Correspondence with Madame d'Épinay, his true ground of recognition by us to-day, has been published in two volumes. In these letters he speaks too much of his money-matters and his postages. He wishes incessantly to appear amusing, sparkling, and he is not every day in the vein: "I am *stupid* this evening. . . . I have nothing *droll* to send you from here. . . . I am not gay to-day, and my letter will not be suitable to repeat." These expressions drop perpetually from his pen, and hurt the naturalness of his letters. There are days, we perceive, when he pinches himself to make his reader laugh. Add to this the inconvenience of frequent, incredible indecencies, even for the age of Diderot and Voltaire, and which have no precedent out of Rabelais. "Let us not yield to the delicate people," Galiani used to repeat; "I wish to be what I am, I wish to assume the tone that pleases me." He used and abused that license.

No one has ever spoken better of France, no one has ever judged it better than the abbe Galiani; one should hear him explain why Paris is the *capital of curiosity;* how "at Paris there is only *l'àpropos*"; how we speak so well of the arts and everything else, while often only half succeeding in them. On the occasion of an Exhibition at the Louvre, and I know not what criticism that had been made upon it, he said: "I remark that the ruling character of the French peeps out always. They are essentially talkers, reasoners, jesters; a bad picture brings forth a good book; thus you will speak of the arts better than you will ever practise them. It will be found at the end of the account, some ages hence, that you will have reasoned the best, and discussed the best, concerning that which all the other nations will have done best. Cherish printing, then; it is your lot in this lower world." This, however, does not prevent him, at another day, from speaking very severely of the liberty of the press which M. Turgot, it was said, thought of granting by an edict, and from wishing it very much restricted, even in the interest of the French mind, which has better play and success when under constraint. "There are empires which are handsome only in their decay," he again says of us. Finally he understands us, he loves us, he is one of our citizens, and we indeed owe to this charming abbe an honorable, choice, purely delicate burial, *urna brevis*, a little elegant urn, which should not be larger than he.

Upon it should be engraved, as an emblem, a Silenus, a head of Plato, a Punchinello, and one of the Graces.

FREDERIC THE GREAT.

THE works of Frederic have not hitherto obtained in France the high esteem they merit. People have ridiculed certain bad verses of that metromaniac prince, which are not worse, after all, than many other verses of the same time which passed for charming, and which cannot be read again to-day; and one has not paid sufficient attention to the serious works of the great man, who would not resemble other great men if he had not really set his seal to numerous pages, historical and political, which he has written, and which form a vast whole. As for the letters of Frederic, one has done them more justice; in reading in the Correspondence of Voltaire those which the king addressed to him, intermingled with those which he received in return, we find that not only do they bear the comparison very well, but that, while equal intellectually, they have also a superiority of view and of sense which is due to force of soul and of character. It is our business to-day to abandon the little ideas of a rhetoric altogether too literary, to recognize the man and the king in the writer, and to welcome him as one of the best historians we possess.

I say *we*, for it was in French that Frederic wrote, it was in French that he thought, it was the French again that he had in mind and whom he addressed in order to be read, even when he wrote down judgments and recited actions which were little fitted to please them. Frederic is a disciple of our good authors, and, in history, he is a pupil, and certainly an original and unique pupil, and in passages a proficient pupil, of the historian of the *Age of Lewis XIV.*

The negligence and incorrectness with which the works of Frederic were previously printed, had something to do with the slight esteem in which those persons seemed to hold them who are not accustomed to judge for themselves upon every subject. One cannot imagine to what an extreme the infidelity and the license of the editors had in this respect been carried. I will cite but a single example, which has remained secret till to-day. In France, in 1759, during the Seven Years' War, one had thought of printing the works of the *Sans-Souci Philosopher* (that was the title which Frederic had taken in his poems and his first literary efforts). But M. de Choiseul, minister, wrote at that date to M. de Malesherbes, director of the library, on the very subject of this project, and on the request which some Parisian publishers had made that they might print the Collection they had obtained of the Works of Frederic:*

"MARLY, December 10.

"It is important, sir, that the king's minister should not be in any degree compromised, nor suspected of having tolerated the publication of the Works of the King of Prussia. So, in case that M. Darget (*reader and secretary of the King of Prussia*) comes to speak to me of the matter, I shall earnestly assure him that I have no knowledge of the printing, and that I am going to get the king's order to prevent its being executed in France. While I am waiting for M. Darget, I hope that the publication will be made, and that all will be said . . ."

* This Collection had been printed in Prussia in 1750 and in 1752; but these two first editions, which were wholly confidential, were limited to a very few copies, destined only for the king's friends.

The publication, at once protected and clandestine, was then made; but it is curious to see how M. de Choiseul set himself to falsifying it, going so far as to point out with his own hand the details of the corrections and modifications to be introduced into it:

"It cannot be permitted" (the Collection), he wrote, "except the greatest precautions be taken that it may appear to have been printed in a foreign country, and this consideration must not be lost sight of in requiring corrections.

"For this reason I have proposed but two sorts of corrections; one sort, those which may be made without one's perceiving them in reading the text. As these changes relate only to some impieties of the most decided character, or to strictures upon great personages, there is no reason to fear that the king of Prussia will complain that the text has been altered, and the public will not be able to discover it. But in suppressing passages, I have carefully avoided making any substitutions; that would be a censurable infidelity.

"The other corrections are the suppressing of proper names, the place of which you will supply with points or stars. This is no more what I call an infidelity, than are the other changes. It is, perhaps, even a regard for the king of Prussia."

One sees that the minister who drove away the Jesuits knew how to practice shuffling when necessary, and secretly to alter a text while declaring that it was not an infidelity. Later, in the publication of the posthumous historic writings of the king of Prussia, exactness, for a thousand reasons, was no better observed, and one may say, in considering the edition which is published to-day at Berlin by order of the Prussian government, and in comparing it with its predecessors, that the works of Frederic appear to-day for the first time in a text that is authentic and worthy of recognition.

The edition undertaken by the Prussian government, and which will comprise not less than thirty quarto volumes, is monumental. It is thus that one day, and soon, France should publish the works of Napoleon, works to-day scattered, or collected without method and without order; not falsified, but, in general, printed almost as negligently as have hitherto been those of Frederic. The monument of Napoleon's tomb will not be complete till one shall have added to it the national edition of his works. Be this as it may, the Prussian government and the reigning king have thought that their honor was concerned in publishing a complete collection of the writings of the man who was altogether the greatest king and the first historian of his country. Some clever savants have been charged with the execution of this project; M. Preuss, historiographer of Brandenburg, is at their head. The historic portion of Frederic's works has justly had precedence over the other writings; it forms seven volumes, of which five are before me. I have made their acquaintance, and I have examined them with all the care of which I am capable.

That I may not have to come back to these details of editions, I may be permitted at the outset to make two or three remarks. The text, typographically, is admirable. The titles are in the highest taste; the portraits are fine: I find nothing to disapprove but the kind of vignettes which terminate the pages at the ends of the chapters, and which make this royal volume resemble at times a book of illustrations: these embellishments, of which the subject is often enigmatical, are not in keeping with the monumental gravity of the edition. As for the text, I have said that it is for the first time exact and faithful; many bold thoughts have been restored, many energetic and vivid phrases which the prudence or the literary prudery of the first editors had effaced or softened. I could have wished, however, that one had not pushed his scrupulousness so far as carefully to restore faults of grammar. Of what use is it, for example, to make the king say that M. du Lowendal *was* marched to a certain point, instead of saying that he *had* marched? Frederic, before publishing his work, would have had these trifles corrected by some of his French academicians at Berlin. Another fault of this edition, and a grave fault, is that it lacks strategic maps and plans of places, which renders the reading of these campaigns tedious and sterile to the majority of readers. Why not join to these histories of Frederic an atlas expressly prepared, of the same kind as that which M. Thiers has executed for his History of Napoleon? Finally, if it is permissible to enter into these minutiæ, which do not fail to have their importance with the reader, I will complain, in the name of France, that there does not exist in Paris a single complete copy of the volumes thus far published. The National Library has but five volumes; the Library of the Institute does not possess one of them. The king of Prussia, who distributes this magnificent edition, has forgotten our Institute of France in his largesses. It is there that the great Frederic would have begun.*

I have said all I wish touching these details, which are in some sort external, and I come from them to the great man whom one is happy in being able at length to study more closely and with confidence in his successive acts and writings. Frederic, in spite of the wrong he has done himself by some of his rhapsodies and speeches,

* Along with the great quarto edition, there is published one of smaller size, for the use of common readers; this small edition, which is sold, is easier to find.

by the placarded cynicism of his impieties and jeers, by that versifying mania which always provokes a smile, is a really great man, one of those rare geniuses who are manifestly born to be the chiefs and leaders of the peoples. When we strip his person of all the anecdotal drolleries upon which the light-minded feast, and when we go straight to the man and to the character, we pause with admiration and with respect; we recognize at the first instant, and at every step we take with him, a superior and a master, firm, sensible, practical, active, and indefatigable, inventive in proportion to his necessities, penetrating, never duped, deceiving as little as possible, constant in all fortunes, governing his personal affections and passions by patriotic sentiment and zeal for the greatness and advantage of his nation; enamored of glory, while judging it; vigilantly careful and jealous of the amelioration, honor, and well-being of the populations which are entrusted to him, even at the very time when he has little esteem for men.

Of Frederic as a captain, it does not belong to me to judge; but, if I have well understood the observations which Napoleon has made on Frederic's campaigns, and the simple recitals of Frederic himself, it seems to me that he was not chiefly a warrior. He has nothing, on that side, very brilliant or fascinating at first view. Often beaten, often at fault, his greatness is shown in learning through trials; especially in repairing his faults or those of fortune by coolness, tenacity, and an immovable evenness of soul. Whatever eulogium good judges may pass upon his battle of Leuthen, and on some of his great manœuvres and operations, they have still more criticisms to make on many and many an occasion. "He was great especially in critical moments," said Napoleon; "it is the finest eulogium one can pass upon his character." This moral character it is which is conspicuous in Frederic as a warrior, and which transcends his martial greatness; it was the case of a strongly-tempered soul and a great mind applying itself to war because it must do so, rather than the case of a born warrior. He had neither the rapid and lightning-like (*foudroyante*) valor of a Gustavus Adolphus or a Condé, nor that transcendent geometrical faculty which characterized Napoleon, and which that powerful genius applied to war with the same ease and the same aptitude that Monge applied it to other objects. Endowed with a superior genius, with a character and a will in unison with his genius, Frederic applied himself to the military art as he applied himself to many other things, and he was not slow in excelling it, in possessing himself of it, in perfecting his command of its instruments and means, although it was not, perhaps, at first, a calling for which his genius fitted him, and he was not in his proper element.

Nature had made him, before all things else, to reign, to be a king, with all the functions which that lofty employment demands; and war being one of the most indispensable of these functions, he devoted himself to it and he mastered it. "One must catch the spirit of his calling," he wrote in jest to Voltaire, amid the Seven Years' War. This has the air of a joke only, yet it is true. In Frederic the will and the character directed the mind in everything.

Generally one did not perceive in any of the qualities of Frederic that primal freshness which is the brilliant sign of the singular gifts of nature and of God. All, in him, seems the conquest of will and deliberation acting upon a universal capacity, which they lead hither or thither, according to different exigencies. He is clearly the great king of his time; he has the stamp of the age of analysis.

One has sought to establish a contradiction between the conversations and writings of Frederic, as an adept in philosophy, and his actions as king and conqueror. I do not find this contradiction so great as some have wished to make out. I lay aside certain essays and certain sallies of Frederic, when very young and prince-royal; but, from the very moment that he understood his part as king, I find him true. And I do not see, for example, in the histories which he has written, a single word which he has not justified in his conduct and in his life. He says:

"A prince, in my opinion, is the first servant and the first magistrate of the State; he should account to it for the use which he makes of the imposts. He raises them that he may be able to defend the State with the troops he maintains; in order to defend the dignity with which he is clothed, to recompense services and merit, to establish in some way an equilibrium between the rich and the debtor classes, to comfort in every way the unhappy of every class, to invest with magnificence all that interests the body of the State in general. If the sovereign has an enlightened mind and a heart that is right, he will direct all his expenditures to the promotion of the public good and the greatest advantage of the people."

This is what Frederic almost always really did, in peace and in war, and he varied from this policy as little as possible. After making every deduction for his faults, for his ambitious acts, and for his personal misdeeds, the sum and substance of his policy remains still what we have just seen, and what he has so well described. To judge him as a politician, we must get rid of the French point of view, of the French illusions, and of what is left to us of the atmosphere of the Choiseul ministry. Open once more Frederic's Memoirs; in writing them he never seeks to varnish the truth. I know of no man who, when he takes his pen, is less a charlatan than he; he gives his reasons, without any coloring whatever; "a borrowed part," he thought, "is difficult to sustain; a person can never well be anybody but himself." In writing the history of his house under the title of *Memoirs of Brandenburg*, he gives us the meaning, the first inspiration, the key of his actions. Prussia had not come really to count for anything in the world, and to put, as he says, its *grain* into the political balance of Europe, till the time of the Great Elector, which corresponded with the prosperous days of Lewis XIV. In reciting the history of that clever and brave sovereign, who to the mediocre fortune of an Elector knew how to unite the heart and the merit of a great king,— in speaking to us of that prince, "the honor and the glory of his house, the defender and the restorer of his country," who was greater than his sphere of action, and from whom his posterity reckon,— Frederic has evidently found his ideal and his model; what the Great Elector was, as simply a prince and member of the Empire, Frederic will be to it as king.

This title, this appellation of king, which was given only to the son of the Great Elector, and, as it were, by grace, appears rather to have degraded than to have exalted the Prussian name. The first Frederic who bore it, a slave to ceremony and etiquette, had rendered the title of Majesty almost ridiculous in his person; he was crushed by it. That first king of Prussia, by his entire life of vain pomp and display, said, without knowing it, to his posterity: "I have acquired the title, and I am proud of it; it is for you to render yourselves worthy of it." The father of Frederic, of whom the son, who was so maltreated by him, has spoken so admirably, and with sentiments not filial, but truly loyal and magnanimous, — that rough, economical, avaricious father, the persecutor of his family and the idolater of discipline, that praiseworthy man, who "had a laborious soul in a robust body," had restored to the Prussian State the solidity which, through the inflation and vanity of the first king, it had lost. But that was not enough; Frederic's father, estimable as he was, in many respects, when closely viewed, was not respected at a distance; even his moderation and the simplicity of his manners had been prejudicial to him. People regarded his twenty-four thousand troops as a parade-show, and as a corporal's grandiose madness. Prussia was not counted among the European powers, and when Frederic, at the age of twenty-eight (1740), mounted the throne which he was to occupy for forty-six years, he had everything to do for his own and the nation's honor; he had to create the Prussian honor, he had to win his spurs as king.

His first thought was that a prince should make his person, and above all, his nation, respected; that moderation is a virtue which statesmen must not always practice strictly, on account of the corruption of the age, and because, when there is a change of reign, it is more expedient to give proofs of firmness than of mildness. He says again, and he tells us frankly, that "Frederic (his grandfather), in erecting Prussia into a kingdom, had, by that vain display, planted a germ of ambition in his posterity, which would sooner or later fructify. The monarchy which he had left to his descendants was, if I may be permitted to explain myself thus (it is always Frederic that speaks), a kind of *hermaphrodite*, which partook more of the electorate than of the kingdom. There was glory in *deciding that condition of things;* and that sentiment was surely one of those which strengthened the king in the great enterprises in which so many motives engaged him." He tells us these motives, and why he anticipated the House of Austria, instead of waiting for it, and letting himself be struck or humbled. He will explain with the same clearness and the same frankness the motives which led him to get the start of his enemies at the beginning of the Seven Years' War, and which decided him to appear the aggressor without being such. These motives, all drawn from the interest of his cause and of his nation, seem in no respect discordant with the maxims of Frederic and with his favorite ideas as philosopher and writer. Knowing men and the things of the world, as he did, he very properly felt that one is not permitted to be a bit of a philosopher upon the throne until he has proved that he knows how to be something else besides. He was not in a humor to play the good-natured part of a Stanislaus. To be more surely a shepherd of his own people, he began by showing to other peoples that he was a lion. All that he willed, he did; he boldly disentangled the position and the function of Prussia, created a counter-weight to the House of Austria, and established in northern Germany a focus of civilization, a centre of culture and of toleration. It is for his successors to maintain it, and to be faithful, if they can, to his designs.

All the persons who have praised Frederic, have made

a reservation touching Poland and the Partition of 1773, which he provoked and by which he profited. Here, as the Polish question is one of those that cannot be treated conveniently and with entire impartiality, I will beg leave to be silent. There is in that Polish name, and in the misfortunes which are associated with it, a remnant of magic which sets men in a flame. Frederic, however, never changed his opinion regarding the character of the Poles as a people: that opinion is energetically expressed in ten passages in his histories, and long before the idea of a partition occurred to him.

In that affair, however, and whatever was the fact regarding the motives which he has himself exposed in all their nakedness, he violated that which the ancients called *the conscience of the human race*, and he took part in one of those scandals which always shake the confidence of the peoples in the protective law of societies. He forgot his own maxim: "The reputation of a knave is as dishonorable to the prince himself, as disadvantageous to his interests." But here the considerable interest of the moment and of the future, the instinct of natural enlargement, won the day. In that, again, he was not so inconsistent as one would believe him to be. His delicacy as a philosopher was not such that it could not accommodate itself to these political procedures. While he had sentiments of relative justice and even of humanity, Frederic, like all his age, was absolutely wanting in ideality; he did not believe in anything that was better than himself. He governed and earnestly cared for the men who were entrusted to his keeping; he made this duty a matter of honor and dignity; but he did not place it upon any deeper foundation. We touch here upon the radical vice of that wisdom of Frederic's, I mean irreverence, *irreligion*. The cynical railleries of his conversations and letters are well known: he had the capital fault, for a king, of jesting, of jeering at everything, even at God. The love of glory was the only thing about which he never jested.*

Strange inconsistency and protest of a noble nature! for if the human race is so foolish and so worthy of contempt, and if there is no thing or person above it, why go and devote body and soul to the idea of glory, which is nothing else than the desire and expectation of the highest esteem among men? It is inconceivable that, looking at everything, as he did, from the higher standpoint of the State and the social interest, Frederic should have regarded religion as one of those neutral grounds where people may meet for after-dinner pastimes and pleasantries. He forgot that he himself, writing to Voltaire, had said: "Every man has in him a ferocious beast; few know how to chain him; the majority let him loose, when fear of the law does not restrain them." His nephew, William of Brunswick, permitted himself one day to show him the inconsistency there was in thus relaxing the religious ties which restrain the ferocious beast. "Oh! against the rascals," replied Frederic, "I have the hangman, and that is quite enough." No, that is not enough; when one has the hangman only, it is insufficient. It is at this point especially that the estab-

* One of the most competent judges, one of the assistants of M. Preuss in the preparation of the works of Frederic, M. Charles de La Harpe, writes to me in regard to this subject: "There are two other things also concerning which he never jested, the *love of country* and *friendship*. This mocking hero is the tenderest and most faithful of friends, and one knows that his passion for his country was such that he deprived himself of everything that he might be able to alleviate its miseries and endow Prussia with useful institutions."

lishment of Frederic fails and is imperilled; he could be a great organizer, he was not a legislator.

But, even setting aside the sovereign's interest, it is offensive to see a great man sully his name by pleasantries of this kind regarding objects which are respectable in the eyes of the great majority; it was, to a certain degree, a violation of the hospitable toleration in which he gloried, thus openly to despise that which he professed to welcome and tolerate. It betrays a relic of native bad taste and of northern coarseness, and one could say with just severity of the letters of Frederic: "There are vigorous and great thoughts, but, close by them, we see beer and tobacco stains upon these pages of Marcus Aurelius." Frederic, who had respect for heroes at least, has said: "Since pious Æneas and the crusades of Saint-Louis, we have seen no example in history of devout heroes." *Devout*, it is possible, taking the word strictly; but religious, one may say that heroes have almost always been; and John Muller, the illustrious historian, who so well appreciated the merits and great qualities of Frederic, was right in his conclusion concerning him, when he wrote: "Frederic wanted only the highest degree of culture, religion, which completes humanity, and humanizes all greatness." *

I will say no more of Frederic to-day, except as a historian. His histories are composed of *Memoirs of Brandenburg*, which contain all that we need to know of the

* M. Henry, pastor of the French church at Berlin, has written a dissertation in which he treats of Frederic's irreligion; without pretending to absolve him in this matter, the worthy writer believes that there has been a great deal of exaggeration of that French side of Frederic, by which he flattered the philosophers of the eighteenth century. He seeks to show that Frederic himself, with a kind of swagger, took pleasure in exaggerating it. M. Henry thinks that this irreligious mockery of Frederic transpired chiefly

Prussian annals anterior to his accession; and four other works, which contain the history of his time and of his reign from 1740 to 1778. The history of the Seven Years' War is one of these four compositions, and that by which he naturally takes a place between Napoleon and Cæsar.

The *Memoirs of Brandenburg* are the only portion which appeared in his life-time. From the preface it is plain that we have to do with a lofty and firm spirit, that has the noblest and soundest ideas upon the class of subjects he handles. "A man," he says, "who does not believe that he has fallen from heaven, who does not date the world's epoch from the day when he was born, must be curious to know what has passed in all times and in all countries." Every man must, at least, care for what has passed before his time in the country which he inhabits. In order that this knowledge may be really profitable, one condition is indispensable,— truth. Frederic wishes for truth in history: "a work written without freedom can be only mediocre or bad." He will speak the truth, then, about persons, about another's ancestors as about his own. But he believes that he should record, touching every matter, only that which is memorable and useful. He gives no heed to curiosities. He leaves to the professors in *us*, fascinated with learned minutiæ, to know of what stuff was the coat of Albert surnamed *Achilles*. He is firmly of opinion that a thing does not deserve to be written except so far as it deserves to be remembered.

on the surface of his soul; that, in yielding himself to it, he yielded chiefly to a bad tone of society, thinking that it would never come to the public knowledge, but that the basis of his royal nature was serious, meditative, and worthy of a legislator who comprehends and would provide for the fundamental needs of every society and of every nation. In a complete and impartial appreciation of Frederic, it is well to take note of the facts to which M. Henry calls attention, and of the point of view to which he refers them.

He runs rapidly over the barbarous and sterile times, and over those of his ancestors of whom one knows only the names or some insignificant dates. "It is with histories," he says, "as with rivers, which become important only at the place where they begin to be navigable." He chooses the French in preference to every other language, because it is, he says, "the most polished and the most widely-diffused language of Europe, and because it appears in some way to have been fixed by the good authors of the age of Lewis XIV." He might have added, because it is the fittest to express the thoughts of a clear-headed, bold, sensible, and resolute genius.

All the little biographies of the primitive Electors, of whom there is nothing great to be said, are sketched with sobriety and with a severe taste. A few sarcasms thrown out by the way, some philosophical sallies, mark the pupil of Voltaire; but these pleasantries are hasty ones, and do not here derogate from the general tone. That tone is simple and manly, and the narration is enriched with curious but forcible reflections, which reveal the chain of causes. When he comes to the epochs of the Reformation and the Thirty Years' War, the historian-king characterizes those great events in a few words, by their general traits and in their real principles; he never fails to distinguish the essential things from the accessories. When he recounts the horrors and the devastations which signalized those sad periods of history, he shows sentiments of humanity and order, sentiments of good administration which are perfectly unaffected, and which he will justify. I have said that the type which he proposes for imitation, the man from whom he justly dates the greatness of his house, is Frederic-William, called *the Great Elector*, he who began to rule Brandenburg at the end of that disastrous Thirty Years' War "which had made of the Electorate a frightful desert, in which one recognized the villages only by the heaps of ashes which prevented the grass from growing in them." He enlarges upon this reign with complacency; he goes so far even as to dare establish a parallel between that little northern prince and Lewis XIV in his glory: saving two or three passages, which are a little flowery and too mythological, saving a slight oratorical accent which betrays itself here and there, this comparison forms a fine page of history, and one that is really noble in tone. It is to be noted that Frederic, in writing, while he is severe in style, is less sober than Cæsar and even than Napoleon; he does not refuse the use of art, especially in that first history of which Gibbon could say that it was *well written*. Having to narrate the campaign of 1679, in which the Great Elector, in midwinter, drove out the Swiss, who had invaded Prussia, he will say: "The retreat resembled a rout; of sixteen thousand Swedes, which they numbered, hardly three thousand returned to Livonia. They had entered Prussia like Romans; they left it like Tartars."

He has sayings which sum up a complete judgment upon men and upon nations. In the portraits of his grandfather, the first Frederic, son of the Great Elector, who was so little like his father, he will say to mark the pomp of that king, who had no less than a hundred chamberlains: "His ambassadors were as magnificent *as those of the Portuguese.*"

His judgments of men are profound and decisive. To heroes he has a visible attraction; he speaks only with respect, and with a deep fraternal instinct, of the Gustavus-Adolphuses, of the Marlboroughs, of the Eugenes; but he is not deceived in regard to greatness, and does not waste words upon it: queen Christiana and her capricious abdication appear to him only whimsical; the duel between Charles XII and Peter the Great at Pultowa appears to him a duel of two of *the most singular men of their century.* Foreigner though he is, he knows how to choose his expressions like a just mind that fits or bends language to its thought. Of that same Peter the Great he will say elsewhere with energy: "Peter I, to govern his nation, worked upon it like aquafortis upon iron."

For painting statesmen and ministers he has those well-chosen and authoritative words which are historical in advance, and which grave themselves on the memory. Wishing to characterize the too vast and too restless genius of cardinal Alberoni, and his too fiery imagination, he says: "If one had given Alberoni two worlds like ours to turn topsy-turvy, he would still have demanded a third." The portraits of the eminent persons whom he knew and managed, are thrown off with the hand of a master, and, as it were, by a man who was clever at this business, and endowed with a natural aptitude for seizing upon vices or ridiculous traits. To give an idea of general Seckendorff, who served at the same time both the Emperor and Saxony, he says: "He was sordid-minded; his manners were coarse and rustic; lying was so habitual to him, that he had lost the use of truth.* It was the soul of a usurer, which passed sometimes into the body of a soldier, and sometimes into that

* This trait recalls the portrait which Xenophon, in his *Retreat of the Ten Thousand*, has traced of Meno, who had come, in the way of lying, even to look upon truthful persons as *ill-bred* persons, *without education.*

of a negotiator." And observe that all this is not after the portrait style, as in histories more or less literary, where the historian stations himself before his model: it is said on the spur of the moment, as if by a business man who thinks aloud and talks.

When he enters upon the affairs of his own time, those which he has directed and in which he has coöperated, Frederic keeps the same tone, or rather he speaks with even more simplicity than in his History of Brandenburg. In speaking of himself, he is neither haughty nor modest; he is true. In speaking of others, even of his greatest enemies, he is just. At the beginning of his reign, narrating that conquest of Silesia which roused the anger of so many persons, and which succeeded at once to his wishes, he discloses his motives nakedly; he indicates his faults and his *schools* in war. Along with measures and calculations dictated by a far-sighted boldness, he recognizes what he owes to "opportunity, that mother of great events," and he is careful to make allowance in every affair for the part which fortune plays:

"That which contributed the most to that conquest," says he, "was an army which had been formed during twenty-two years by an admirable discipline, and which was superior to the rest of the soldiery of Europe (*note the homage to his father*); some true citizen generals, some wise and incorruptible ministers; *and finally a certain good fortune which often waits upon youth and denies itself to advanced age*. If that great enterprise had failed, the king would have passed for a rash prince, who had undertaken what he had not strength to accomplish; success caused him to be regarded as clever as well as lucky. Really it is only fortune which determines reputation; he whom she favors is applauded; he whom she disdains is blamed."

The History of the Seven Years' War is admirable for its simplicity and truth. The author does not limit himself to strategic operations,— he depicts the Courts of Europe during that time. In reciting the events of the war, he is sober, rapid, not entering into personal details, except in a few cases, where he cannot help paying a tribute of gratitude to his brave troops or to some valiant companion in arms. I recommend the reading of the sixth chapter, which treats of the campaign of 1757, that campaign so full of vicissitudes and reverses, in which Frederic, reduced to despair, won his easy and brilliant victory of Rossbach, and his masterly and *classic* victory of Leuthen. If we join to this narrative, so noble and so simple, the letters which he wrote to Voltaire during the same period, we shall see Frederic at the most brilliant time, at the crisis from which he came forth with the most heroic and glorious perseverance. It is here that we truly recognize the philosopher and the stoic in the warrior. The gravest reproach which he makes against the Austrian Court is that "it follows the brute instincts of nature; puffed up in prosperity and cringing in adversity, it never has been able to attain to that wise moderation which renders men impassive to the blessings and the ills which chance dispenses." For himself, he is resolved, in the greatest extremities, never to yield to chance or to *brute nature*, but to persevere so well in the path of great souls that he will finally make Fortune blush with shame.

On coming out of this war, in which so much blood was spilled, and after which everything was placed upon its former footing, saving the devastations and the ruins, Frederic loves to dwell upon the futility and emptiness of human schemes: "Does it not seem astonishing," he says, "that all that is most refined in human prudence, joined to force, is often the dupe of unexpected events or of sudden chances? and is it not plain that there is a certain *I know not what*, which sports contemptuously with the projects of men?" One recognizes here a recollection of Lucretius in some of his finest verses: *Usque adeo res humanas vis abdita quædam.* . . . Napoleon, undertaking the campaign of 1812, wrote to the Emperor Alexander: "I understood that its lot was cast, and that that invisible Providence, whose rights and empire I recognize, had decided upon this matter as upon so many others." It is the same thought; but there is in Napoleon's reflection a flash more of inspiration, there is, so to speak, a mysterious reflection brought back from Tabor, which the thought of Frederic lacks. That accomplished king needed to mount one step more upon the height to receive on his brow the ray that gilds and that also which dazzles.

Frederic, nevertheless, reads the human heart rightly, and shows himself to be a just moral observer and a practical prophet when he adds:

"Time, which heals and effaces all ills, will soon, no doubt, give back to the Prussians their abundance, their prosperity and their first splendor; the other powers will likewise reëstablish themselves; then other ambitious men will stir up new wars, and cause new disasters; for that is the peculiarity of the human mind, that examples correct nobody; the follies of fathers are lost upon their children; every generation must commit its own."

Perhaps at another day I shall speak of Frederic as a dilettante, a lover of the Fine Arts and of Belles-Lettres. I have also some unpublished details thereupon, which, on occasion, will serve me as a pretext.

December 2, 1850.

II.

I HAVE tried in the preceding essay to set forth Frederic, as king and politician, in his highest and truest character, — the historic, not the anecdotal Frederic. It is thus that he himself thought that great men should be finally judged,— without amusing ourselves with the accessories, — by rising to the point which governs their contradictions and their caprices. The inner and private life of Frederic, however, is fully known; every part of his character has been revealed; we have his letters, his verses, his pamphlets, his whims and facetiæ, his secret disclosures of every kind; he did nothing to suppress them, and it is impossible not to recognize in him another very essential person, which is at the man's very heart. One may say that if, in Frederic, the great king was duplicated by a philosopher, he was also complicated with a man of letters.

The great cardinal Richelieu was so too; to have composed a fine tragedy would have been a thing almost as sweet to his heart, and would have appeared to him a work almost as glorious, as to triumph over the Spaniards, and to maintain the allies of France in Germany; the laurels of the *Cid* would not let him sleep. At the close of the Seven Years' War, when D'Alembert went to visit Frederic at Potsdam, and spoke to him of his glory,—" He told me with the greatest simplicity," writes D'Alembert,"that there was a fearful deduction to be made from that glory; that chance counted in it almost for all; and that he would much rather have composed *Athalie* than have waged all that war." There is certainly something of the philosopher in this way of judging military triumphs; but there is always something of the man of letters in the preference thus given to *Athalie*. I know not whether Frederic would not have contradicted himself, in case an evil genius had taken him at his word, and he had really had to choose between the Seven Years' War and *Athalie;* or rather I am very sure that the king, in the end, would have won the day; but the poet's heart would have bled within him, and it suffices for us, to qualify him as we do, that he could have hesitated for a single instant.

When we study Frederic in his writings, in his Correspondence, especially that which he had with Voltaire, we recognize, it seems to me, an evident fact: there was a man of letters preëxisting in him before all, before even the king. What he was before everything else, naturally, and so to speak, most unaffectedly and primitively, was still a man of letters, a *dilettante*, a virtuoso, with a lively taste for the arts, with especially a passionate worship of genius. He had only to abandon himself to his inclinations to overflow in that direction. His position as king, his love of honorable glory, and the great capacity with which he was endowed, directed him to other employments, which had for their aim social utility and the greatness of the nation: he thought that "a good mind is susceptible of all sorts of forms, and that it brings the proper aptitudes to everything it would undertake. *It is like a Proteus which changes its form without difficulty, and which appears really to be the object it represents.*" Thus he appeared to have been born for everything he had to do as king; he was up to the height of his task. "The strength of States," he thought, "consists in the great men to whom nature seasonably gives birth in them." He wished to be and he was one of those great men; he worthily fulfilled his function as a hero. The nation which the Great Elector had sketched before him, he formed and completed by giving it a body and by impressing it with unity of spirit; Prussia did not really exist till it went out from his hands. Such is the part of the great Frederic in history; but, at heart, his secret or even slightly secret tastes, his real delights, were to reason upon every subject, to follow out his thoughts as a philosopher, and also to cast them upon paper, whether seriously or in jest, as a rhymer and a writer.

He had been educated by a Frenchman named Duhan, a man of merit, who had inspired him with love for our language and literature. He had been initiated, after a kind of tradition which was yet correct enough, by the French refugees in Berlin. That desire of glory which nourished the young soul of Frederic, and which sought also its object, made him naturally turn his eyes toward France. The age of Lewis XIV, now completed, gradually extended its influence over all Europe. Brandenburg was slower than the other nations; there was nothing astonishing in that; but Frederic felt humiliated by it, and he believed that it was for him to inaugurate that new era of Renaissance in the North. While his father lived, this purely literary desire of Frederic prevailed over his other thoughts, and engaged him in some proceedings, some advances, in which the future king forgot himself a little. He was prince-royal and twenty-four years old when he began the Correspondence with Voltaire (1736). Voltaire was living then at Cirey, with Madame du Châtelet. He received from the young prince of Prussia, not a complimentary letter, but a real passionate declaration. One may smile to-day at that first letter, so awkward, and more than half Teutonic, in which Frederic mingles his admiration for Wolff with his admiration for Voltaire, and in which he speaks to the latter in the name of human kindness, and talks of the "*support which you offer*," says he, "*to all those who devote themselves to the arts and sciences.*" Through this singular style of Frederic's first letters the noblest thought finds its way. Looking at Voltaire from afar, and judging of him by his works alone, embracing him with that youthful enthusiasm which it is honorable to have felt at least once in one's life, Frederic proclaims him the only heir of the great age which has just ended, "the greatest man in France, and a mortal who does honor to speech." He admires him and salutes him, as Vauvenargues will soon likewise salute him, without getting a glimpse of the faults of the man, simply on account of the beauties of his mind and the graces of his language. He declares himself, consequently, to be his disciple, his disciple not only in his writings but in his actions; for, deceived by the distance and by the gilded mists of youth, he sees in him almost a Lycurgus or a Solon, a legislator and a sage.

Do not, however, be too ready to smile at this. Never has one more clearly perceived than that young prince what literature might be in its highest inspiration, how much it contains that is elevated and useful, and how much of its glory is durable and immortal. "I count it as one of the greatest blessings of my life that I was born a contemporary of a man who has so distinguished a merit as yours." This sentiment breaks out in all this phase of the Correspondence. Voltaire is charmed, Voltaire is complimentary; he thanks, he praises, he enchants;

we should not say truly that he is secretly laughing, and doubtless he did not then laugh much, at certain solecisms and swelling tones' which often accompanied these northern praises. According to him that young prince makes verses *like Catullus in the time of Cæsar;* he plays upon the flute like *Telemachus;* he is *Augustus-Frederic Virgil.* Enough, replies Frederic, who has the advantage here in respect to good sense and good taste, morally speaking: "I am, I assure you, neither a species of great man nor a candidate for greatness. I am but a simple individual who is known only to a small part of the continent, and whose name, according to all appearances, will serve only to decorate some genealogical tree, to fall afterward into obscurity and oblivion." Such is his self-judgment, and he was right at that date; this man of twenty-five feels that he is nothing yet, and that he has not even made a beginning. "When persons of a certain rank," he remarks, "complete half of a career, people award them the prize which others do not receive till they have finished it." He is indignant at this difference in standards, as if one deemed princes to be of an inferior nature to other men, and less capable of an entire action.

One day Voltaire has the impudence to say to him that he, Frederic, writes better French than Lewis XIV, that Lewis XIV was ignorant of orthography, and other wretched things of that kind; as if Lewis XIV was not one of the men in his kingdom who spoke the best, and as if one of the greatest praises that could be given to that excellent writer, Pellisson, was not his having been on more than one occasion the worthy Secretary of Lewis XIV. Here, again, Frederic checks Voltaire, and gives him a lesson in tact: "Lewis XIV," says he, "was a prince great in an infinity of ways; a solecism, an orthographical error, could not sully in the least his reputation, established by so many deeds which have immortalized him. He had the right in every sense to say: *Cæsar est supra grammaticam.* I am not great in any way. It is only my application which may one day, perhaps, make me useful to my country; and that is all the glory to which I aspire." One loves to meet, amid the insipidities and occasional ridiculous extravagances in this beginning of the Correspondence, more than one of these passages in which the future king already peeps out,— the superior man, who, although he has the *rage* for rhyming and for producing his first works, will know how to triumph over it by a higher passion, and who will never be a rhetorician on the throne. In everything, even in these plays of the mind, Frederic always ends by laying the greatest stress on action, on social utility, and the country's good; he is a genius who amuses himself while waiting for something better, who will continue to amuse himself and to make merry in the intervals of the roughest toils, but who will always aspire, by force of a firm will, to reach a practical and useful greatness. There is a time for him to laugh, to play the flute, to make verses, and a time to reign. The man of letters may sometimes balance the king, and frolic before him, but it is only to give way to him, when it is necessary, at the precise hour. One may say of him that never did one of his talents, never did one of his passions or even of his manias, interfere with one of his duties.

Considered as matters of taste, there were many things to be noticed. The rude and slightly coarse nature of the Vandal betrayed itself in Frederic even athwart the intellectual man and the *dilettante* eager to learn and to please. It is not merely language and expression which fail him here and refuse to obey; it is often delicate tact which is wanting. Every time he speaks to Voltaire of Madame du Châtelet, he finds it very hard to avoid being ridiculous: "I respect the ties of friendship too much," he writes to Cirey, "to wish *to tear you away from the arms of Emily.*" When he wishes to be polite, it is with this levity. Frederic can think of nothing more graceful than to send as a present to Voltaire a bust of Socrates, the sage who was preëminently patient; which would have looked like an epigram, if at that time he had better known his poet. But that Socrates recalls to Frederic Alcibiades, and hence more than one equivocal and dangerous allusion, in which, however, Voltaire does not disdain to participate. All this savors of the Goth and the Horule, who have great minds, but minds whose polish is only superficial, and in which more than one corner is not polished at all. That rough diamond will require some time to disengage itself from its matrix.

Nevertheless Frederic improved rapidly; he improves visibly in this Correspondence, and there comes a time when he masters and manages his French prose in a way to challenge the criticism of Voltaire. As to his verses, we must despair of him; for this form of expression, his throat will always remain hoarse and hard, and he will never correct himself. He will say, for example, without difficulty:

"Les myrtes, les lauriers, soignés dans ces cantons
  Attendent *que, cueillis* par les mains d'Émilie, . . ."

or, again:
  "Que vous dirai-je, O tendre Ovide?
  Vous *dédidtes l'Art d'aimer.*"

These are his smallest faults. Let us end this chapter on Frederic's verses. He knew very well that this madness was in him a weakness and an object of ridicule; that people praised him to his face, only to call him Cotin behind his back. "That man," said Voltaire one day, showing a pile of papers from the king, "do you see? is Cæsar and the abbe Cotin." An eminent English historian, Mr. Macaulay, improving upon this, called Frederic a compound of *Mithridates* and *Trissotin*. Frederic knew or had a misgiving of all that, yet yielded, nevertheless, to his rage for rhyming. Being very amorous in his early youth of a young girl who loved verse, he had been bitten by the tarantula, but though entirely cured of one ill (that of loving young girls) he was never cured of the other. One could say nothing to him upon this subject, in the way of objection or expostulation, which he had not said a hundred times to himself: "I have the misfortune," said he, "to love verse, and often to make very bad verse. That which should disgust me, and repel every reasonable person, is precisely the spur which most pricks me on. I say to myself: 'Unhappy little poet! thou hast hitherto been unable to succeed; coúrage!' . . ." He will say to himself also: "Whoever is not a poet at twenty, will not become such while he lives. . . No man who was not born a Frenchman, or who has not lived a long time at Paris, can possess the language in the degree of perfection which is necessary for writing good verse or elegant prose." He will compare himself to vines "which always have a flavor of the soil in which they have been planted." But, finally, this occupation amuses him, it diverts and rests him in the intervals of great affairs, and, even to the last, he will rhyme. He also composed some music after the Italian taste, *solos* by hundreds, and he played on the flute, we are told, to perfection; which did not hinder Diderot from saying: "It is a great pity that the mouth-piece of that beautiful flute should be spoiled by some grains of Brandenburg sand."

In Germany where they write dissertations on everything, they have discoursed on the books and the libraries of Frederic, upon the authors whom he preferred, and they have drawn conclusions concerning the nature and quality of his tastes. From the fact that he calls D'Alembert, in his letters, my dear *Anaxagoras*, one has gone so far as to suppose, for example, that he had a certain predilection for the philosophy of Anaxagoras. These are the refinements and subtleties of commentators. In order to be informed of the real intellectual tastes of Frederic, it is sufficient to hear him himself, as he describes himself to the life, in his Correspondence. He knew antiquity only by translations, and by French translations; he did not therefore judge well, except in the gross, those things which resist that kind of transport from one language into another. The poetic beauty of the ancients escaped him altogether; he did not even suspect it. He judged some historians well, who were proper subjects for his study and meditation; and yet when we see him lavish the title of *Thucydides* on Rollin or even on Voltaire, we are forced to confess that he does not appear to have any notion of the peculiar manner which constitutes the originality of that great historian. He would judge better of Polybius, in whom the subject matter is most important; a really meritorious critic (M. Egger) calls my attention to the fact that

Frederic as historian and Polybius have some real and very striking correspondences. The reflections with which Frederic terminates his recital of the Seven Years' War, closely resemble a page of Polybius: "At a distance of two thousand years, there is the same way of judging of human vicissitudes, and of explaining them by tricks of cleverness mingled with tricks of fortune,"—only the historian king is more sparing of reflections. Frederic judged certain ancient moralists and philosophers well also, and even some philosophic poets in whom thought predominated, like Lucretius: "When I am afflicted," said he, "I read the third book of Lucretius, and that comforts me." Yet even into that which was the subject of his familar readings, he was so far from looking closely, as regards erudition, that he chanced inadvertently to class Epictetus and Marcus Aurelius in the list of *Latin* authors. Among the moderns, he esteemed Locke and Bayle most highly, those *breast-high* philosophers, whom he was tempted to place a little too near or even above the great, imaginative authors, like Leibnitz or Descartes, whose errors offended him. He did not hesitate to ridicule the transcendental geometry as useless, and he went so far in this matter as to be called to order by D'Alembert. His studies were directed most willingly to practical morality and social science; in that he resembled Voltaire, who was himself as practical as a writer can be, and he might have said like him: "I go to the fact; that is my motto."

Touching German literature, Frederic is hardly in doubt; he is very sensible of its faults, which were without compensation down to that date,—heaviness, diffuseness, the division of dialects,—and he indicates some of the remedies. He has, however, a presentiment of some fine days at hand for this national literature, and he predicts them: "*I announce them to you, they are going to appear!*" He does not seem to suspect that they have, in fact, begun to shine at the end of his life, and that Goethe has already come. But can one be astonished that Frederic has not noticed *Werther*?

To sum up: everything like manly and firm thought went straight to his sensitive and vigorous mind. In all other things, it is too clear that he was more or less out of his element; in all that one may call invention or poetry, he made only rough attempts, native sallies, which burst forth especially in his conversation, but which under his pen became feeble or turned heavily to imitation. In his admiration for Voltaire there was a certain amount of truth and justice, and there was also a certain amount of error and illusion. He was marvellously sensible of *the gaiety of that brilliant imagination.* He enjoyed that lively, familiar, sportive genius. "It is not given to everybody," said he, "*to make the mind laugh.*" No one can better describe that species of attraction, of luminous and flashing talent peculiar to Voltaire. Toward the end, while wishing him *pleasanter* sentiments, he saluted him still as "the finest organ of reason and of truth." All this is as well felt as it is justly expressed. But when Frederic admired in Voltaire the preëminently great poet, when he saw in the *Henriade* the *ne plus ultra* of epics, and when he put it above the *Iliads* and the *Æneids*, he showed simply his lack of an ideal, and at what point, on that side, his horizons were limited. The great objects of comparison had kept out of his range and out of his sight; he spoke upon that matter precisely like a man who had neither seen nor conceived, at any day, the supreme and real beauty.

"What pleasures surpass those of the mind?" cried Frederic at twenty-five,— mind, that is to say, the brilliant reason, reason sportive and lively. He thought always thus, and the whole secret of his passion for Voltaire is there. That passion (this is truly the word for it) was, moreover, reciprocal: Voltaire cannot dissemble it; he himself, the great coquet, was smitten with Frederic, and in the witty but miserable libel, so unworthy of confidence, which he wrote after his flight from Berlin, to avenge himself upon the king, he cannot help saying, in speaking of the Potsdam suppers: "The suppers were very agreeable. I know not whether I am deceived; *it seems to me that there was much wit* there; the king had it, and made others have it." Note well the attraction, even in his anger. See the irresistible fascination which they exercised upon each other, and which survived even friendship! In the second part of the Correspondence, when they renew it after the quarrel, we find they have assumed entirely different characters. Every illusion has vanished, and nothing more remains but that lively relish of talent, which manifests itself still. Moreover the primitive and youthfully enthusiastic Frederic has disappeared; he has given place to the philosopher, to the superior and worldly-wise man, who no longer gropes his way anywhere. The king also makes himself oftener felt. They speak truths on both sides, and (rare thing) they bear them. Voltaire tells some to the king, and Frederic pays him back: "You have behaved very badly to me," writes he to Voltaire. . . . "I have pardoned you all, and I even wish to forget all. But if you had not had to do with *a fool who was in love with your fine genius*, you would not have got off so well at every other. . . ."

Nevertheless, after these severe words, too strong not to be just,— after these words, the king, as the fool in love with the brilliant mind, easily betrays himself again when he adds: "Do you need some sweet things? In good time; I will tell you some truths. I regard you as the finest genius whom the ages have produced; I admire your verses, I love your prose, *especially those little detached pieces of your literary Miscellanies*. Never has any author before you had a tact so fine, a taste so sure, so delicate, as you have. You are charming in conversation; you know how to instruct and to amuse at the same time. You are the most bewitching creature that I know, and capable of making yourself loved by everybody when you will. You have so many graces of mind that you can offend and at the same time merit the indulgence of those who know you. Finally, you would be perfect if you were not a man."

Let any one say now whether he who had such a liking for Voltaire, and who found these French ways of insinuating sweet things after the bitterness, was not the man of his time who showed the most ability when confronted with Voltaire.

When one has read a certain *Portrait* of Voltaire by Frederic (1756), a *Portrait* traced with the hand of a master, with unerring penetration and without embellishment, one understands still better the meaning of the language which he has just used,— that that seductive genius has such graces that he speedily lays hold again of the very persons whom he has offended, and who know him.*

I believe that I have kept within the bounds of truth, in saying that the intellectual attraction of these men for each other survived even their friendship; for it is evident, when we read in good faith the whole series and the end of that Correspondence, that their friendship itself has not died, that it has revived with some of the old charm mingled with reason, and that it is founded, not simply on amusement, but on their serious and higher qualities. At the same time that he combats the always irascible and choleric instincts of the now aged Voltaire, Frederic exalts and favors, as far as possible, his beneficent and humane tendencies. He takes pleasure in praising, in encouraging as a defender of humanity and toleration, the man who clears and repeoples the almost abandoned soil of Ferney, as he himself has peopled the sands of Brandenburg; in a word, he recognizes and he embraces the great practical poet as his fellow laborer in social work and in civilization. With a remnant of veneration, and, if one will, of yet touching idolatry, Frederic, in all the comparisons he makes of the two, always gives the advantage to Voltaire, and that, too, in a heart-felt tone whose sincerity is above suspicion. Speaking of that future of perfected reason of which he perceived hardly the dawn, and of which, thoroughly sceptical as he was, he did not utterly despair as regards the future of humanity, he says: "Everything with man depends upon the time when he comes into the world. Although I have come too late, I do not regret it: *I have seen Voltaire;* and if I see him

* It appears to be proved to-day that that remarkable Portrait of Voltaire, found among Frederic's papers, was not his composition: in copying it with his own hand, he limited himself to ratifying its truth.

no more, I read him and he writes to me." From such accents one might divine, though he did not tell it, the passion which was still the profoundest and the most radical in Frederic, that which Voltaire while living personified in his eyes: "My last passion will be that for Letters!" It had been the first also.

The intercourse of Frederic with D'Alembert was of quite a different nature from his intimacy with Voltaire; it was never as lively, but it was long and enduring. It was not simply a natural liking which drew Frederic to D'Alembert: "We princes have all selfish souls, and we never make acquaintances except when we have some private views, which look directly to our profit." Frederic had early thought of drawing D'Alembert to Berlin to make him president of his Academy. That purpose became quite serious after the death of Maupertuis, and when Frederic had come out of the Seven Years' War. I have before me the manuscript and unpublished Collection of Letters written by D'Alembert to Mademoiselle de Lespinasse during his sojourn with the king of Prussia. In June, 1763, D'Alembert went after Frederic, who was then in his Westphalian States; joining him at Gueldres, he traveled as one of his suite as far as Potsdam. D'Alembert had already seen Frederic several years before; on seeing him again, he was surprised to find him greater than his reputation. Frederic had the characteristic peculiar to great men, of surpassing expectation even at the first sight. He begins by chatting four hours in succession with D'Alembert; he speaks to him with simplicity, with modesty, of philosophy, of Letters, of peace, of war, of everything. At that date, that is to say, three months only after peace was concluded, Frederic had already rebuilt four thousand five hundred houses in the ruined villages; two years after (October, 1765), he will have rebuilt not less than fourteen thousand five hundred. We observe, at the very outset, with D'Alembert, this organizing and even pacific side of the warrior. The amiable, familiar, and seductive side of Frederic is perfectly indicated in the Recital of our traveller; the prudent and modest guest has not had time or a desire to perceive some faults which often impaired that groundwork of wisdom and of agreeableness.

Honors do not turn the head of D'Alembert: he is touched, but not intoxicated. While on his way to the Brunswick States, he has dined at the table of the ducal family, and has been styled *Marquis:* he has submitted to the title after a slight protest. Apparently, he says, that was etiquette. With Frederic there is no etiquette, and all passes as with a private man, a man of genius. D'Alembert would have little to do to become necessary to Frederic by his conversation, as Frederic would be to D'Alembert. It was no longer the time of brilliant suppers at Potsdam, of which Voltaire had seen and contributed to the last five days: the familiar guests of that time, the friends of the king's youth, at that second epoch, were dead or grown old. The king was not merely the pleasantest man in his kingdom; if we except the Lord Marshal, he was the only one. "He is almost the only person in his kingdom," says D'Alembert, "with whom one can converse, at least can have that kind of conversation of which one knows but little out of France, and which becomes a necessity when one has known it once." D'Alembert is inexhaustible upon the king's affability and gaiety, the lights which he brings to bear upon every subject, his good administration, his care for the welfare of his people, the justice and the *justness* which mark all his judgments. Touching Jean-Jacques, he says: "The king talks, it seems to me, very well about the works of Rousseau; he finds heat and force in them, but very little logic and truth; he professes to read only for self-instruction, and the works of Rousseau teach him little or nothing."

To D'Alembert, whose estimable character he appreciated at the outset, Frederic shows himself purely as a philosopher; one sees him as he would have liked to be seen in the second half of his life, if gout and ill-humor had not irritated him too much, and if he had had about him some worthy person to sympathize with and listen to him:—"His conversation runs sometimes upon literature, sometimes upon philosophy, very often even upon war and politics, and sometimes upon contempt of life, of glory, and of honors." This is the circle of human subjects which he loved to treat habitually, sincerely, and always in a moralizing way; but literature and philosophy were still the topics of which he loved to chat above all others, in order to unbend, after he had done his duties as king. All the good qualities of Frederic are set in relief in this Recital, and D'Alembert, elsewhere circumspect, cares not to see any others during these three months of his visit. He knows, however, how to resist the caresses and the delicate offers of the king. One day when he was walking with him in the gardens of Sans-Souci, Frederic gathers a rose and presents it to him, saying: "I should very much like to give you something better." That *better* was the Presidency of his Academy. It is singular to see thus connected the Presidency of an Academy and a rose. D'Alembert remains wise, he remains a philosopher and a friend to the end, and faithful to Mademoiselle de Lespinasse. He returns to France grateful, with his heart forever won to Frederic, but not vanquished.

All must be told: some years after, Frederic communicated, one evening, some of his verses to Professor Thiébault, a good grammarian and academician, whom D'Alembert had procured for him, and inadvertently suffered himself to go so far as to show a very biting epigram which he had composed against D'Alembert himself; that caustic king could not deny himself the malicious pleasure of noting something ridiculous which he had hit upon in that honorable character. It was a capital fault of Frederic; he did not easily deny himself the pleasure of saying disobliging things to people or of writing pungent things about them. In the present case he soon repented having shown his epigram to Thiébault, and he enjoined secrecy; the good D'Alembert never knew anything of it. But surrounded, as he was, at home with courtly wits and all more or less dull, Frederic was less scrupulous with them. As soon as he had discovered their weak side, he pricked them pitilessly in their vulnerable points; he made them his butts, he took pains to show his contempt for humanity in their persons, and he thus acquired the reputation of a bad man, when he was really only a terrible satirist of society. The wittiest of these dull courtiers and of these false friends, such as the able Bastiani, secretly avenged themselves on the king by reviling him to strangers. M. de Guibert has reported to us in his *Journal of Travel* one of these confidential disclosures full of baseness and of perfidy, regarding which he shows himself too credulous. The misfortune of Frederic was to be surrounded at all times, and especially toward the end of his life, only by second-rate people of letters, whose not very elevated character afforded too ready facilities to his princely sports. Worthy men, who had respect for themselves, like D'Alembert, would have compelled him in his turn to respect them. The estimable Thiébault, in his modest way, knew how to do this.

Returned to France, D'Alembert continued to correspond with Frederic; and (if one forgets the epigram which was never known), the Correspondence gives evidence on both sides of much reason, of genuine philosophy, and even of friendship, so far as it could then exist between a private person and a monarch. Let us not forget that D'Alembert also had his weaknesses; we know already that the philosophers of the eighteenth century had not much love for the liberty of the press, except when it promoted their own interest; one day D'Alembert was insulted by some gazetteer who edited the *Lower Rhine Courier*, in the States of Frederic; he denounces him to the king. Here it is Frederic who is the true philosopher, the true citizen of modern society, and he replies:

"I know that a Frenchman, a countryman of yours, daubs regularly two sheets of paper a week at Cleves; I know that people buy his sheets, and that a fool always finds a greater fool to read him; but I find it very difficult to persuade myself that a writer of that temper can prejudice your reputation. Ah! my good D'Alembert, if you were king of England, you would encounter many other lampoons, with which your very faithful subjects would furnish you to try your patience. If you knew what a number of infamous writings your dear countrymen have published against me during the war, you would laugh at this miserable scribbler. I have not deigned to read all these works which are the offspring of the hate and envy of my enemies, and I have recollected that beautiful ode of Horace: '*The wise man continues unmoved*'. . . ."

He continues to paraphrase the *Justum et tenacem*. . . . We recognize in this admirable lesson the disciple of Bayle on the throne. At another day it will be the disciple of Lucretius. D'Alembert is plunged in sorrow, a deep and very legitimate sorrow: he has lost Mademoiselle de Lespinasse; he is going to lose Madame Geoffrin. That geometer's heart, so sensitive to friendship, does not fear to overflow into the soul of Frederic,— to pour into it its grief, and almost its sobs, and the king replies to him as a friend and as a sage, by two or three letters of philosophical consolation, which should be quoted in full. A lofty and tender epicureanism breathes through them, that of a Lucretius speaking to his friend:

"I compassionate the misfortune which has happened to you, in losing a person to whom you were attached. The wounds of the heart are the most painful of all, and, in spite of the fine maxims of the philosophers, it is only time that can heal them. *Man is an animal that has more feeling than reason.* It has been my misfortune to have had too bitter an experience of what one suffers from such losses. The best remedy is to do violence to one's feelings, to divert one's attention from a painful thought which is too deeply rooted in the mind. Some geometrical occupation should be chosen which demands much application, to dispel as well as one can the fatal ideas which are incessantly renewed, and which it is necessary to banish as far as possible. I would propose to you better remedies, if I knew of any. Cicero, to console himself for the death of his dear Tullia, threw himself into literary composition, and wrote several treatises, some of which have reached us. Our reason is too weak to vanquish the pain of a mortal wound; we must yield something to nature, and confess to ourselves that at your age, as at mine, one must console himself with the thought that he will not be long in rejoining the objects of his regrets."

He then engages to come and pass some months with him: "We will philosophize together on the nothingness of life, on human philosophy, upon the vanity of stoicism and of our whole existence." And he adds, with that mixture of the warrior-king and the philosopher which would seem contradictory if it were not touching here, that "he will feel as much joy in tranquillizing him *as if he had won a battle.*" Such letters well atone for some blunt expressions which one might find in the same collection, and which recall at times the presence of the master; they are a reply to those who, judging Frederic only by his harsh words and by his epigrams, deny that he had, even at the close of his career, sentiments of affection, of humanity, and, I dare say, of goodness, even that he had had real and lively sentiments of friendship in his youth. For myself, on whatever side I regard him, even in the years when his faults were most marked, I can, on the whole, but come to a favorable conclusion, and say, as Bolingbroke said of Marlborough: "He was so great a man that I have forgotten his faults." In the present case, the great man had, in spite of all, some goodness and some humanity, and a basis of heart.

In a select edition of Frederic's works, which should be made for the use of people of intellect and taste, in order to avoid the trash whose proximity always spoils the best things, I would have admitted only his Histories, two or three of his Dissertations at most, and his Correspondence; there would be already quite enough of his verses, which are scattered through his Letters, without adding others. We should thus have, in all, a dozen volumes of strong, sound, agreeable, and entirely instructive reading. Let us drop those names, so often applied to

Frederic, and which would be injurious or flattering,— the too debatable names of the Emperor Julien and Marcus Aurelius; let us not employ, on the other side, the name of Lucian, of whom he would only furnish parodies and strange travesties; but, if we would give him a *classic* designation, let us define him in his best productions as a writer of the most marked character, whose temper is wholly his own, but who, in the habit and turn of his thought, resembles at once Polybius, Lucretius and Bayle.

December 16, 1850.

INDEX.

A

Ampire, M., on the epochs of pulpit eloquence in France, 70.
Arnold, Matthew, as a critic, 70.
Augustine, Saint, ingenious comparison by, 210.
Authors, little known of the greatest, 63.

B

Baron, the actor, on Massillon, 94.
Beaumont, Madame de, her acquaintance with M. Joubert, 189–194; her *salon*, 194.
Bossuet, 44–88; on Lewis XIV, 5; his training of the Dauphin of France, 30; his increasing fame, 44; his political and religious views, 45; his tone like that of Moses, 45, 46; works of Lamartine and Poujoulat on, 46, 47; M. de Baussuet's biography of, 47; the abbe Victor Vaillant's study on his sermons, 48; his birth and parentage, 49; his precocity, 49; his love for the Bible and for Homer, 50; becomes canon at Metz, 50; purity of his youth, 50; sees Richelieu, 51; becomes a student at the college of Navarre, 51; his rapid rise at Metz, 52; analysis and criticism of one of his early sermons, 52–59; on the heresy of the Marcionites, 53; on the civil discords of France, 58; his early style, 59; his personal appearance, 59–63; his Panegyrics on Saint Gorgon and Saint Paul, 64, 76, 77; preaches at Court, 65; his sermons on All Saints' Day criticised, 66–69; on true joy, 68, 69; his resemblance to Æschylus, 70; of Lewis XIV, upon his style, 70–74; compared with Bourdaloue, 74–76; his sermons upon "Ambition," "Honor," and the "Love of Pleasure," 77–80; his repetitions, 79; on the freaks of fortune, 79, 80; his use of obsolescent words, 80; his funeral orations, 80; contrasted with Massillon, 120; his treatise on "The Knowledge of God," 132–136; his method of reasoning compared with Pascal's, 132–136; eloquent extract from, 133; on Divine Providence, 223.
Bourdaloue, compared with Bossuet, 75, 76.
Buffon, on severity of style, 93.
Burton, author of the "Anatomy of Melancholy," 63.

C

Caylus, Madame de, her "Recollections," 146.
Chateaubriand, on the Memoirs of Lewis XIV, 20; compared with Rousseau, 147, 150, 151; encouraged and advised by Joubert, 189; his best pieces, 203; compared with Bernardin de Saint-Pierre, 204; Sainte-Beuve's lectures on, 36.
Choiseul, French Minister, his alterations of the text in the Works of Frederic the Great, 249, 250.
Clarendon, Lord, causes of his fall, 223.

Conversation, histories of, 72.
Conversions, religious, Massillon on, 110.
Corneille, on the deceptiveness of example, 222.
Cousin, his exaggerations and prejudices, 70, 71; his errors regarding Lewis XIV, 71, 72.
Criticism, literary, Sainte-Beuve's theory of, 54–66; Wordsworth on, 65; its excellence in France, 66, 67; character of British, 67–70.

D

D'Alembert, his acquaintance with Frederic the Great, 283–289; satirized by Frederic, 286; his correspondence with Frederic, 286–288.
D'Haussonville, Viscount, quoted, 15, 16.
Daguesseau, Chancellor, on "Pascal's Thoughts," 134.
Doubts in religion, Massillon's sermon on, 105, 106.
Droz, M., his "Art of Being Happy," 75, 76.
Dryden, John, few facts known of his history, 63.
Dubois, archbishop of Cambray, 119, 120.

E

Ennui, Massillon on, 114.
Eugene, Prince, Fenelon on, 38, 39.
External influences, their influence on men of genius overestimated, 61, 62.

F

Fenelon, 22–43; his fondness for La Fontaine's Fables, 22; compared with La Fontaine, 22–24; naturally tolerant, 24, 41; his character as bishop, 24, 25; portrayed by Saint-Simon, 27, 28; his influence upon the duke of Burgundy, 28, 29; compared, as an educator, with Bossuet, 30; his "Spiritual Letters," 31, 32; his sweetness of temper, 32; on piety, 33; his letters to the chevalier Destouches, 33–40; on the ancient and modern styles, 35; his letter on the death of the duchess of Burgundy, 36; his letter on the death of the duke of Burgundy, 37; his dislike to being under obligation, 38; on the prince Eugene, 38, 39; his account of a dangerous accident, 39, 40; his gaiety, 40; on La Motte's translation of the "Iliad," 41; his chief weakness, 41; his "Telemachus," 42; characterized as a literary man, 43; his love of Horace, 49, 50; his treatise on "The Existence of God" analyzed, 128–130; his mode of reasoning compared with Pascal's, 131, 132.
Frayssinous, the abbe, his lectures on religious doctrine, 107.
Frederic I, of Prussia, 256.
Frederic William 1, of Prussia, his character, 257.
Frederic the Great, 248–290; the different editions of his works, 248–252; his character, 253; his military abilities, 253, 254; a great king, 254; his opinion of a prince's duties, 255, 257; his truthfulness, 256; his participation in the Partition of Poland, 259; his lack of ideality, 259; his irreligion, 260, 261; character of his histories, 261–268; his preference of the French language, 263; his sketches of the Electors of Prussia, 263; his style, 264; his judgments of men, 264, 205; his sayings about Peter the Great, Cardinal Alberoni, and General Seckendorff, 265; his indebtedness to good fortune, 266; his History of the Seven Years' War, 266–268; his opinion of the Austrian Court, 267; his reflections upon the futility of human schemes,

267, 268; his love of letters, 269, 270, 283; his remark on human versatility, 270; his correspondence with Voltaire, 271–275, 280, 281; his admiration and overestimate of Voltaire, 272, 273, 279, 281; his self-estimate in youth, 273, 274; his opinion of Lewis XIV, 274, 275; his practicality, 274; his lack of delicacy, 274, 275; his rage for rhyming, 275, 276; his love of music, 277; his classical knowledge, 277; his resemblance as a historian to Polybius, 278; his favorite authors and studies, 278; his supposed Portrait of Voltaire, 281; his intercourse with D'Alembert, 283; the latter's opinion of him, 285; his opinion of Rousseau, 285; offers the Presidency of the Berlin Academy to D'Alembert, 285; his epigram on D'Alembert, 286; his satirical habits, 286, 287; his letter on the treatment of lampoons, 287; his letter of sympathy to D'Alembert, 288, 289; final estimate of, 289, 290.

Frenchmen, their impulsiveness, 220; characterized by the abbe Galiani, 239, 247; their sunny temperament, 23.

G

Galiani, the abbe, Ferdinand, 227–247; his birth, 227; his early works, 228; made an abbe, 228; his residence at Paris, 228, 229; characterized by Grimm and Marmontel, 229; his buffooneries and jests, 229, 230; his description of himself, 230; his love of Paris, 231, 242; his witty sayings, 231, 232, 234, 243, 244; his apologues, 232; his confutation of atheism, 232, 233; his philosophic views, 235, 236; his views of incredulity, 236, 237; an advocate of toleration, 237; admired by Diderot, 237; his "Dialogues upon the Grain Trade," 238, 239, 240; his opinion of the French and their language, 239, 247; his observations on economists and statesmen, 240; criticised by the abbe Morellet and Turgot, 241; his classification of reasonings, 241, 242; becomes Secretary of Commerce at Naples, 243; his studies, 243; his opera bouffe, 243; his noble qualities, 244; his paradoxical character, 242, 244, 246; his death, 246; his correspondence, 246.

Geoffrin, Madame, 162–184; her *salon*, 162, 163, 169–171; her birth, 163; her account of education, 164; her love of Paris, 165; anecdotes of her husband, 165; witty sayings of, 166, 171, 173, 174, 178, 183; her personal appearance, 166; her style of dress, 166, 167; her indebtedness to Madame de Tencin, 167; contrasted with her, 169; her dinners for artists and men-of-letters, 169; her *salon* compared with those of Madame du Deffand and Mademoiselle Lespinasse, 170; her habit of scolding, 172, 177, 178; described by Sir Horace Walpole, 172, 177; her resemblance to Fontenelle, 173; her beneficence, 172–175; her egoism, 174, 175; her good sense, 177; her note to David Hume, 178; her mental and moral peculiarities, 179, 184; her journey to Poland, 180, 181; attacked by the dramatists and by Montesquieu, 182; her religious habits, 182, 183; her last sickness, 183; her death, 184; compared with Madame Recamier, 184.

Gibbon, the historian, his merits and defects, 74.

Globe, the Paris organ of the *Doctrinaires*, its contributors and its character, 17.

Goethe, on French and German criticism, 17; saying of, 27; on classicism and romanticism, 48.
Grimm, Jacob, on the abbe Galiani, 229.
Guizot, 205-226; his "Discourse on the History of the English Revolution," 205, 206, 219-225; his writings a linked series, 206; his persistence, 207; not a *littérateur*, 207, 208; his qualities as a writer, 208; the founder of a historic school, 209; his "History of Civilization in Europe," 209, 212, 213; his philosophy of history considered, 212; his "History of the English Revolution" criticised, 214-216; compared, as a historian, with Hume, 216; his extreme gravity of style, 216, 217; his qualities as an orator, 217-219; his admiration of the English government, 220; his condemnation of revolutions, 221; his excessive use of Providential intervention in history, 223, 224.

H

Hallam, Henry, as a critic, 69, 70.
Havet, M., his edition of Pascal's "Thoughts," 123, 139, 140.
Henry IV, King of France, his style, 18; saying of, 116.
Historians, not necessarily able politicians or statesmen, 213; Montaigne on, 225; hints to, 226.
History, difficulties attending its study, 210-213; its illusions, 211; dangers of generalizations in, 212-214; the true philosophy of, 222; the intervention of Providence in, 223-224, 225; of what it should treat, 226.
Hume, David, compared, as a historian, with Guizot, 216; his opinion of the abbe Galiani, 238.

I

Idle hours, their value to a writer, etc., 44.

J

Joubert, Joseph, 185-204; on Fenelon, 32; his birth, 185; his "Thoughts and Letters," 185, 186; his character, 186; a pupil of Diderot, 187; his dislike for sensationalism, 188; on the Athenian taste, 188; his aid to Chateaubriand, 189; his acquaintance with Madame de Beaumont, 189-194; his letters to her, 191-193; his excellencies and faults as a writer, 195-197, 201, 202; on literary style, 197-200; his observations on force in literature, 198, 199; his mannerism, 200; his conversation, 203; his comparison of Saint-Pierre and Chateaubriand, 204.

L

La Fontaine, compared with Fenelon, 22, 24.
Lamartine, his description of Bossuet, 60, 61; the same criticised, 61-63; on the comparative popularity of Bossuet and Bourdaloue, 75.
Lamennais, his intimacy with Sainte-Beuve, 30, 31; his "Words of a Believer," 31.
Lampoons, Frederic the Great on the treatment of, 287.
Lessing, saying of, 52.
Lewis XIV, and his writings, 1-21; his looks and character in youth, 3-5; Bossuet on, 5; educated by events, 6; Mazarin on, 6; Saint-Simon on, 7, 9; his qualifications as a sovereign, 8, 12; on the blessings of royalty, 9; rules without a minister, 10; loves application, 10; on the study of history, 11; conservative in his views, 12; on treaties, 13; his "slow and sure"

policy, 13; on the qualities needed by a sovereign, 14; did violence to the genius of the French monarchy, 15; his mistakes, 15, 16; on following one's instincts, 16; his Memoirs, 16-17; anecdote of, 17; his style, 17, 18; a good story-teller, 18; his speech at the siege of Lille, 19; on his glory, 19; his self-estimates, 20; Chateaubriand on his Memoirs, 20; his influence upon French literature, 21; his admiration for Bossuet's preaching, 73; his influence upon Bossuet, 71-74; Cousin on the lateness of his influence, 71, 72; Frederic the Great's opinion of him, 274.

Lewis XV, his conversation, 18.

M

Macaulay, T. B., as a critic, 68, 69.
Maine, the Duchess of, her egoism, 79, 80.
Maintenon, Madame, on Fenelon's "Spiritual Letters," 31, 32.
Marmontel, his description of Massillon, 121; his opinion of the abbe Galiani, 229.
Massillon, 84-122; his precocity, 85; his early education, 85; his early irregularities, 85, 86; his retreat to the abbey of Septfonts, 86; ordained as priest, 86; his popularity in Paris, 87; his sermons at court, 87; his *Petit Carême*, 87, 113-118; his manner in the pulpit, 89, 90; his sermon before Lewis XIV on All Saints' Day, 90, 91; his art of exposition and style, 91-93, 96, 97; by whom he will be admired, 93, 94; described by Baron, the actor, 94; his sermon on "Trifling Faults," 95-97; his indebtedness to Racine, 98; his sermon on "Afflictions," 98; on human happiness, 99; the effects of his eloquence, 99-101; his sermon on "The Small Number of the Elect," 99, 100; Lewis XIV on his preaching, 100; his defects, 101; his funeral discourses, 101-103; his oration at the funeral of Lewis XIV, 102, 103; his sermons at Court, 104-108; his sermons on "Doubts about Religion," and on "The Reality of a Future Life," 105, 106; his portraiture of Spinosa, 106; his sermon on "The Sinning Woman," 108; humbled by praise, 109; on sudden conversions, 110; criminations of, 110-112; his sermon on "Slander," 112; on ennui, 114; on the duties of kings, 115; praised by Voltaire, 117; made bishop of Clermont, 118; becomes a member of the French Academy, 118; censured for taking part in the consecration of Cardinal Dubois to the archbishopric of Cambray, 119, 120; renounces preaching, 119; his tolerant spirit, 120; his "Moral Paraphrases of the Psalms," 120; contrasted with Bossuet, 120, 121; described by Marmontel, 121; his death, 122.
Mazarin, Cardinal, on Lewis XIV, 6.
Men of genius, their self-ignorance, 19, 20; their peculiarities and eccentricities, 58-60; contrast between their writings and their lives, 64, 65.
Minds, classified by a French philosopher, 202.
Montaigne, criticised by Rousseau, 144; on historians, 225.

N

Napoleon I, on Providence, 268; Sainte-Beuve's opinion of him, 76, 77; his style as a writer, 78, 79; saying of, 79.

O

Orleans, the duchess of, on the morals of France, 104.

P

Pascal, 123-140; his natural qualities, 123; his "Thoughts upon Religion," 124; restoration of the original text of the "Thoughts," 125; not simply a reasoner, 126; his method of combating unbelief, 127; the same compared with the methods of Fenelon and Bossuet, 128-136; his disdain of half-proofs, 131; on miracles, 135; his love for little churches, 135; his definition of faith, 135; his affectionate character, 135, 137; upon the agony of Jesus Christ, 136; how his writings should be studied, 137, 138; the uses of his works, 138.
Philosophy of the eighteenth century, its spirit, 14.
Physiological studies, moral effects of, 15.
Pope, Alexander, characterized by Sainte-Beuve, 73.
Poujoulat, M. his "Lettres sur Bossuet" noticed, 46, 47, 82, 83.
Progress, modern, 139.
Providence, its intervention in history, 222-224.

R

Revolution of 1848 in France, Sainte-Beuve's notes on, 34, 35; the Revolution of 1789, 138.
Richelieu, his love of letters, 269.
Romantic School of writers in France, 18.
Rousseau, 141-161; his influence on the French language, 141, 142, 147; his "Confessions," 142, 160; on autobiographies, 143, 144; his language criticised, 145, 148, 149; contrasted with Chateaubriand, 147; his lack of taste, 149; his moral qualities, 149; contrasted with the "René" of Chateaubriand, 150, 151; his sensibility, 151; a regenerator of language, 153; his love of nature, 153; his portrait of Madame de Warens, 153, 154; his sense of reality, 154; his criticism on the novelist Richardson, 155; his influence on French literature, 156; his "discovery of reverie," 157; his pedestrian journeys, 158, 159; his treatment of the picturesque, 160; his style and his imitators, 160, 161; his follies and vices, 158, 161.

S

Sainte-Beuve, C. A., his life and writings, 9-86; his funeral, 9, 10; difficulty of characterizing him, 10, 46, 47; his critical labors, 10, 11, his devotion to literature, 11, 12; his birthplace and parentage, 12, 13; character of his father and mother, 12-14; his education in Paris, 14; his earliest philosophical opinions, 14, 15; his early poverty, 16; the benefits of his medical studies, 16, 17; becomes a contributor to the Globe, 17; his acquaintance with Victor Hugo, 18; embraces the doctrines of the Romantic School, 18; becomes a member of *Le Cenacle*, 18; his work on the French Poetry of the 16th Century, 19; his "Life, Poems, and Thoughts of Joseph Delorme," 19-23; compared with Wordsworth, 21; his "Consolations," and its reception and character, 23, 26; merits and defects of his poems, 25; his "August Thoughts" (*Pensées d'Août*), 25, 26; his ignorance of his own genius,

26; contributes to the *Revue de Paris*, 26; goes back to the *Globe*, 26; fights a duel with Dubois, 27; his frequent changes of opinion, 27–30, 47, 50 51; his defense of the same, 29; his intimacy with Lamennais, 30; his contributions to the *Revue des Deux Mondes*, 31; his novel, "*Volupté*," 31, 32; he declines the Cross of the Legion of Honor, 32; his lectures at Lausanne, 32; his "History of Port Royal," 32, 33; appointed keeper of the Mazarin Library, 32; his frugal life, 33, 34; becomes a professor at the University of Liège, 34; his notes on the Revolution of 1848, 34, 35; his lectures on Chateaubriand, 36; appointed Professor of Latin in the College of France, 38; hissed by the students, 38; made Senator of France, 37; his defense of Renan, 37; devotes himself to criticism, 38; elected Member of the Academy, 38; becomes a contributor to the *Constitutionnel*, 38; brilliancy and popularity of his "Monday-Chats," 38–40; improvement in his style, 40; the labor expended upon the "Monday-Chats," 41, 44; his wide range of themes, 42–44; his recognition of the value of idle hours, 44; his method of preparing a "Monday-Chat," 45, 46; paradoxes in his character, 47; his abhorrence of fixed rules and formulas, 47; his definition of a "classic," 48; his impartiality as a critic, 48, 49; his definition of criticism, 49, 50; his hatred of dogmatism, 50; objection to his views, 51–53; his psychological method, 15, 16, 53; his theory of literary criticism expounded, 54–57; wherein it differs from that of M. Taine, 57, 58; objections to his critical theory, 58–66; his criticism of M. Taine's method, 62; the merits of his "Monday-Chats," 66; his freedom from sentimentality and cynicism, 70; his qualities as a critic, 70, 71; his aphorisms, 71, 72; his thoughts on "the art of being happy," 75, 76; his criticism of Napoleon, 77, 78; his comment on a saying of Napoleon's, 79; his dislike of literary "sensationalism," 80; his estimate of the present age, 70, 71; on human deterioration, 81; on the effect of circumstances on character, 81; one of his "Thoughts," 82; how he overcame the mannerism of his early style, 83; not an eloquent writer, 83; his apparent lack of earnestness, 84; his final views of religion, 85; his introduction to Lacordaire, 86.

Saint Paul, Bossuet on his powers of persuasion, 77.

Saint-Simon, on Lewis XIV, 7, 9; his genius as an observer and painter of character, 26, 27; contrasted with La Bruyère, 27; his portraiture of Fenelon, 27, 28.

Salons, the art of forming them, 162, 163; notices of Parisian, 169, 170, 193, 194.

Slander, Massillon on, 112.

Spinosa, described by Massillon, 106.

T

Taine, M., his method of criticism noticed, 62; his opinion of Sainte-Beuve's critical essays, 66; his style, 74, 75.

"*Télémaque*," Fenelon's, criticised, 42.

Tencin, Madame de, 167, 168.

Thiers, the historian, his comparison of the English and French soldier, 77, 78.

Voltaire, saying of, 51; his admiration of Massillon's *Petit Carême*, 117; his style, 141; his opinion of the writing of Frederic the Great, 273; his regard for the latter, 280; their correspondence, 271, 275, 280, 281.

W

Walpole, Sir Horace, his portraits of Madame Geoffrin, 172, 177.
Wordsworth, William, his genius contrasted with that of Sainte-Beuve, 20–22; his views on literary criticism, 66.
Writing, the great art in, 82.

www.ingramcontent.com/pod-product-compliance
Lightning Source LLC
Chambersburg PA
CBHW030400230426
43664CB00007BB/679